Ancient Inca

This book offers a detailed ε
through the lens of archaeol
accounts of native Andeans. Throughout the Andes, public works
ordained by the emperors of the Incas dominate and transform the
natural landscape. Cities, temples and fortresses of stone, marvelously
engineered roads cut through sheer mountain slopes, massive agricultural terraces, and hydraulic works are emblematic of Inca power.
In this book, Alan L. Kolata examines how these awesome material
products came into being. What were the cultural institutions that gave
impetus to the Incas' imperial ambition? What form of power did the
Incas exercise over their conquered provinces far from the imperial
capital of Cuzco? How did the Incas mobilize the staggering labor force
that sustained their war machine and built their empire? What kind of
perceptions and religious beliefs informed the Inca worldview?

Alan L. Kolata is the Bernard E. and Ellen C. Sunny Distinguished
Service Professor of Anthropology at the University of Chicago. Since
1978 he has led ongoing interdisciplinary research projects study-
ing human-environment interactions in the Lake Titicaca basin of
Bolivia, on the north coast of Peru, and most recently in Cambodia.
He has received multiple large-scale research grants from the National
Science Foundation, the National Endowment for the Humanities,
the National Oceanic and Atmospheric Administration, the Inter-
American Foundation, and the John D. and Catherine T. MacArthur
Foundation, among others. His books include *The Tiwanaku: Portrait
of an Andean Civilization*, *Valley of the Spirits: A Journey into the Lost
Realm of the Aymara*, and a major two-volume research monograph
entitled *Tiwanaku and Its Hinterland: Archaeology and Paleoecology of an
Andean Civilization* of which he is the editor and principal author. At
the University of Chicago, he has served as chair of the Department of
Anthropology, director of the Center for Latin American Studies, and
academic director of the University of Chicago Center in Paris. His
professional awards include the Manuel Vicente Ballivián Foundation
Gold Medal for distinguished service to Bolivian science, presented
in conjunction with the National Academy of Sciences of Bolivia and
the Ministry of Education and Culture of the government of Bolivia;
the Puma de Oro, the maximum distinction conferred by the Bolivian
National Institute of Archaeology; and the Simon Bolivar Foundation
Distinguished Service Award.

Case Studies in Early Societies

Series Editor
Rita P. Wright, New York University

This series aims to introduce students to early societies that have been the subject of sustained archaeological research. Each study is also designed to demonstrate a contemporary method of archaeological analysis in action, and the authors are all specialists currently engaged in field research.

The books have been planned to cover many of the same fundamental issues. Tracing long-term developments, and describing and analyzing a discrete segment in the prehistory or history of a region, they represent an invaluable tool for comparative analysis. Clear, well organized, authoritative, and succinct, the case studies are an important resource for students and for scholars in related fields, such as anthropology, ethnohistory, history, and political science. They also offer the general reader accessible introductions to important archaeological sites.

Other Titles in the Series Include:

Ancient Mesopotamia
Susan Pollock

Ancient Oaxaca
Richard E. Blanton, Gary M. Feinman, Stephen A. Kowalewski, and Linda M. Nicholas

Ancient Maya
Arthur Demarest

Ancient Jomon of Japan
Junko Habu

Ancient Puebloan Southwest
John Kantner

Ancient Cahokia and the Mississippians
Timothy R. Pauketat

Ancient Middle Niger
Rod McIntosh

Ancient Egyptian Civilization
Robert Wenke

Ancient Tiwanaku
John Janusek

The Ancient Indus
Rita P. Wright

Ancient Central China
Rowan K. Flad and Pochan Chen

A doorway at the site of Machu Picchu reflects the importance of stone in the Inca world, as well as the exceptional artistry with which craftsmen conceived and carved this elemental material. (Photo © Edward Ranney, from *Monuments of the Incas*, by John Hemming, Thames and Hudson, Ltd., London, 2010)

Ancient Inca

Alan L. Kolata
University of Chicago

CAMBRIDGE UNIVERSITY PRESS
Cambridge, New York, Melbourne, Madrid, Cape Town,
Singapore, São Paulo, Delhi, Mexico City

Cambridge University Press
32 Avenue of the Americas, New York, NY 10013-2473, USA

www.cambridge.org
Information on this title: www.cambridge.org/9780521689380

First published 2013

Printed in the United States of America

A catalog record for this publication is available from the British Library.

Library of Congress Cataloging in Publication data
Kolata, Alan L.
    Ancient Inca / Alan L. Kolata.
        p.   cm. – (Case studies in early societies)
    Includes bibliographical references and index.
    ISBN 978-0-521-86900-3 (hardback) – ISBN 978-0-521-68938-0
    (paperback)
    1. Incas – History.   2. Incas – Antiquities.   3. Incas – Social life and
    customs.   4. Andes Region – Antiquities.   I. Title.
    F3429.K63   2013
    980'.01–dc23   2012021364

ISBN 978-0-521-86900-3 Hardback
ISBN 978-0-521-68938-0 Paperback

Contents

Figures and Tables

Figures

Tables

Acknowledgments

As most authors will understand, writing this book was a labor of love, but one that demanded more time than I ever imagined. I appreciate the preternatural patience of Rita Wright, my friend and colleague, who commissioned me to write this overview of the Inca and then waited much longer than I had promised to see it come to fruition. I wish to thank Beatrice Rehl and the production staff of Cambridge University Press in New York for their meticulous work in bringing this book to its final, published form.

My graduate students in the Department of Anthropology at the University of Chicago have collaborated with me to articulate many of the theoretical concepts and interpretive directions in evidence throughout this book. In recent years, the roster of my current and former graduate students with whom I have most intensively worked on matters Andean includes Jonah Augustine, Zachary Chase, Nicole Couture, Anna Guengerich, Steven Kosiba, David Pacifico, Steven Scott, Edward Swenson, and Tien-Ann Tshih.

In particular, I deeply appreciate the substantive contribution of Zachary Chase and Steven Kosiba, with whom I shared many hours of vigorous, fruitful debate that resulted in the elaboration of the concepts of hegemony developed at length in the first chapter of this book. They are truly coauthors of this section of the chapter, and I acknowledge with deep appreciation their friendship and the intellectual stimulation they have provided me over the past few years.

I also wish to acknowledge Anna Guengerich's exceptional service as my research assistant during the latter stages of the production of this manuscript. Anna read the manuscript with skill and sensitivity to eliminate flaws of many kinds, ensuring that the text was coherent, consistent in its arguments, and as technically impeccable as possible. She handled all of the critical details concerning manuscript format and content, including citations, footnotes, maps, illustrations, and reproduction permissions, with efficiency and grace. In this latter regard, I also wish to thank the institutions and individuals who responded to Anna's requests and generously extended permission for the reproduction of the extraordinary graphics and images incorporated here.

Finally, I wish to dedicate this book to my wife, Anna, and my daughter, Justine, who traveled with me many times to Bolivia and Peru. They lived there for months on end enduring the rigors of high altitude, intense cold, driving rain, hurricane-force winds, sudden dust storms, lip-cracking aridity, and some of the most terrifying roads in the world. They also came to experience the intense, hallucinatory beauty of the Andean world and the deep generosity and spirituality of the Aymara people among whom we lived. Sharing all of this with Anna and Justine, the hardships and the beauty, makes this a life worth living.

Preface

In the fall of 1492, as the small fleet of Christopher Columbus approached landfall in the Caribbean, far to the southwest a native lord of the Andes was preparing to take dominion over the largest empire ever forged in the Americas. In that year, the Inca Wayna Qhapaq, the last independent heir to a remarkable Andean culture grounded in aggressive religious and cultural proselytism, found himself the supreme lord of a domain of startling proportions. The Incas' own name for their empire reflected their belief that they had conquered the known world: Tawantinsuyu, the "Four Parts Joined," or the Realm of the Four Quarters. The lands of this realm incorporated a dazzling and sharply juxtaposed series of physical landscapes that ranged over the territories of five modern Andean republics: Peru, Bolivia, Chile, Argentina, and Ecuador. The world of the Inca contained an astonishing array of radically different environmental zones, replete with brusque contrasts in climate, vegetation, topography, soil, and other more subtle biological and physical associations. This wild diversity of terrain, and therefore of ecological potential, represented both a significant impediment to the achievement of regional political integration and an exceptional concentration of natural resources with the potential to underwrite imperial-scale economies. Despite the physical difficulties of the terrain, Inca armies were able to extend the power of their lords from the tortuous, dissected mountain slopes and valleys of highland Peru to the perpetually arid coasts strung along the western margins of the South American continent, and from the humid, subtropical enclaves encrusted in the great eastern flanks of the Andean massif to the cold, austere, and seemingly endless high plains of the Lake Titicaca basin. The social obstacles that confronted the Inca political, economic, and military apparatus in its drive to power were no less bewildering in their diversity or daunting in their complexity. The Inca Empire, at its apogee, incorporated more than two hundred separate ethnic groups, most speaking mutually unintelligible languages. Their emperors strained to conquer, and then to administer, societies that covered the entire spectrum of human organization from small, mobile bands of hunters and gatherers who inhabited isolated areas in the densely forested regions of eastern Ecuador and Peru to the powerful, immensely wealthy indigenous states of the Pacific coast and the Andean high plateau, such as the kingdoms of the Chimú, Chincha, Lupaca, and Colla peoples.

Despite these formidable environmental and social barriers to empire, within the evanescent space of three generations during the fifteenth and early sixteenth centuries, the Incas succeeded in transforming themselves from a congeries of small, ethnically related social groups jockeying for power in the mountainous regions around Cuzco in southern Peru into the greatest single Native American political entity ever to emerge. Extending their authority over an area of some forty-eight hundred kilometers in length from north to south, they ruled over several million people and developed a massive imperial infrastructure, the material remains of which still inspire awe and admiration. No other Native American society, not the Aztec, Maya, Toltec, or Teotihuacán in Mesoamerica, ever forged an empire of such scope and social complexity. What, then, was special about the ancient Inca and their world?

Throughout the Andes, public works ordained by the emperors of the Incas dominated, and at times transformed, the natural landscape. Cities, temples and fortresses of stone, marvelously engineered roads cut through sheer mountain slopes, and, most especially, massive agricultural terraces and hydraulic works were emblematic of Inca power and productive capacity. Yet it is not so much these awesome material products of the Inca Empire that claim our curiosity but, rather, the social processes that brought them into being. What, for instance, were the cultural institutions that structured and gave impetus to the Incas' imperial ambition? What form of power did the Incas exercise over their conquered provinces far from their imperial capital of Cuzco? How did they mobilize the staggering labor force that was required to sustain their war machine while simultaneously erecting and maintaining extensive and monumental public works? What kind of perceptions, thought processes, and beliefs informed the Inca worldview, confirming in their own minds their right to rule other nations? What impact did the radical social transformation that the Incas experienced in their move toward statehood and imperial power have on the structure of the Inca nation itself and on other ethnic groups that they subjugated? These are the principal questions that will orient this book.

Answering these questions engages us in an exploration of the social history and the cultural dynamics of civilizations throughout the Andes. The imperial achievements of Tawantinsuyu were not simply the brilliant invention of the kings of Cuzco, the triumph of civilization over barbarism, as Inca court propagandists would have us believe. They had not occurred in a cultural vacuum. The roots of Inca civilization, much like those of their Mesoamerican counterparts, were firmly planted in the deep bedrock of earlier cultural traditions. Before the Incas, the political history of the Andes had been marked dramatically by the ebb and flow of other, more ancient states and empires. The Wari and Tiwanaku of the Andean highlands and *altiplano* had left an enduring legacy of state expansion in the same regions that the Incas would conquer some five hundred years later. Many of the organizational tools that the Incas used to bind local populations to the yoke of their government had been devised and elaborated in the centuries before the Inca by these early predatory states, and they had long been common currency in the pan-Andean repertoire of state formation. Similarly, on the desert coast of northern Peru, the kingdom of Chimor was once ruled by a dynasty of divine kings who had forcefully commanded the resources and the obeisance of a large population generations before the Incas even had pretensions to imperial rule. The richly decorated palaces and royal sepulchers at Chan Chan, the remarkable capital city of Chimor, had been the scenes of unimaginable exhibitions of kingly power and wealth when the first leaders of the Incas had been nothing more than competing petty warlords living in crudely fortified compounds. The ideology and practice of divine kingship, like other institutions that became indelibly associated with the Incas, were clearly not exclusive to the lords of Cuzco. The Inca inherited a rich stream of existing cultural beliefs, social institutions, political strategies, technological capacities, and economic systems that shaped the essential contours, if not the precise course, of their history.

The story of the Incas, who in 1492 were in the midst of extending their domain in the Andes, was the final pre-Columbian chapter of a complex saga of human adaptation over several millennia in a context of formidable environmental and social challenges. We will come to understand the Incas and their empire in terms of continuing interactions between individual and collective social agents pursuing their own interests and enduring sociocultural structures that shaped Andean societies over many generations. That is, we will come to know Inca society and history as the complex product of individual and collective agency and deeply embedded Andean social structures. This book, then, will do double duty, providing detailed descriptions and analyses of Inca history, social organization, political economy, statecraft, and religious ideology, while offering an interpretive framework of Inca society and politics derived from comparative social theory. As we shall see, the social structures, political concepts, economic systems, religious practices, strategies of power, and cultural dispositions of the Inca have general comparability to those of other indigenous states and empires, but they also possess unique features that make exploring the Realm of the Four Quarters a particularly fascinating study in social analysis.

A Note on Orthography

Many of the terms used in this book are Quechua, the language spoken by the Inca. In part because Quechua originally existed only as a spoken language, a great deal of variation in spelling continues to exist. Many scholars use an older system of standardization, based on Spanish orthography, and some terms may be recognizable to the reader in this form, such as "*quipu*" for "*khipu.*" In most cases, this book adopts spellings in accordance with the most recent system of standardization (post-1970s). Only those terms that are well known in their Hispanicized version retain these spellings here – including "Cuzco" and, of course, "Inca" (now often spelled "Inka").

1   Into the Realm of the Four Quarters

On September 24, 1572, clad in mourning and riding a mule bedecked in black velvet, Tupac Amaru, the last Inca king (Figure 1.1), slowly descended the vertiginous, stone-paved streets of Cuzco to its expansive main square. The streets, patios, parapets, and rooftops of the city, once the imperial capital of Tupac Amaru's illustrious forebears, teemed with Indian subjects as well as with Spanish citizens come to bear witness to an epochal event. Accompanied by a phalanx of four hundred native guards brandishing lances to push back the jostling crowd, the king solemnly mounted a scaffold newly erected in the square. On reaching the summit, Tupac Amaru silenced the boisterous crowd with a simple gesture. He then pronounced his final discourse, received the heartfelt consolation of his conquerors' priests, and laid his head on a chopping block. With little hesitation, the executioner seized Tupac Amaru's hair, exposed the king's neck, swiftly struck his head off "with a cutlass at one blow," and then held the severed head "high for all to see" (Hemming 1970:449).

Eyewitness accounts to this act of regicide concur that upon seeing the bloody head of Tupac Amaru suspended from the executioner's hand and later speared on an iron pike, the assembled throng of some fifteen thousand Indians broke into uninhibited "cries and wailings" (Toledo [1572], cited in Hemming 1970:449–450). This spontaneous outburst of lamentation and the subsequent worship of the king's lugubrious remains by his erstwhile subjects alarmed Viceroy Francisco Toledo, the supreme political authority in what had become Spanish Peru. After only two days, Toledo ordered Tupac Amaru's royal head removed from public display, rightfully perceiving that the natives' unconstrained eruption of despair and adoration of the king's mortal remains might become a threat to public order and a potential source of sedition and rebellion.

Toledo's campaign to eradicate the last vestiges of Inca rule did not end with the execution of Tupac Amaru. He implacably persecuted natives who claimed any measure of royal blood, or who had been ennobled by the Inca. Toledo secretly immolated the mummified remains of

1

1.1. Tupac Amaru, the last ruler of Tawantinsuyu, executed in 1572 by order of Viceroy Francisco Álvarez de Toledo, Count of Oropesa. (Copyright Museo Nacional de Antropología, Arqueología, e Historia)

Tupac Amaru's immediate royal predecessors, Titu Cusi and Manco Inca. In a complex sequence of initial collaboration, subsequent diplomacy, and eventual rebellion, Manco Inca had fled the onslaught of the Spanish conquest begun in 1532 and established a reduced but effective state of resistance in Vilcabamba, a densely forested, virtually trackless land to the northeast of Cuzco. Although the Spanish *conquistadors* had irrevocably seized effective political power in Inca Peru with their cunning, lightning-fast capture and subsequent execution of the Inca emperor Atawallpa on July 26, 1533, his proximate descendants, Manco Inca, Titu Cusi, and finally Tupac Amaru, managed to sustain an extended campaign of resistance to the new Spanish overlords who had humiliated, abused, and slaughtered the Inca noble families and their one-time subjects. They launched a series of harrowing guerilla-like actions and open-field battles in the countryside to harass and kill Spanish military forces, juridical authorities, priests, economic agents, and native collaborators. These last three kings of the Inca defended the small but autonomous bastion of Inca power in Vilcabamba with considerable tenacity and new tactical skills born of increasing recognition of the desires, military capabilities, and cultural proclivities of the Spanish invaders. They repeatedly sent emissaries to the Spanish authorities seeking recognition of their personal authority and right to ancestral properties and privileges, while simultaneously maintaining a state of resistance in the isolated hinterlands just beyond the reach of complete Spanish territorial control. Decades of negotiations seeking the final capitulation of these last independent members of the Inca royal dynasty yielded continued frustration for the Spanish Crown and deep unease among the citizens of Cuzco, who feared a devastating repeat of the full-scale Indian assault on the city led by Manco Inca in 1536. However, Toledo's arrival as viceroy in Peru in 1569 and his single-minded determination to eradicate the Inca dynastic line root and branch finally changed this seemingly intractable state of affairs.

The viceroy well understood the dangers to the Spanish Crown's new dominions in Peru embodied in the continuing existence of autonomous Inca nobles possessed of a palpable mystique of power and the still real capacity to mobilize thousands of Indian subjects. On Palm Sunday, April 14, 1572, Toledo acted decisively against this threat by declaring a war of "fire and blood" against the rebellious, "reprobate" Inca (Hemming 1970:424). By assembling military expeditions of overwhelming force and by exercising an iron will to annihilate the remnant of free Inca in Vilcabamba, Toledo rapidly accomplished his goal. Part of the Spanish expeditionary force under the command of Captain Martín García de Loyola finally tracked down Tupac Amaru, who was retreating from the front lines of the confrontation deeper into the jungles of Vilcabamba with his *qoya* (queen) and a few of his remaining military commanders and personal retainers. García de Loyola dragged Tupac Amaru in chains from the cloud forests of Vilcabamba to Cuzco, where the triumphal military expedition arrived on September 21, 1572, to the celebratory relief of Cuzco's Spanish citizens. Three days later, after a sham trial for sedition and rapid instruction in the elements of the Catholic faith, Tupac Amaru met his ignominious fate on the scaffold and with him the final, embodied remnants of the Inca Empire irrevocably disappeared.

But the power of indigenous mentalities, cultural dispositions, and social practices lingered long after the humiliation, immiseration, and extermination of Inca nobles. Throughout his tenure as viceroy, Toledo assiduously sought to destroy the icons of Inca religion and to eradicate indigenous religious practices. A genuine religious impulse to convert Indian "heathens" to Catholicism, and thereby bring them to salvation, may have been one of Toledo's motivating forces in his campaign to extirpate idolatry. Yet, a more compelling explanation of Toledo's relentless iconoclasm was the immediate political imperative to impose an orthodox, hierarchical social order that required the repression of heterodox practices. He intuitively understood that indigenous religious beliefs and social practices were a deep well of potential, long-term resistance to Spanish authority. Even more astutely, he realized that particular material objects, and the expression of religious sentiment mediated through objects, was the conceptual key to the meaning of Inca religion. Toledo assumed that destroying those objects held sacred by the natives would eradicate heterodox beliefs and practices by eliminating the oracular vehicles of their expression. Ironically, as we shall see, Toledo was preceded in this assumption by the Inca kings themselves, who had organized their own campaigns to extirpate the sacred objects (*wak'as*) of the natives they had subjected. Toledo was particularly anxious to locate the Inca idol of Punchao, the cast gold image of the young sun god that had a mimetic heart of dough fabricated from the desiccated fragments of the actual hearts of dead Inca kings placed in a golden chalice inside the statue's body (Hemming 1970:450). When Punchao was finally located in the custody of one of Tupac Amaru's generals in Vilcabamba, the idol was seized, stripped of its dazzling gold medallions, and dispatched to King Phillip of Spain. Viceroy Toledo recommended that the idol be sent to "His Holiness," the Roman Catholic pope, "in view of the power of the devil exercised through it, and the damage it has done since the time of the seventh Inca" (Toledo [1572], cited in Hemming 1970:450). This passage reveals just how much Toledo appreciated the efficacy and inherent political potency of religious objects. Moreover, his clandestine destruction of Inca royal mummies speaks volumes about his shrewd political instincts. Toledo clearly recognized the objects of power in the indigenous Andean world; even more critically for his purposes, he grasped the cultural power of objects.

How was it, then, that the decapitated head of an Inca king, heir only to a shattered empire, commanded such undiminished awe? Why were the desiccated corpses of former kings objects of such intense worship? What force compelled many subjects of the Inca to continue performing their assigned tributary duties to the vanquished state well after the

Spanish conquest of the realm? Why, in short, did the Inca have such a hold on the labor, imagination, and fealty of many, if not all, of their former subjects, even after it became painfully clear that they had irrevocably lost their domain to foreign invaders? Toledo intuited the presence of deep currents of social power that represented a potential challenge to Spanish authority sublimated beneath the surface of the Inca's abject military defeat. To definitively supplant the Inca so recently dominant in the Andes, Toledo sought to understand, and then to eliminate, the sources of that social power, whether these derived from the prestige of living noble lineages or from inert, yet deeply meaning-laden material objects.

The task of this book is similar to the challenge Toledo faced. To understand the Inca, we must understand the essence of social power in their world. How did the Inca themselves conceive of power? What beliefs, objects, social relations, economic forces, and political instruments did the Inca deploy to extend and consolidate their power? What roles did violence, coercion, diplomacy, sociality, religious sentiment, and the compulsive desire for renown, for wealth, and for power itself play in the story of the Inca Empire's emergence? In order to grapple with these questions, we must first analyze the nature of social power itself. Only then can we proceed to explore the specific fields of power that structured the Inca world and shaped the historical trajectory of their imperial ambitions.

The Elementary Forms of Social Power

Holding and exercising power of different forms and intensities lies at the heart of empire – the latter necessarily entails the former. But what kinds of social power did the Inca recognize, privilege, and deploy? How did they succeed in concentrating power to such a degree that in less than a century they were able to assemble the most extensive political entity that ever existed in the pre-Columbian Americas, far larger than any of the Aztec, Toltec, or Maya city-states in Mexico? What social, economic, political, and ideological forces converged in the Inca ruling classes that permitted them to transform their social order from a relatively small, bounded, and not notably powerful ethnic group, one among many in the south-central highlands of Peru, into a predatory state operating over a vast geopolitical space? What motivated them to do so? What, in other words, were the means and the ends of Inca social power? To understand the particular kinds and applications of power that underwrote the Inca drive toward political supremacy in the ancient Andean world, we must first consider the elementary forms of power more generally.

What is social power? How is it produced and circulated? What impact does the application of social power have on the parties involved in any power-laden transaction?

Broadly speaking, power is the capacity to produce causal effects, to transform an object, state of being, or social relationship through purposeful, intended actions. As John Scott notes, social power "is a form of causation that has its effects in and through social relations" (Scott 2001:1). In this sense, social power involves human agents, whether individuals or collectives (kin networks, classes, interest groups, political parties), exerting some kind of force, whether positive (persuasion, incentives) or negative (violence, coercion), on other agents to achieve a desired effect. In the sense I use the term here, one deeply relevant to class-stratified, hierarchical societies such as the Inca Empire, social power entails a dyadic relationship between "principals" (or paramount agents) and "subalterns" (subordinate agents).[1] The causal effects of such a dyadic relationship do not necessarily flow in one direction, that is, from a more powerful principal to a less powerful subaltern. The relationship can be a much more subtle form of mutual interdependence in which the beliefs, desires, actions, and social practices of subalterns can cause principals to alter their behavior to achieve a desired outcome. In other words, most forms of social relations entail a game of power in which each side of the dyad implements specific strategies to influence the behavior of the other. The rules of this power game, however, do not constitute a level playing field. By definition, dominant agents possess strategic social and political advantages that permit them to assert their will more fully and frequently than subalterns.

We can define two elementary forms of social power: interpersonal power and institutionalized, or state, power. These forms of social power are interdependent, but they operate on different scales. As the social theorist Michel Foucault observed, interpersonal power relates intimately to institutionalized structures of domination: "if we speak of structures or mechanisms of power, it is only insofar as we suppose that certain persons exercise power over others" (Foucault 1982:225). Both of these forms of social power are highly relevant to an analysis of the Inca.

The deployment of interpersonal power to effect social and political transformations is particularly characteristic of emergent, nonbureaucratic, and precapitalist state formations. Interpersonal power operates at the scale of face-to-face interaction; it is embodied power that relies on the personal characteristics of individuals asserting their desires in

[1] See Gramsci 1971:52.

immediate communication with others. The prominent sociologist Max Weber analyzed one dimension of interpersonal power in terms of the phenomenon of charisma, and the nature of charismatic leadership. This dimension of interpersonal power is central to understanding the emergence and rapid expansion of the Inca Empire. According to Weber, charismatic authority depends on special "gifts of mind and body" that permit an individual to appear extraordinary and imbued with supernatural or divine authority: the charismatic leader "must work miracles, if he wants to be a prophet. He must perform heroic deeds, if he wants to be a warlord" (Weber 1978:1114). Charismatic domination develops in contexts in which an individual exerts a kind of magnetic attraction on followers, who view the leader as having extraordinary skills and capacities to organize and motivate others, whether in politics, religion, the military, or any other collective social endeavor.

Charismatic leaders have a sense of a personal, often divinely inspired, mission that drives them in pursuit of their goals. According to Weber, the leader "seizes the task for which he is destined and demands that others obey and follow him by virtue of his mission," and the charismatic leader's domination of others finds justification "by virtue of a mission believed to be embodied in him" (Weber 1978:1112, 1117). The charismatic leader has the capacity to inspire deep emotions of awe, fervor, and reverence in followers because of both exceptional personal characteristics and a collective belief in this embodied, charismatic mission. Jeanne d'Arc, the fifteenth-century French religious visionary and military leader, was a classic example of a charismatic leader. But charismatic leaders can sustain their power of domination only if followers continue to have faith in the leaders' ability to perform extraordinary feats in service of their mission. Charisma is an evanescent personal quality completely dependent upon collective belief. If the leaders fail to continually "work miracles" or "perform heroic deeds," their charisma dissipates and their followers rapidly disappear. In this regard, charismatic leadership is a metastable form of rule that requires of the leader exquisite sensitivity and constant personal attention to his or her followers' attitudes and behaviors. An inherent flaw in charismatic leadership as an instrument of governance is the problem of succession. As a highly personal form of social power, charisma cannot be readily transferred from one person to another. A charismatic king will not necessarily beget an equally charismatic son or daughter to succeed him. In this sense, charisma as a pure form of interpersonal power is idiosyncratic and of a relatively short duration – limited to a single lifetime. Moreover, any attempt by a charismatic leader to routinize or institutionalize this personal form of social power inevitably transforms it into something other than charisma. Followers of the original charismatic leader and charismatic mission may lose faith in its efficacy, and the intense emotional bonds necessary to sustain this mission will dissolve. Routinization, institutionalization, and depersonalization of leadership are all anathema to charismatic authority.

Norbert Elias's observations on the distinction between charismatic and absolutist forms of kingship offer further insight into the nature of this form of leadership: "The charismatic ruler, unlike a consolidated [absolutist] government, usually possesses no established administrative apparatus outside his central group. For this reason, his personal power and individual superiority within the central group remain indispensable to the functioning of the apparatus. This defines the framework within which such a ruler must rule" (Elias 1983:124–126). Moreover, according to Elias, the charismatic ruler is "constantly required to prove himself directly in action and to take repeated risks.... [S]uccess in mastering incalculable crises legitimizes the ruler as 'charismatic' in the eyes of the central group and the subjects in the wider dominion. And the 'charismatic' character of the leader and his followers is maintained only as long as such crisis situations constantly recur or can be created" (Elias 1983:125–126). Charismatic kingship necessarily creates and re-creates a crisis mode of leadership. Personal acts of royal risk taking, or at least actions that the public perceives as entailing risk, are conceived in terms of an extraordinary capacity for engagement and personal intervention on the part of the charismatic leader. The grounds and warrants of charismatic royal power are in personal political action, public visibility of the ruler to the ruled, habitual resolution of crises, and the maintenance of social cohesion among the nobility. In sharp contrast, royal power in the absolutist state is grounded in universally and permanently defined legal conceptions, legitimized by legal text, not by personal action. The personal intervention and risk of the ruler is minimized, as is the need for continuous social interaction between the ruler and the ruled. Elsewhere I have argued that Andean, and specifically Inca, kingship as a form of charismatic power depended on a deeply ingrained cultural pattern of sociability (Kolata 1996, 2003). The mode of consciousness of this kind of power was subject oriented rather than the legally enmeshed frameworks of absolutist rule. Subject-oriented rule demanded constant engagement, or the perception of engagement, with subjugated populations at all levels of the social hierarchy by the king himself, by his representatives, or by his supernatural avatars. That is, the legitimacy of Inca kings required a peculiarly intense and continuous form of social exchange. This social exchange was not framed solely in terms of a circulation of commodities in tribute or gift form, but rather consisted of

a constantly shifting and strategically deployed manipulation of obligation, solidarity, social power, and instrumental resources. I will explore
these features of Inca kingship grounded in interpersonal, charismatic
authority in greater detail later in this book.

The second elementary form of social power is institutionalized
power. Some prominent theorists, including Max Weber (1978), envi-
sion power as a zero-sum game in which social power relies upon inherently hierarchical relations of domination and subordination: one side of
the dyadic pair achieves a favorable outcome only at the expense of the
other. Weber was particularly concerned with the process of the institutionalization of power, and the organizational vehicles for the application
of power. The classic framing structure for this perspective is that of the
authority embedded in the premodern and modern bureaucratic states
of Europe. Weber specifically concentrated on the means that states use
to deploy power and concluded, along with Leon Trotsky, that "every
state is founded on force." He further refined this view by defining states
as "a human community that (successfully) claims the monopoly of the
legitimate use of physical force within a given territory" and as "a relation of men dominating men, a relation supported by means of legitimate (i.e. considered to be legitimate) violence" (Weber 1958:77–78).
In such a relation, Weber argued, the distribution of power is inherently
asymmetrical: some agents will possess and implement more power than
others, and there will be a continual struggle for power that results in
clear winners and losers in the game. The principals in a dyadic power
relation are those individuals who hold the capacity through force to
constrain the actions and alternatives open to a subaltern. This concept
of social power emphasizes the fundamentally asymmetrical, coercive,
and repressive aspects of principals over subalterns.

When thinking about power, most people intuitively subscribe to a
concept similar to that articulated by Weber: power is force, or the threat
of force, applied by one party over another to extract some benefit, to
punish some infraction, or to constrain the other party's possibilities for
action. But, as Weber emphasized, for a state to succeed, the monopoly of force required to exercise power must be perceived as legitimate
by its citizens. Without this recognition of legitimacy, the state would
devolve into an anarchic, Hobbesian "war of all against all," destabiliz-
ing the very monopoly of power that underwrites the authority of the
state in the first instance. This, then, presents a conundrum: how can
violence, or the threat of violence, ever be perceived and accepted as
legitimate? This is a paradox that has various resolutions in terms of the
presumptive ends of power. The state may justify violence to maintain
internal security; to defend sovereign territory and natural resources; to

promote a "civilizing mission" among weaker, less developed states; or, in contemporary terms, perhaps to defend cultural ideals of "individual freedom of choice" or "universal human rights." All states attempt to justify their monopoly over the application of force through some claim to defense, security, and the need to create a pacified territory in which citizens can conduct productive pursuits unmolested. In other words, the legitimacy of a state's monopoly over force can be sustained only if citizens are persuaded of its necessity, even when the resulting application of force fetters their capacity for individual freedom of action. Why would citizens consent to subordinate themselves to the power of the state? One simple answer would be fear: fear of violence or coercion from the state's agents, or fear of violence from other sovereign powers. Whatever the state's claims to legitimacy may be, the salient watchwords for this conception of social power are differential capacity for autonomous action, hierarchy, domination, discipline, coercion, and extraction. These characteristics certainly comprised some dimensions of the Incas' power regime, but they are not sufficient to explain entirely how the Inca held and exercised social power.

Another influential vein of social thought analyzes power relations from a different, though potentially complementary, non-zero-sum game frame of reference. From this perspective, social power is not exclusively concentrated in concrete organizational forms or organs of the state. Rather, power is broadly diffused throughout society, in individuals and institutions, even if the most efficacious forms of power are not evenly distributed. This is the vision of power exemplified by Michel Foucault. Unlike Weber, Foucault focused on the diffused strategies and technologies of power that all social actors, principals and subalterns alike, reproduce, deploy, and often resist. As John Scott observes:

According to this view, power is the collective property of whole systems of cooperating actors, of the fields of social relations within which particular actors are located. At the same time, it stresses not the repressive aspects of power but the facilitative or "productive" aspects. Of particular importance are the communal mechanisms that result from the cultural, ideological, or discursive formations through which consensus is constituted.... [A]ll can gain from the use of power, and there need be no losers. (Scott 2001:9)

Whether it is true that we can imagine a consistent "win-win" proposition in any serious application of power, and that "there need be no losers," it is evident that for power to persist in some relatively stable form the consent of the governed is required. Consent can be coerced through acts or threats of force by the military, the police, judicial authorities, or other agents of discipline, or consent can be manufactured through

"cultural, ideological, or discursive formations." The former type of consent (which, of course, is not willing consent) is unstable and at some
point unsustainable since it relies on a strategy of imposition, the constant application of acts of force, violence, and coercion on unwilling,
alienated subjects. This state of "consent" is inherently limited since
unceasing subjugation of populations distributed across large geopolitical spaces requires virtually inexhaustible resources in the form of
standing armies, fortresses, garrisons, prisons, and a costly political
apparatus of surveillance. The means of sustaining unwilling consent in
subject populations rarely, if ever, justifies the ends of power to advance
the interests of the elite, ruling classes. Just as importantly, forcefully
imposed consent becomes, in time, a fertile breeding ground for revolu-
tionary sentiments, acts of subversion, and rebellion.

The latter type of "manufactured consent," derived from collective
cultural understandings, embeds consent in a fabric of shared values,
social structures, cultural predilections, and habitual practices. Even if
the social world inhabited by subject populations is inherently unequal,
a dominant class can often obtain the willing consent of subalterns
through ideologically formed strategies of socialization that "natural-
ize" the social order. This is the fundamental insight of Antonio Gramsci
(1971), who elaborated upon the concept of hegemony to explain the
apparent paradox of subalterns willingly acquiescing in their own subordination. Here I would note that, even in a Weberian zero-sum game
model, the power of a principal over a subaltern in the ongoing struggle for dominance consists most profoundly in the capacity to convince
subalterns that their interests lie in doing something that is, in fact, more
beneficial to the principals than to themselves, or even something that
may be "harmful to them or contrary to their deeper interests" (Scott
2001:3). That is, both persuasion and force can accomplish the same
ends of state power: ensuring compliance to the principals' desires. Of
the two, persuasion (and, as we shall see, the accompanying transformation of historical consciousness that is part and parcel of persuasion) is
often the more effective. Subalterns become invested in the system of
power relations even when they fully recognize their subordinate status.
They firmly believe that they draw sufficient material, emotional, and
even moral benefits from the institutionalized power relationship to justify their consent to subordination. Just as in the case of consent imposed
by force, fabricating the consent of the governed through persuasion
requires considerable economic resources since effective persuasion
most often demands a structure of incentives to induce and constantly
reinforce that consent. Dominant elites must pay close attention to the
material and moral claims and expectations of their subjects in order to

maintain their subalterns' acquiescence and active participation in the prevailing system of power relations. Both paramounts and subordinates are enmeshed in an interdependent system of expectations, obligations, claims, and behaviors. To ensure effective consent of the governed, the ruling classes must fund a system of incentives that often takes the form of strategic material rewards, such as grants of land, privileged access to strategic natural resources, costly religious festivals, state-sponsored pageants, public monuments, development of new infrastructure (roads, bridges, irrigation canals, agricultural terraces, and the like), and other elaborate, highly visible social benefits. The enormous economic costs of responding to the accelerating expectations of subjects while often simultaneously sustaining military campaigns of conquest can easily bankrupt a king and his court. History is replete with examples of penniless kings forced to go hat in hand for gifts and loans from wealthier subjects in order to maintain some semblance of power. Persuasion, like unrelenting force, has its costs, revealing the underlying fragility and evanescence of power. Although the game of power is not simply a cold calculation of costs and benefits, both paramounts and subordinates continually recalibrate their positions and their own interests within the framework of the constraints and opportunities that the prevailing power structure affords.

Expanding on the insights of Weber, Foucault, and Gramsci, I analyze these subtle kinds of power under the general term "hegemony," although my understanding of the term is not identical with that developed by Gramsci. I will define a number of distinct variants of hegemony and hegemonic processes grounded in the lineaments of social power defined by both Weber and Foucault. That is, as I define them, these hegemonic processes work as a dialectic of force and persuasion, domination and consent in such a way as to obscure the apparent contradiction between these seemingly opposed strategies of power. Historically, no state has relied on a single strategy of power. We see rather an event-contingent application of force and persuasion, domination and consent in various intensities and modalities depending on the political context. Power is never applied abstractly, in pure forms, but in various strategic combinations according to concrete, often shifting circumstances. In other words, social power is always situational. As we shall see, this more ample concept of social power in terms of hegemonies and hegemonic processes holds great relevance for understanding the Inca Empire's sources and applications of power.

What is the relationship between power in its elementary forms and the cultural phenomenon we refer to as hegemony? Hegemony specifically entails the production of political subjects embedded in a social hierarchy characterized by principals and subalterns (cf. Gramsci 1971:52). We might also be tempted to employ the analogous Hegelian terms of "master" and "slave," but this overstates the power of principals to produce intended causal effects on subalterns, and simultaneously understates the capacity and agency of subalterns to themselves produce intended causal effects on principals. Colloquially speaking, hegemony is a two-way street, even if the paramount agent who possesses the capacity to constrain the behavior of subordinate agents often heavily influences the rules of engagement. As John Scott notes: "[T]he exercise of power and the possibility of resistance to it establish a dialectic of control and autonomy, a balance of power that limits the actions of the participants in their interplay with each other" (Scott 2001:3). Yet Gramsci observed that the production of hegemonic power is never complete; it is always developing, linked to a process in which collective agents seek to fulfill a project of domination. Since the "dialectic of control and autonomy" involves the establishment of an interdependent relationship between opposing groups, a common idiom of practices, discourses, and symbols often emerges. As a result, sociocultural boundaries develop that serve to confine and frame possible actions. This does not mean that such a process necessarily leads to the oppressive constraint of human action and agency. Possibilities for action emerge out of a hegemonic process, just as others are eliminated. With regard to how individual subjects may perceive their choices for action, the process is both creative and constraining.

Contemporary anthropological applications of hegemony are deeply influenced by Gramsci's use of the concept to refer to the historically particular relationship between class formation and state consolidation in capitalist, industrial Europe. Unfortunately, much like Marx's concepts of value or class, hegemony has become an a priori expectation within anthropological research, something that analysts seek within any political process or period. If hegemony is to be a useful concept, it cannot be resolved into a single formula or "ideal type." However, it can be usefully partitioned into a set of heuristic categories that may then be the basis for further analytical comparison. Such categories are linked to specific kinds of claims to sovereignty, resulting in the production of particular kinds of political subjects.

Despite its ubiquitous application, hegemony remains a nebulous concept. Often hegemony refers to both a *period* of political domination and a *process* of establishing political domination. Although ideas of hegemony have been applied in a variety of ways, most anthropologists deploy the concept in one of two ways: either as "hegemony over" or as "hegemony between." Each of these applications entails different notions of political subjectivity – that is, different ideas of the degree to which subjects may reflect upon the conditions of their subordination. The concept of "hegemony over" is often employed in archaeological research to characterize hegemony as a historical period in which one class or group of people has come to dominate others politically. For instance, many scholars speak of Inca hegemony over other social groups forcibly incorporated into a centralized system of governance.[2] But this application does not address the invaluable Gramscian notion that hegemony is always a project in process, something never truly completed or fully congealed in social institutions. Instead, researchers applying the concept in this way focus on hegemony as an established program of political control and extended domination over people and territory – a formulation derived ultimately from a Weberian-style zero-sum game model. This interpretation of hegemony assumes that a dominant class is conscious of their motives and has implemented knowledge of how society should be organized, that is, that they have the capacity to reflect upon their claim to political dominance. The universality of this assumption is not self-evident. Instead of assuming ancient states to have "held" hegemony over others, we should consider how government agents attempt to establish dominance by claiming their political sovereignty over a specific territory or people. I will link such state projects seeking to attain "hegemony over" to two specific kinds of hegemony, which I term "laminar hegemony" and "viral hegemony." But I also emphasize that a project to establish "hegemony over" is rarely sustained as originally envisioned. Such projects often become significantly altered or even derailed by protracted, low-intensity conflicts and, at times, running battles among elites, self-interested state agents, and subaltern groups. In other words, various significant words, symbols, practices, objects, and places may originally be associated with an overt claim to sovereignty. These signs, substances, and practices inevitably become bound up in a hegemonic process through conflict, cooperation, resistance, collaboration, and emergent mutual recognition among all the players in the social arena.

"Hegemony between" specifically refers to the contested process during which one class seeks to implant and implement particular ideas and projects for the reorganization of the world. In this sense, hegemony refers less to a set of concrete ideas that correspond to a claim of sovereignty and more to the political process through which such ideas are born and disputed (Laclau and Mouffe 1985). Throughout such a process, different parties struggle over the definition of the symbols,

[2] E.g., D'Altroy 2002.

practices, objects, and places that both govern and organize everyday experience. "Hegemony between" considers such cultural and material substances to be hegemonic in that they are recognized to be politically salient by all parties involved, even though they may mean different things to different parties. This definition of hegemony refers to an ongoing process of struggle for meaning and resulting mutual recognition in which the contenders are acting as classes for themselves – as groups that have identified their own collective interests. In contrast to the "hegemony over" application, which often foregrounds a period of seemingly unchanging political sovereignty, the "hegemony between" application concentrates on a dynamic process through which certain symbols, practices, and places emerge as politically charged instruments that are claimed to be representative of a social order. This application underscores Gramsci's salient point that hegemony is never complete; it is a process through which different groups and political subjects are defined relative to the positions that they take on key issues.

Laminar and Viral Hegemonies

To understand the nature of hegemony at any given moment, one must recognize and account for the historical specificities of preexisting structures of power, authority, and rule. The creation and extension of hegemony can follow any number of structural pathways, depending on the nature of various externalities. In short, the conditions of possibility for and the specific character of hegemonic power directly depend on changes in the principles and structures of government prior to and throughout the process of hegemonic emergence. One can readily imagine, for instance, that it matters considerably for such an analysis if the historical trajectory of state formation and governance initially entailed the forceful imposition of direct control over territories, resources, and populations by some form of dominant political, economic, and military power, or if, instead, governance was sustained through indirect networks of political alliance, social exchange, and commodity circulation via trade and mutually accepted tributary or clientage relationships. A third possibility entails some dynamic combination of mutualism, articulation, and perhaps inadvertent co-constitution of political power by otherwise autonomous social groups.

Here I introduce three concepts that will further clarify the processes by which hegemonies may emerge. First, I elaborate on *laminar hegemony*, a concept used to describe the forceful imposition of governing principles. Second, I discuss *strategic viral hegemony*, a concept used to describe an explicit state strategy to incorporate people as citizens,

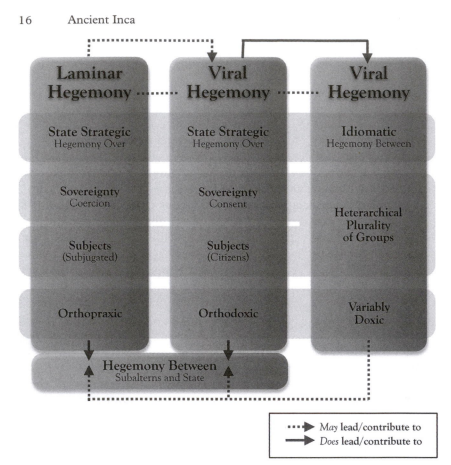

1.2. Laminar and viral hegemony

principally through the generation of consent. Finally, I consider *idio-matic viral hegemony*, a concept used to describe how ostensibly local yet idiomatically generalized political claims may condition the emergence of hegemonic symbols, practices, objects, or places (Figure 1.2). I separate these concepts for purely analytical purposes and stress that most, if not all, governmental strategies or political processes embed some elements of all three concepts. That is, these forms of hegemony possess both spatial and temporal variability. A given state formation, for instance, may simultaneously exercise or produce laminar and viral forms of hegemony in different territorial, temporal, and sociocultural contexts. This is particularly likely for expanding states and empires as the course of conquest, incorporation, and encapsulation of subject populations proceeds. As we shall see, this was certainly the case in the formation and consolidation of the Inca hegemonic process. Similarly, a state characterized by a laminar form of hegemony may over a period of time (e.g., decades or generations) produce a viral form of hegemony with specific material and ideological consequences.

Laminar Hegemony

Laminar hegemony refers to a state strategy that seeks to establish a period of "hegemony over" by setting into motion a process of coercive and disciplinary subjugation. Laminar hegemony seeks to produce compliant, subjugated populations, not autonomous citizens. Coercion and discipline become privileged instruments of power within this form of hegemony, even though governmental mechanisms that beget consent may also be employed. Here, territorial annexation, the imposition of externally derived laws and regulations, and often a powerful colonial ideology of a "civilizing mission" are central to the dynamics of governance. A necessary institutional correlate of this state strategy is the potential or actual deployment of military and police power. The physical embodiments of this power include chains of strategically placed fortresses, garrisons, and fortified walls, but also new colonial towns imposed in the countryside, often with streets laid out in visually transparent grid or radial forms to enhance the state's capacity for the surveillance, tracking, and taxing of subject populations. The strategy of laminar hegemony, in other words, reflects the militaristic logic and logistics of empire.

In a state formation structured according to a political strategy of laminar hegemony, the effects on the historical consciousness of subjugated populations may not be deeply transformative, but may remain fluid and potentially evanescent. The material presence or physical artifacts of the superordinate state rarely dominate local landscapes. Foreign-occupied military garrisons, and foreign-conceived and foreign-imposed colonial new towns either are few and far between or are entirely absent. I use the term "orthopraxy" to describe the everyday behaviors and experiences of subjects that are produced by a state strategy of laminar hegemony. By orthopraxy I mean social forms of practice that come close to the dominant patterns of behavior without adopting the underlying meaning or worldview inscribed in such practices. Subjects of laminar hegemony behave (publicly at least) in a fashion consistent with the expectations of state authorities. They may do so to avoid punishment or, perhaps just as likely, to extract social, political, or economic benefits from the dominant elite and state institutions. James Scott's analysis of domination and its relationship to the behavior of dominated subjects makes a similar point about orthopraxic behavior in terms of the power of "public transcripts," or sociopolitical narratives, that undergird and justify power relations:

The theatrical imperatives that normally prevail in situations of domination produce a public transcript in close conformity with how the dominant group would wish to have things appear. The dominant never control the stage absolutely, but their wishes normally prevail. In the short run, it is in the interests of the subordinate to produce a more or less credible performance, speaking the lines and making the gestures he knows are expected of him. (Scott 1990:4)

The performative behavior of local subjects is strategically mimetic and does not constitute thoroughgoing assimilation or conversion. In this sense, Scott (1990) refers to the "hidden transcripts" that subordinates relate and perform in the context of their more intimate social relations with family, friends, and peers. Such hidden transcripts often conflict with the public performances demanded by the prevailing power relationship. Over time, orthopraxic behavior can generate an uneasy and fluid synthesis of foreign (ostensibly dominant) and local (ostensibly subordinate) beliefs; express its own system that may partially incorporate, transform, or even reject foreign elements; and, importantly, constitute its own political strategy. So, even if they are at least partially transformed by foreign concepts and institutional practices as they interpenetrate them, local practices are recognized and represented as "local" by subjects. In this way, orthopraxy is a form of situational, pragmatic social practice formed in the crucible of unequal power relations. Yet, by initiating a process of "hegemony between," orthopraxy may condition the possibility for certain symbols, practices, objects, and places to become perceived as naturalized political phenomena.

This does not mean that in a complex state formation structured through the exercise of laminar hegemony social impacts on subject populations are negligible. Taxation of labor or products will often be onerous, even though institutional forms of extraction may remain local. Surplus inevitably flows away from the local communities into the coffers of both the local authorities (as was likely the case prior to foreign domination) and the distant, foreign elites. Although social, and especially economic, impacts on subject populations are considerable, they may be periodic, not chronic, and framed in terms of very specific social domains. At least initially, they do not seep into daily social practice or necessarily transform people's understanding of themselves or of their place in the world, even though such state installations may later be perceived as naturalized political representations. That is, a strategy for laminar hegemony may gradually develop into a process of viral hegemony (see Figure 1.2).

Viral Hegemony

The term "viral hegemony" refers to the manner in which cultural ideas and practices may become deeply embedded in a "body politic," flowing through the circulatory system of subjugated populations to the extent that they are no longer conceived to be a co-creation of social agents external and internal to the local society, but are perceived as the normative way of being. That is, viral hegemony involves the emergence of a set of political programs culminating in a situation in which the social significance of certain symbols, practices, objects, and places is no longer explicitly challenged, questioned, or even thought to be political. They become taken for granted as the natural order of things. As Comaroff and Comaroff observe, "[H]egemony ... exists in reciprocal interdependence with ideology: it is part of a dominant worldview which has been naturalized and, having hidden itself in orthodoxy, no more appears as ideology at all" (Comaroff and Comaroff 1991:25).

Owing to its covert power of insinuation, viral hegemony stands in contrast to laminar hegemony, the latter consisting of overt assertions to sovereignty over subjugated groups without the internalization of "naturalized" principles or practices. I distinguish two kinds of viral hegemony, strategic viral hegemony and idiomatic viral hegemony, by noting whether the emergence of hegemony is tied to an explicit political project (strategic) or to multiple, differentiated political claims (idiomatic).

Strategic Viral Hegemony

"Strategic viral hegemony" refers to a context in which a state attempts to dominate populations without actually administering them directly. In this instance, power and influence are exercised not by the unilateral imposition of administrative regulations, or by a centrally controlled bureaucracy, but by the strategic application of force – tactical force, not generalized military oppression – and by the "demonstration effects" of cultural superiority and awesome displays of material wealth, sumptuousness, conspicuous consumption, and superior military capability (Sahlins 2004). The intrusive, material presence of the state in local communities is much reduced, and often absent altogether, in favor of the co-optation of local institutions and facilities; displays of superiority (the demonstration effects) are frequently limited to capitals, where they may impress and overawe the local people.

In the dialectic of force and persuasion, strategic viral hegemony involves a claim to state sovereignty over people and territory, yet privileges interagent social relations based on negotiation, consensus, and affiliation. Here, forceful coercion by foreign authorities recedes before the state's structure of incentives to collaboration. The most powerful of these incentives is the extension of full citizenship to local populations, moving them from the status of "subjugated subjects" to that of "subject-citizens." Extreme cases of viral hegemony can produce a kind of society-wide Stockholm syndrome in which subject populations move their perception of newly dominant authorities from fear and loathing to identification, collaboration, and emulation. Short of extending the grant of citizenship, states of this viral form deploy a full range of inducements, including the right of subject populations (or perhaps more accurately their political leaders) to enter into lucrative trade agreements; massive capital and labor investments in regional infrastructure such as roads, warehouses, ports, and intensive agricultural systems; establishment of religious foundations with a full panoply of rites and festivals that incorporate local populations into broader social worlds; and grants of marriage alliances with high-ranking foreign authorities, among many more such incentives for cooperation and collaboration. Of course, such incentives are never equally distributed among subject populations, but are concentrated among local elites, congealing into long-term structures of social inequality and wealth stratification. Unless local elites collaborating with foreign authorities circulate some of the social and economic benefits of cooperation to the broader population, social ruptures between the haves and have-nots can emerge and weaken the causal effect of the hegemonic practices. In some instances, such ruptures can induce counterhegemonic resistance that pits foreign and local elites against the broad masses of the subjugated population. In such cases, urban riots and agrarian revolts may emerge along with other, subtler, forms of resistance to threaten the political stability of state power (Scott 1990).

By employing a strategy of viral hegemony, a state seeks to create conditions in which historical consciousness may be so thoroughly transformed that the dominated and the dominators come to broadly share the new ideology of social relations and governance. The project is to create a situation in which the political subjugation of local populations becomes naturalized. I use the term "orthodoxy" to describe the everyday behavior and experiences of subjects of a state strategy of viral hegemony. Behavioral orthodoxy is intimately associated with a viral process that attempts to transform historical consciousness. Habitual social, economic, religious, and ideological practice is intimately bound to belief.

Believers become citizens; citizens become believers. Subjects aspire to the values promoted by state authorities, often through religious practice. New communities of worship and social belonging are among the most effective vehicles for the transformation of historical consciousness that, in political terms, can be glossed as the transformation of subjects into citizens. In the world of orthodoxy, behavior and belief become isomorphic: subjects of the state do what they believe, and they believe what they do. Subjects become stakeholders and, in the process, willing agents of the state's social, economic, political, and cultural agendas and its status quo. In the calculus of cost versus benefits, orthodox citizens may profit from conforming their behavior to the dominant beliefs and practices of the state. Yet, such agents may also influence or transform the governmental apparatus by insisting that politics adhere to certain local conceptions of norms and belief. Since strategic viral hegemony involves the transformation of historical consciousness, such a strategy will entail the development of a matrix for political action that may continue even after a state has dissolved. I use the term "idiomatic viral hegemony" to refer to such a matrix.

Idiomatic Viral Hegemony

In contrast to strategic viral hegemony, idiomatic viral hegemony is not directly linked to any explicit state political strategy of regional consolidation or domination. The term "idiomatic viral hegemony" refers to the process by which hegemonic ideas, symbols, practices, objects, and places may emerge through an actual or potential struggle between different local agents or polities that are situated within a broader region. In other words, much like its strategic counterpart, idiomatic viral hegemony involves the naturalized or unquestioned acceptance of certain political ways of being. Throughout a process of idiomatic viral hegemony, such ideas and practices are simply thought of as being essential to "how politics is done," even if different social groups are using the same symbols, practices, things, or places to make markedly different kinds of political claims. In short, the distinction between strategic and idiomatic viral hegemony is a difference in scale and kind. While the former term refers to how hegemony emerges as the product of a state's claim to regional sovereignty, the latter term refers to the manner in which hegemonic political ideas and practices may emerge from the interaction of different politically autonomous social groups. These groups may then develop a shared set of sociocultural idioms allowing for the potentially antagonistic, yet also inadvertently unifying, mutual recognition of each group's authority, boundaries, identity, and sovereignty. In contrast to the other forms of hegemony, the emergence of idiomatic viral hegemony is not the intended effect of political claims to sovereignty; rather, it is the general outgrowth of a politics framed by plurality, heterarchy, and oftentimes opposing or mutually incompatible political claims.

The empirical correlates of such a process of idiomatic viral hegemony conform to our expectations of the kinds of material signatures that may be associated with a protracted process of "hegemony between." We should expect to see settlement patterns that are centered on local, authoritative places throughout a region. Although no one of these localized settlement clusters may seem to dominate the others in size or elaboration, each authoritative place should share certain key attributes, such as perimeter walls; well-defined and delimited economic resources (irrigated agricultural terraces, exclusive pasturelands, hunting and fishing grounds, and the like); links to mortuary complexes; and forms of internal organization that foreground key architectural elements like plazas. Such common attributes signify that a shared culture of politics characterized the region, even if each social group seems to have maintained some degree of political autonomy. A relevant Andean example of this form of idiomatic viral hegemony concerns historical processes occurring in the Late Intermediate Period from ca. 1000 to 1400, just prior to the emergence of Inca imperial expansion (see Chapter 2). This period in the south-central Andean highlands was characterized by political balkanization as well as the development of a shared regional framework allowing for the recognition of political authority (Kosiba 2009). A historical process of idiomatic viral hegemony may serve as a precursor to regional state formation and the implementation of more formalized strategies of hegemonic governance, as occurred with the emergence of the Inca state. On the other hand, a process of idiomatic viral hegemony may also result from the dissolution of states, during which different localized authorities vie for power and struggle for recognition by mobilizing the symbols and practices of the once-dominating state. Such a process may partially explain the efficacy and rapidity with which the Inca constituted their empire. In a matter of a few generations the Inca redeployed recognized instruments of coercion and induced consent that had been worked out by prior Andean states and empires. The effect of idiomatic viral hegemony on political consciousness and subjectivity differs from what we have seen within the strategic forms of hegemony. In this instance, subjects are both self-defined and socially recognized as localized actors that may be members of specific politically autonomous ethnic or social groupings. Yet, since a common vernacular of political practice emerges within a process of idiomatic viral hegemony, shared and mutually recognizable categories of subjects will be produced.

Power and Culture in Hegemonic Forms

In Gramsci's concept of hegemony, subaltern classes are "incomplete" and cannot conceive of, possess, or practice culture in any coherent way independent from politically dominant groups (Gramsci 1971:52–55). But historical encounters between expansive and local polities provide trenchant examples not of "culture[s] of resistance" but of the "resistance of culture" (Sahlins 2005; Wernke 2007:130). That is, power is not necessarily the sine qua non of all social interaction. My suggested approaches to the conceptualization of hegemony do not refer to all cultural practices and manifestations; hegemony and culture are not coterminous. However, hegemonic dynamics will always work through or within particular cultural means and media. Our task here will be to identify the specifically Inca cultural means and media that permitted Inca kings and their collaborators to shape one of the most effective hegemonic powers in the indigenous Americas. Throughout this book, I will use the conceptual tools provided by my foregoing definitions, categorization, and analysis of power and hegemonic processes to explain the Inca imperial achievement. Laminar, viral, strategic, and idiomatic forms of hegemonic processes were all implicated at different times and in different places in the course of the Inca's construction of their expansive, yet evanescent empire. As we shall see, scholars of the Inca disagree on the degree to which the Inca Empire constituted a self-identifying sociological and geopolitical category with a developed, or at least a developing, sense of unity and belonging among its subjects. The analytical concepts concerning the nature of social power and hegemonic processes developed here will help clarify this issue and will yield deeper insight into the fundamental nature of the Inca Empire as a historical and sociocultural phenomenon.

Analytical Categories

Before exploring the specifics of Inca culture and history, however, we must reflect on two other issues of social theory relevant to a nuanced understanding of the Inca. The first of these has to do with the tendency of scholars of the Andes to essentialize Andean peoples and their experiences, and to frame the analysis of Andean societies in terms of their utter "uniqueness." The second issue concerns the analytical categories that we use to describe and understand Inca beliefs, social practices, and institutions.

Few historical overviews of the Inca choose to grapple intensively with the broader theoretical implications of this society's political, social, economic, and religious structures and practices, or to place Inca-specific sociocultural phenomena in a comparative context. Two notable exceptions include Patterson's (1991) thoroughgoing Marxist analysis of the Inca Empire, and Zuidema's (1990) extensive structural analyses of Inca kinship, calendar systems, rituals, and semiotics. Most scholars of the Inca prefer to provide extended descriptions of Inca myths, political institutions, social organization, religious practices, physical settlements, and historical events based on the accounts of sixteenth-century Spanish chroniclers and on more recent archaeological investigations. These empirical and descriptive studies of the Inca are extremely valuable in themselves, and I will make considerable use of the synthetic information they provide.[3] But my strategy in this book will be different from previous overviews of the Inca. I intend to make sense of the Inca world and Inca cultural achievements in terms of general social theory, as well as in the context of some cultural comparisons with other premodern states. Unfortunately, cross-cultural comparison has not been favored by most scholars of the Inca, who appear to subscribe to a notion of Andean exceptionalism that assumes peoples in this region of the world (writ large across space and time) possess a unique, enduring set of interrelated cultural proclivities: a common fund of perceptions, values, symbols, and social, spatial, and material practices. The salient attributes of this presumptive Andean essence, a concept that has come to be termed *lo andino,* include the organization of political economies according to the socioenvironmental logic of verticality, social structures based on competitive and complementary dual organization, communal labor shaped by principles of reciprocity, and personal relationships between the human and physical world that are expressed in kinship terms. The *lo andino* perspective also assumes that the indigenous peoples of the Andes possess an almost preternatural capacity for resilience in the face of social and environmental shocks. I will explore all of these attributes throughout this book. These distinctive cultural tendencies and practices are inevitably intertwined with what is viewed as the singular geographical and ecological essence of the Andean natural environment.[4] One can readily understand why many scholars of the Andes subscribe to the *lo andino* paradigm. Among highland Andean peoples there are undeniable continuities from the pre-Hispanic past to the present in terms of basic forms of social structure, such as the *ayllu* and moiety forms of kinship and spatial organization that I will analyze in Chapter 3;

---

[3]   See, for example, D'Altroy 2002; Julien 2000; Rostworowski 1999; Rowe 1946.
[4]   For seminal essays, see Murra 2002.

the belief systems revolving around the complex concept of *wak'as*, or holy places and objects, that I discuss in Chapter 5; agricultural practices; and other cultural dispositions. There are also many historical ruptures and cultural transformations. But certain structural continuities are so striking that many Andeanists have adopted the *lo andino* concept as a convenient portmanteau explanation of the long-term persistence of core cultural beliefs and practices. Despite an argument that the *lo andino* paradigm carries a valuable "assumption of historical particularism" (Silverman 1992; D'Altroy 1992:9–10), the pervasive nature of the concept has actually impeded studies of historical particularities by proffering prefabricated and explicitly pan-Andean cultural explanations for local or regional historical and material data (Gelles 1995; Van Buren 1997). These reduce particular historical contexts to a generic Andean structure, a deterministic Andean "order of things." That is, the *lo andino* paradigm artificially flattens the contours of Andean lived, historical experience. At the same time, adherence to an unmediated *lo andino* perspective as an explanatory model inhibits broader anthropological comparisons of Andean data with data from other areas and cultures, encapsulating Andean scholarship (as well as peoples – past and present – living in the Andes) in an imagined, internally coherent discourse that is literally incomparable. The problem is not that the *lo andino* concept is entirely wrong, but that it has become the standard model for explaining virtually all Andean cultural and historical experience, having been converted into a kind of procrustean bed that excludes alternative explanations.

If we are to explore the historical experience of Andean peoples, and the Inca specifically, we must take into account social change, multiple processes of human agency, and the role of material conditions in human relations. The degree of structure in history should be empirically examined, not assumed. Structure does not determine individual or group agency, but it does impose sets of constraining circumstances (social, cultural, environmental). Here, one cannot help but cite Marx's famous dictum: "Men make their own history, but not in circumstances of their own choosing" (Marx 1852). Uncritically applied, the *lo andino* paradigm offers us the worst of all worlds: insufficient scope for individual human agency, bound up with the paradoxical notion of structures and constraining circumstances that are putatively unique to Andean historical experience. For this reason, I will explicitly place Inca social institutions, cultural practices, and lived, historical experiences in a cross-cultural perspective that will permit us to discover what, in fact, was unique to the Inca, and what was common to other premodern states, particularly in the ancient Americas.

Finally we must consider the issue of the categories that I will use to analyze Inca civilization. Many scholars have recognized that the indigenous, precapitalist states of the Americas (and, for that matter, of the premodern world in general) cannot be adequately understood through the use of contemporary Western analytical social categories such as economics, politics, religion, and social structure (D'Altroy 2002). These premodern societies did not make clear distinctions between politics and religion, for instance, so that kings and royal lineages were simultaneously warlords, holders of political office, and religious authorities – the high priests of the realm. Similarly, practices of production, such as intensive agriculture and herding, were not perceived as strictly instrumental practices, but as expressions of spirituality and habitual ritual practice as well. Further, society-wide social structures did not have an ontologically distinct status from other forms of associations, such as communities of religious worship, or voluntary affiliations of kin, fictive kin, and neighbors that shared labor, communal meals, and recreation. In other words, the distinct Western social categories with which we are most familiar in the contemporary capitalist moment were not relevant to the Inca understanding of their world. In that world, religion, politics, and economics merged and interpenetrated in terms of both habitual social practices and their meaning to the Inca. Many sacred sites and objects (*wak'as*) were fully enmeshed in systems of economic production. For instance, springs as sources of irrigation water facilitated economic activities, but they also served as sanctified origin points for the kin groups that cultivated the surrounding lands. The curated bodies of ancestors were holy objects that lineages worshipped and to which they sacrificed the first fruits of their harvests, but they were also the source of legitimacy and a tangible, public emblem of the right of lineages to occupy and cultivate their ancestral lands. They were simultaneously religious objects and the equivalent of property titles to productive resources. Rivers, trees, and carved rocks were all objects of religious devotion, yet they also functioned as political boundary markers, delimiting land, water sources, and traditionally recognized territory. Social structure, economics, politics, and religion were mutually interpenetrating and mutually implicatory. Although the chapter titles at the core of this book reflect Western analytical terms (the "Social Order," the "Economic Order," the "Moral Order," and the "Political Order"), they are not meant to imply that these different kinds of "order" had any separate reality for the Inca themselves. Rather, I use these designations to bring a narrative coherence to my analysis. In the course of this analysis, I will tack back and forth across these categories in each chapter to illustrate the complicated ways in which the Inca merged, in belief and practice, activities that we generally consider as discrete, bounded, and individually recognizable entities: economy, religion, politics, social structure. Perceiving just how these practices and beliefs interpenetrated in Inca society will reveal much of the distinctiveness and analytical interest of this civilization to our modern eyes.

2 Imperial Narratives: Sources and Origins

Epistemology and Historiography

How do we know what we know about the Inca Empire? On what methodological grounds and with what sources of information can we write a convincing historical narrative of the Inca people and their extraordinary social and political achievements? The Inca themselves left no written record of their history and social institutions based on a conventional alphabetic script. They relied instead on other media to record their deeds and to administer their empire. Inca technologies of reproducing and transmitting information included painting figural and abstract images on wooden plaques and *keros* (ceremonial drinking vessels) or weaving them into textiles. *Cantares*, or traditional songs, preserved the myths, legends, and histories of individuals and Inca noble lineages, especially the heroic deeds of the royal dynasty (Julien 2000:163; Niles 1999; Tomlinson 2007). Highly trained, professional cantors memorized the songs for performance during important public and lineage-based ceremonies, ensuring their transmission across generations. The Inca also encoded complex numerical data, such as census records, tribute tallies, and calendars, as well as literary and historical narratives, in *khipu*, or elaborately knotted, multicolored cords that were produced and interpreted by specialists called *khipu kamayuqkuna* (see Figure 3.14). Scholars have struggled to understand the code of the *khipu*. Despite recent progress based on analysis of binary structural attributes of the knot and cord arrays, these indigenous mnemonic devices produced by the Inca and their subjects remain undeciphered (Ascher and Ascher 1981; Quilter and Urton 2002; Urton 1998, 2003). The relatively small number of preserved pre-Columbian *khipu* (around six hundred survived the Spanish conquest); the apparent lack of standardization of information in conventional, repetitive forms; and the fact that *khipu* were produced and interpreted by an indigenous class of specialists (*khipu kamayuq*) who incorporated memorized, context-specific oral information into the code of individual *khipu* records indicate that these artifacts will never provide us with an emic history of the Inca Empire, that is, a history as perceived and recorded by the Inca themselves. To write Inca history and to reconstruct the social, economic, religious, and political institutions that they developed, we must rely principally on information derived from sources external to the Inca. Inevitably, any history of the Inca Empire will be based on categories and data derived from outside observers – an etic history – and will not be one written exclusively from the perspective of the Inca people as they actually lived and experienced their world.

In the absence of decipherable, written testimonies produced by the Inca, we have three substantive sources of knowledge about their world prior to contact with Europe: archaeology, ethnohistory, and ethnography. Yet how we choose to use and to critically evaluate these three sources of evidence to generate new knowledge about the Inca further complicates our empirical and interpretive enterprise. Archaeology offers us considerable empirical insight into the material basis of the Inca Empire, including human settlement structure, density, and distribution; principles and techniques of urban planning; technological dimensions of agricultural production; patterns of the fabrication and circulation of craft objects; evidence of mass consumption, commensalism, and related ritual practices; and much else that generated a tangible material signature. Ethnohistorical evidence, based principally on Spanish-authored chronicles, memoirs, administrative reports, litigation documents – all the literary production of the early Spanish colonial period beginning with the conquest of the Inca in 1532 – provides us with the lion's share of our specific information on dynastic histories, on social, economic, and religious institutions and practices, and on indigenous mentalities and dispositions. Ethnography, including nineteenth-century historical accounts, offers indirect, generic, but still useful information on certain deeply rooted, indigenous Andean institutions and practices that can serve as sources for hypotheses that can be tested by archaeological and ethnohistorical evidence. Here is where the strength of the *lo andino* perspective can be brought to bear on our analysis of the pre-European Andean world. We do know that certain social structures, environmental perceptions, and cultural dispositions, particularly the *ayllu*-moiety-*wak'a* complexes, persist into the twenty-first century, even though these institutions and modes of perception have undergone extensive transformation in the course of a half-millennium of encounters with the European world. Although not directly applicable to explaining the social world of the ancient Inca, these perduring forms of organizing social life and conceptualizing the relationship between the sacred and secular worlds offer us insights by analogy, as sources of plausible hypotheses about the deep structure of Inca society, and as one means of interpreting the material record left by the Inca.

Each of these kinds of information on Inca history, social institutions, economic organization, religious beliefs, and political practices presents interpretive challenges. In the absence of contemporary written texts, archaeological research cannot provide us with an event-based historical narrative of the Inca Empire, or reveal the critical strategies, thought processes, motivations, or decisions of individuals in Inca history. Ethnography offers us even less Inca-specific information given the enormous temporal and cultural divide between the Inca and contemporary Andean people. The most we can expect from ethnography is to use the observed, deeply rooted mentalities and practices of contemporary populations for hypotheses and analogical inferences with which to interpret ancient Inca society. The enormous corpus of sixteenth- and seventeenth-century documents produced during and after the Spanish conquest of the Inca remains our principal source for writing and interpreting Inca history. But such texts are not immediate, exact, or unambiguous renderings of an Inca history. They vary enormously in literary genre, authorial intent, and historiographical significance, reflecting the mutable political, social, and historical circumstances under which they were produced. The most information rich of these documents include chronicles of the conquest of the Inca Empire by Spanish soldiers, clergy, and functionaries; diaries, travelogues, and memoirs written in the aftermath of conquest; appeals to the Spanish court for grants of property rights, labor, and resources; administrative edicts generated during the long process of European colonization; synthetic "histories" of the Inca based on interviews of native informants commissioned by Spanish administrators to justify domination over and appropriation of the Inca Empire; and detailed descriptions of Inca "idolatry" intended to facilitate eradication of Inca religious sentiments and practices that might be a potential source of sedition and, in theory, to accelerate conversion to Christianity.

Even if we could recover with perfect fidelity the cultural memories of the principal actors in the Inca Empire, such recollections would not provide an unmediated, comprehensive account of the *res gestae*, the things that actually occurred in the course of the empire's history. The events and actions deemed worthy of preservation in the Inca's orally transmitted memories, performances, and graphic media changed over time, so that there was never one objective, unvarnished history of the empire that all parties considered accurate and faithful to the "truth" of events. As in many imperial societies, historical truth in the Inca realm was in the eye of the beholder. Only the victors made history. For instance, Pedro de Cieza de León, the exceptionally perceptive Spanish soldier and chronicler of the Inca, observed that if an Inca king "had been so successful that he left behind laudable fame and deserved to live forever in their memory because of his bravery and good government, they would send for the great *khipu camayoc*, who kept the accounts and could tell the things that had taken place in the kingdom ... and if any of the kings turned out to be a coward, given to vices, and a braggart without having expanded the empire's dominion, they would order that little or no memory of him be kept" (Cieza de León 1976:187). As Kosiba astutely observes, the Inca elite often went much further than simply editing out the memory of their predecessors and rival claimants to the throne "by forcibly erasing the claims and memories of rival factions – killing their members and confiscating their land. In short, if there was an Inka sense of their 'history,' then it certainly was a politically charged and ever-changing history, and not the static, generalized and monolithic meta-narrative of [Inca] history that was often rendered by the Spanish" (Kosiba 2009:55). The constant rewriting of dynastic history by Inca kings, courtiers, and claimants to the throne complicates the task of reconstructing the events and processes that led to the emergence, expansion, and consolidation of the Inca Empire. We are forced to reconstruct Inca history through multiple self-serving, often contradictory, redactions produced by this king or that noble faction, conveyed through authors writing principally in European languages and with a conceptual framework alien to indigenous mentalities. The persona, social status, political power, and strategic interests of our informants profoundly shape the history that we can write. So, of necessity, any history of the Inca Empire will be fragmentary and multiperspectival.

Equally problematic for the task of writing Inca history, all of the chronicles, memoirs, interviews, inquisitions, administrative documents, and other kinds of texts produced in the course of European colonization were shaped by the subjective perspectives, biases, political agendas, and individual intentions of their authors, whether of Spanish, *mestizo*, or indigenous origin. For instance, Juan de Betanzos, the influential Spanish chronicler and master translator of Quechua – the Inca lingua franca – married into a faction of the Inca royal family and, based on their firsthand testimony, wrote his great narrative of Inca history. Betanzos's wife, originally named Cuxirimay Ocllo, was the niece of the last independent Inca emperor, Wayna Qhapaq. Shortly before the Spanish conquest of the Inca in 1532 and when she was just ten years old, she married King Atawallpa. After Atawallpa's execution by the Spanish, Cuxirimay Ocllo, baptized into the Christian faith as Doña Angelina Yupanque, became Francisco Pizarro's mistress, bearing the conquistador two sons before

Pizarro himself was assassinated in 1540. Betanzos's subsequent marriage to Doña Angelina brought him wealth and unfettered access to the memories of his wife and her kinfolk. As a result, Betanzos's richly detailed narrative of Inca history presents the particular political perspective of his affines, recording their self-interested memories and testimonies as if they were an "official" rendering of Inca history. Not surprisingly, in Betanzos's narrative, the figure of King Pachakuti, the progenitor of Doña Angelina Yupanque's lineage, becomes an unalloyed culture hero responsible for virtually all of the extraordinary organizational and political achievements of the Inca Empire.

A similar instance of history writing influenced by the author's subject position is that of Pedro Sarmiento de Gamboa. Sarmiento claimed to have written an objective history of the Inca realm by interviewing dozens of native informants and cross-checking their recollections of pivotal individuals and historical events. In reality, Francisco Toledo, newly installed as viceroy of Peru, had commissioned Sarmiento to write a history that would explicitly portray Inca kings as tyrants who had usurped the power of indigenous "natural lords" and therefore had no legal justification to rule. In other words, Sarmiento's manuscript was not a dispassionate, objective narrative of the Inca, but a purpose-driven history written in the service of the Spanish Empire and the specific regime of regulations and governance instituted in the colony by his viceregal patron.

Clearly such texts cannot be read as if they were a transparent or objective record of Inca history. Rather, they must be critically evaluated and interpreted through an explicit methodological and theoretical frame of reference. In this respect, two principal approaches have emerged among scholars of the Inca: one can be referred to as the "historicist" perspective, and the other as the "structuralist" perspective. These two schools of thought have sharply divergent understandings of the value of these sixteenth- and seventeenth-century documents for writing a verifiable, narrative history of the Inca; they also operate with distinct, contrasting hermeneutics.

Scholars subscribing to the historicist perspective believe that close, comparative reading of various Spanish chronicles, memoirs, litigation documents, and administrative texts reveals consistencies, convergences, and, occasionally, telling discrepancies in the texts that reflect true historical events, as well as elements of the personal biographies of Inca kings and other influential actors in the empire. Scholars taking this perspective, pioneered by the ethnohistorian John Rowe (1946, 1967, 1982, 1986), believe that by aligning the accounts of different chroniclers, careful comparative readings can extract a reasonably accurate, fact-based, and chronology-driven history of the Inca familiar to conventional Western standards of historiography. Proponents of the structuralist perspective, on the other hand, contest the methodological validity and historical accuracy of the historicist's approach. Because of the many constraints on deriving a conventional, fact-based history of the Inca, including the absence of native texts and the Incas' own lack of interest in recording an "objective" history of their past, structuralist scholars of the Inca, notably R. T. Zuidema, the most influential proponent of this approach, read the chronicles and indigenous testimonies as metaphoric renderings of deeply seated Inca (and more generally indigenous Andean) organizational structures, institutions, and mentalities rather than as faithful records of actual individual actions and past events. Structuralist scholars[1] seek not to reconstruct some putatively objective history of the Inca, which they believe to be unattainable, but instead use the chronicles and other Spanish documentary evidence to derive an interpretation of the deeply embedded organizing principles, cultural attributes, and social values that shaped life in the Inca Empire.

The approach of this book is essentially structuralist. I will seek here an analytical and institutional history of the Inca, not a history of events and the lives of particular individuals. This does not mean, however, that I take a strictly structuralist perspective that no conventional historical narrative composed of reconstructed events or the actions of identifiable individuals is possible for the Inca. One cannot deny that the Inca Empire emerged from the effects of specific individuals and decision makers responding strategically to political events and historical contingencies. The traces of their actions on the expansion and consolidation of the empire can be plausibly reconstructed, if not absolutely verified, through the memories and oral accounts of native informants interviewed by the Spanish. Although the Inca were not concerned with time reckoning in terms of an unbroken, linear accumulation of years, but rather emphasized seasonal and annual cycles, native informants encountered by the Spanish certainly had the ability to remember individuals and events extending back at least one or two generations. If we accept that people have the capacity to recall with reasonable fidelity salient events in their parents' and grandparents' lives, then the testimonies given by Inca informants in the early decades after the Spanish conquest in 1532 offer the opportunity to sketch a plausible, event-based, chronological narrative of the late history and eventual destruction of the Inca Empire.

[1] See, for example, Duviols 1973, 1979; Pease 1978, 1981, 1982; Sherbondy 1982, 1992; Zuidema 1964, 1982a, 1983a, 1983b, 1989a, 1989b.

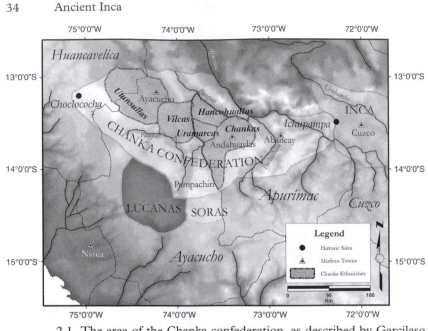

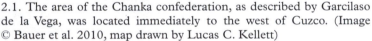

2.1. The area of the Chanka confederation, as described by Garcilaso de la Vega, was located immediately to the west of Cuzco. (Image © Bauer et al. 2010, map drawn by Lucas C. Kellett)

The historicist scholar John Rowe (1945), relying principally on the chronological inferences of the Spanish cleric Miguel de Cabello Balboa (1951), established a standard historical account of the emergence of the Inca Empire that begins with the ascension to the throne of King Pachakuti in 1438, ostensibly as the result of a resounding victory in an interethnic war between the Inca and the powerful, confederated military forces of the Chanka people, who lived to the northwest of the Inca homeland (Figure 2.1). Subsequent military expansions and political consolidation of the empire are attributed in this standard account to the reigns of Pachakuti's descendants: Thupa Inka Yupanki (ca. 1471–1492), Wayna Qhapaq (ca. 1493–1527), Waskhar (ca. 1527–1532), and Atawallpa (ca. 1527–1533) (Figure 2.2). The latter two royals reigned simultaneously as rival half-siblings engaged in a bitter civil war for supremacy that ended with a short-lived victory by Atawallpa, who, at the moment of his exceedingly bloody victory over the forces of Waskhar, was himself captured and executed by Francisco Pizarro in 1533.

Although several of our Spanish sources record the names and associated deeds of kings who lived prior to Pachakuti, we can have little confidence in the historical veracity of any presumptive preimperial dynasties

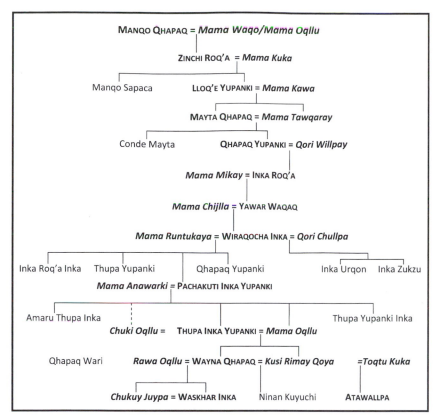

2.2. Genealogy of Inca kings with principal queens and royal offspring. (Adapted from D'Altroy 2002)

of the Inca. Beyond this three-generational threshold, human memory and the oral transmission of events lose resolution. Even if we assume that the *khipu kamayuqkuna* faithfully recorded events and historical narratives and succeeded in training subsequent generations of specialists in reading the contents embedded in individual *khipu*, the encoded information would have been the self-interested product of particular political factions, nobles, and kinship groups, not an unambiguous source of "true" history – *res gestae*. For instance, the epochal battle between Pachakuti and the war chiefs of the Chanka ethnic group that putatively set the Inca on the path to imperial domination of the Andes may, in fact, have been a mytho-historical rendering of a more protracted period of interethnic conflict in which the Inca eventually emerged victorious over a period of several generations, not simply the sudden, glorious

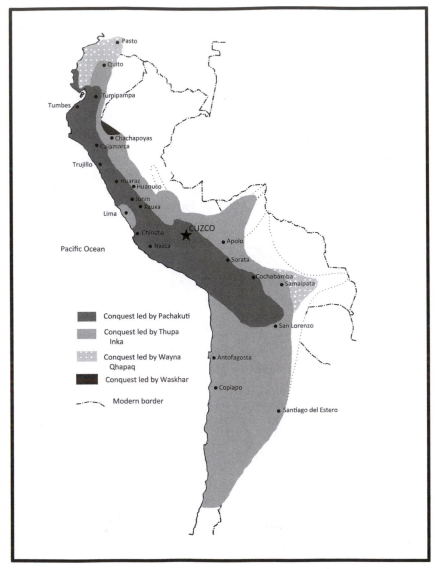

2.3. The successive expansion of the Inca Empire between the reigns of Pachakuti and Waskhar, as reconstructed by Martti Pärssinen from multiple historical documents. (Adapted from D'Altroy 2002)

result of Pachakuti's indomitable will to power (Rostworowski 1999:28–29; D'Altroy 2002:65).

Reconstructing Inca history in terms of conventional Western historiography is fraught with ambiguity and constrained by a lack of detailed contemporaneous testimony. Yet scholars working from the historicist perspective have made a plausible argument, mostly corroborated by archaeological evidence, that beyond its immediate Cuzco-centered heartland, the Inca Empire emerged rapidly, in the space of a few generations, beginning in the mid-fifteenth century (Figure 2.3). This frenetic, expansionary phase of late Inca history between about 1450 and 1525 may, indeed, have been the product of three great warrior-kings: Pachakuti, his son Thupa Inka Yupanki, and his grandson Wayna Qhapaq (Pärssinen 1992). There is ample historical precedent for well-organized and hyperaggressive warlords expanding their control suddenly across vast stretches of territory, subduing dozens of ethnic groups. Here one thinks of the spectacular career of Timuchin, better known by his title, Chinggis (or Ghengis) Khan, architect of the vast Mongolian Empire. Born in the 1160s, Timuchin gradually unified disparate Mongolian tribal groups and in 1206 was elected "Universal Ruler." By the time of his death in 1227, just twenty-one years after ascending to the throne, he had created one of the most expansive preindustrial empires the world has ever seen, extending across vast stretches of Eastern Europe into northern China and, by 1241, from Siberia to Vietnam. Chinggis Khan's lightning-quick conquest was enabled by his superior military strategy based on a highly trained, mobile cavalry organized into decimal units for ease of communication and logistical coordination on the battlefield. As we shall see, the Inca developed similar organizational, logistical, and strategic tools that facilitated their own rapid expansion across the Andes. But before analyzing the instruments of Inca social power, I will briefly sketch the spatial and temporal framework of their political history from their emergence as a recognizable polity in the thirteenth century.

Inca Emergence

Like all empires, that of the Inca did not develop in a cultural or historical vacuum. Centuries prior to the Inca's assumption of imperial power, other ethnic groups had created expansive, predatory states and generated instruments of concentrated social power upon which the Inca later elaborated. At least two earlier episodes of imperial power can be recognized in the archaeological record: that of the people of Wari centered near the modern Peruvian city of Ayacucho, and that of the partially contemporaneous Tiwanaku people in the Andean *altiplano* (Figure 2.4). In the period from ca. 500 to 800, the people of Wari expanded throughout the Andean highlands from the edge of the Andean *altiplano* near the border between Peru and Bolivia into the northern highlands of Peru. Based principally on graphic martial iconography incorporated into

2.4. Expansive Andean polities prior to the Inca Empire: Tiwanaku, with its capital at the city of Tiwanaku (AD 400–1100); Wari, with its capital at Wari (Huari) (AD 600–1000); and the kingdom of Chimor, with its capital at Chan Chan (AD 1000–1475)

textiles, ceramic vessels, and other forms of portable objects, most scholars of the Wari attribute their expansion to violent military conquest. Archaeological evidence reveals a highly stratified society organized into distinct social classes and military orders with the capability of mobilizing collective human labor on a massive scale. Wari nobility founded administrative centers throughout their domain. These colonial towns

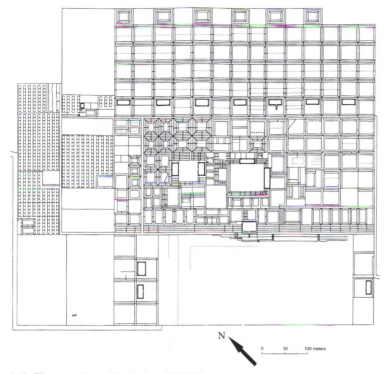

2.5. The pre-Inca Wari site of Pikillacta, near Cuzco. (Adapted from McEwan 2005)

were often built on the precisely executed plan of a modular, orthogonal grid, suggesting a desire on the part of the architects to impose "legibility" on the urban environment in order to closely monitor and manipulate the circulation of information, goods, and people (Isbell and McEwan 1991; Schreiber 1992). Principal examples of Wari colonial new towns that shared spatial canons facilitating surveillance and population control include the extensive, stone-built cities of Pikillacta, some 250 kilometers southeast of Wari's capital (Figure 2.5), and Viracochapampa, located 700 kilometers north of the capital (McEwan 2005) (Figure 2.6). Apart from architectural designs intended to manipulate the flow of people and goods, Wari administrators also employed the complex *khipu* accounting devices associated most closely with Inca administrative techniques. Similarly, like the Inca, the people of Wari also developed technically complex agricultural systems based on irrigated terraces for the production of prestige crops, especially maize, as

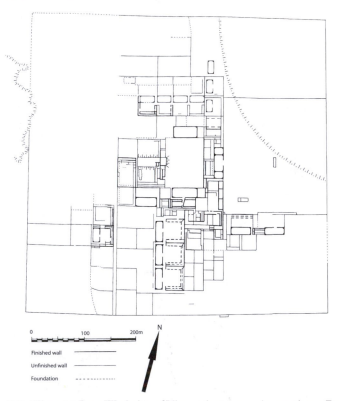

0   100   200m   N

Finished wall   ————————
Unfinished wall   ————————
Foundation   - - - - - - - - -

2.6. The pre-Inca Wari site of Viracochapampa, in northern Peru near Huamachuco. (Adapted from Isbell and McEwan 1991)

well as highland and coastal road networks that articulated different subject groups and territories. Although constructed on a less massive scale, these Wari infrastructural projects were clear precursors of Inca technical achievements produced some five hundred years later (Isbell 2008; Schreiber 1992). That is, Wari organizational, logistical, and infrastructural structures and processes likely served as significant historical models or templates for the architects of the Inca imperium, facilitating the Inca's rapid geopolitical expansion.

Wari imperial expansion can readily be analyzed in terms of my concept of laminar hegemony. As noted earlier, the Wari Empire created and circulated objects in multiple media infused with ubiquitous representations of warriors and other graphic martial iconography, established strategically placed military garrisons, and imposed colonial towns designed as instruments of social control and economic extraction in

the countryside of subject populations. This is precisely the material signature one would anticipate from a political system that perpetuated a
laminar form of hegemony. Whether Wari's laminar form of hegemony
developed over time into a more deeply engrained form of viral hegemony that transformed the historical consciousness of subject populations to the point at which the social hierarchy and worldview imposed
by the Wari Empire was "naturalized" and accepted as an unquestion-
able ontological structure is still an open question. This can be resolved
only by more systematic archaeological and art historical research, particularly into the material culture produced and propagated over generations in the households of subject populations. Such research could
help us understand if the Wari worldview, political structure, and "way
of being" had penetrated into the households of subject populations
throughout its realm and transformed itself into an orthodoxy that
no longer appeared as an explicit ideology of the self-interested elite.
Populations in the Inca Empire were subjected to the coercive, laminar
forms of hegemony similar to that imposed by Wari, but, over a period of
two or three generations, at least some Inca subjects became enmeshed
in viral forms of hegemony in which Inca rule came to be understood
as the natural "order of things." These subjects became willing collaborators and, despite their status as social inferiors, were able to extract
distinct material advantages by manipulating the obligations and claims
inhering in their political relationships with the Inca.

At approximately the same time that Wari was beginning to expand
politically and militarily throughout the central Andean highlands,
Tiwanaku had emerged as the principal hegemonic power in the Lake
Titicaca basin and *altiplano* regions of the southern Andes (Kolata 1993,
1996, 2003). Wari and Tiwanaku share significant elements of religious
iconography, particularly the image of the "Gateway God" that appears
in its most prominent, complex, and elegant forms in the monumental stone sculptures of Tiwanaku (Figure 2.7). This pre-Inca deity was
assimilated into Inca concepts of a creator deity called Viracocha, as well
as the manifold celestial and solar complex focused on the deity called
Inti, explored in greater detail in Chapter 5 (Demarest 1981). Evidently,
a considerable component of Tiwanaku's political power derived from its
key role as a center of religious expression and pilgrimage. The extensive
spatial distribution and temporal persistence of its religious iconography
implies that Tiwanaku's political authority entailed the emergence of both
strategic and idiomatic forms of viral hegemony, rather than the imposition of a coercive, laminar hegemony. The prestige of Tiwanaku religious
beliefs and practices contributed significantly to the consolidation of its
political authority throughout the Andean *altiplano*, obviating the need

2.7. The "Gateway God" with attendants from the Gateway of the Sun at the site of Tiwanaku. This deity shares similar characteristics with the later Aymara deity Thunupa and with the Inca deity Inti-Illapa. (Image from Posnansky 1945)

for excessive, sustained military force. Yet this is not to say that Tiwanaku constituted a kind of peaceful theocracy operating exclusively within a social network that relied on political consensus and shared religious practice. Substantial archaeological evidence reveals that the Tiwanaku ruling elite did not shy from exerting strategic violence through spectacular displays of decapitation and human sacrifice (Kolata 1993, 2003:chapter 7). Whether tactical warfare was also part of the Tiwanaku elite's repertoire of political instruments remains unclear, though this is likely given the evidence currently at hand. In the case of preindustrial states such as Tiwanaku we must always be aware of the interplay of force and persuasion, of laminar versus viral forms of hegemony and how these interacted and interpenetrated over space and time.

Well after the city of Tiwanaku fell into ruins in the mid-twelfth century, the Inca still considered it and the nearby islands of Lake Titicaca among the most sacred locales in their realm, attesting to the enduring cultural prestige of Tiwanaku in Andean religious belief and practices. Inca kings commissioned large agricultural terrace and shrine complexes on the Islands of the Sun and Moon in Lake Titicaca that were previously the sites of important Tiwanaku ritual activity (Bauer and Stanish 2001; Seddon 1998). Inca rulers appear to have made a particular effort to identify themselves with Tiwanaku and Lake Titicaca as wellsprings of religious and ideological identity. Some scholars have even raised the possibility that Inca nobility originated from earlier dynasties who reigned at Tiwanaku and in the Lake Titicaca basin, and that the Inca "secret" court language was a dialect of Aymara, one of the principal indigenous languages of the *altiplano* (McEwan 2008; Torero 2002). The extent to which the Inca political achievement built upon Wari and Tiwanaku antecedents is still unclear and remains the focus of intense speculation and some empirical research. But the evidence does indicate that the Inca drew upon more ancient cultural streams to construct, organize, and govern the Realm of the Four Quarters. That is, the Inca Empire, despite (or perhaps because of) the extraordinary rapidity of its emergence, could not and did not develop in a vacuum.

Once the Inca began their own phase of imperial conquests, they encountered a range of societies from small-scale hunting and gathering groups in the tropical forests east of the Andes to powerful kingdoms and nascent empires on the desert coasts of Peru whose technological, social, and ideological concepts, practices, and innovations heavily influenced the conquerors. John Rowe (1948) argued that a prime example of exogenous cultural impact on the Inca derived from their conquest of the kingdom of Chimor, a complex polity that emerged on the desert coast of northern Peru during the period between ca. 1000 and 1470. The kingdom of Chimor was an enormously wealthy, intensely hierarchical society governed by a series of divine kings and allied aristocratic lineages centered in the political and religious capital of Chan Chan near the modern Peruvian city of Trujillo (Kolata 1990, 1997). Chan Chan was literally a city of kings. Social life in the city revolved around elaborate protocols of courtly etiquette and ritual attended by aristocratic families constantly jockeying to enhance their political power and social prestige by demonstrating their proximity to the royal household. The social order of both the capital and the larger kingdom was marked by strict sumptuary laws that indexed and publicly displayed the enormous social distance between the governing noble houses and the popular classes who constituted the labor force for Chimor. The deep class division between aristocrats and commoners was inscribed in the very ontological and cosmological concepts of a kingdom in which nobles were believed to descend from one set of stars and commoners from another (Rowe 1948). Perhaps the most extravagant cultural displays produced in the kingdom of Chimor were intended to intensify

2.8. This doorway at the site of Tambo Colorado reveals the blending of cultural traditions that was entailed in the creation of the Inca Empire. Although constructed in a traditionally Inca trapezoidal form, it is made of adobe bricks, an ancient construction material that had long been a trademark of coastal societies such as Chimor. (Image courtesy of author)

the awe, reverence, and courtly spectacle that adhered to the person of the king, and by extension to his royal household. Each of the kings of Chimor constructed opulent palaces incorporating elegantly appointed interior plazas intended for hosting the feasts, court rituals, and shared discourses that fueled the commensal politics of the realm. These palaces contained capacious, secure storehouses that held the tributary wealth of precious commodities that flowed to the capital, as well as a lavish mortuary compound designed to house the king and many of his relatives and retainers who accompanied him in the afterlife. The overwhelming material wealth of Chimor, reflected in its magnificent public monuments, well-tended royal estates, expansive multivalley irrigation systems, multiple administrative citadels, and vast troves of splendidly crafted ceremonial clothing, gold masks, scepters, drinking vessels, table wares, and countless other precious objects used by the aristocratic households in displays of power and authority, clearly had a significant cultural and, most likely, psychological impact on the Inca nobility. After Thupa Inka Yupanki conquered the kingdom of Chimor sometime between 1470 and 1475, he seized Minchançaman, the last independent monarch of Chimor, as a hostage and conveyed him to Cuzco in a triumphal procession that included many royal kinsmen, aristocratic retainers, and craftsmen of luxury goods, as well as enormous quantities of portable treasure. Rowe believed that this encounter with the sophisticated courtly society of Chimor provided the Inca nobility with new cultural models that resulted in a rapid intensification of emergent class differentiation in Cuzco and the elevation of the Inca king from a particularly powerful, influential warlord to a unique political being (the Sapa Inca) imbued with the aura of the divine (Rowe 1948). Upon vanquishing the kingdom of Chimor, Inca kings could certainly be no less magnificent in displaying and deploying their social power than the lords of Chan Chan. To understand the rise of the Inca to political prominence and the nature of the social world they created, we must be aware of these rich cultural crosscurrents that served as sources of social inspiration and creativity (Figure 2.8).

The Cuzco Heartland

Recent archaeological research in the Cuzco region reveals that the Inca began their protracted project of political domination of neighboring polities and ethnic groups during the period between ca. 1000 and 1400 at the same time that the kingdom of Chimor was coalescing far to the north. In the conventional chronological framework deployed by Andean archaeologists, these four centuries are referred to as the Late Intermediate Period and, in the specific region of Cuzco, as the K'illke Period (Bauer 2004; Bauer and Covey 2002; Covey 2006). Archaeologists working in the area around Cuzco have documented a broadly shared K'illke Period settlement pattern characterized by multiple dispersed villages intensively utilizing local natural resources for their subsistence, well-being, and social reproduction. These villages constructed, defended, and exploited agricultural production zones of dry-farmed and irrigated terraces, adjoining pasturelands, forests, streams, springs, lakes, and ponds. Material evidence, such as shared ceramic motifs and inventories (Figure 2.9), suggests that these villages cooperated as well as competed with each other at different times, resulting in loosely knit, volatile coalitions that changed in intensity and duration according to the exigencies of political circumstance. That is, the social world of these villages in the Cuzco region prior to the mid-fifteenth-century imperial expansion of the Inca was shaped and reshaped in the crucible of intense competition as well as strategic cooperation. In order to obtain access to valued resources, these villages, at times opportunistically linked in ethnic confederations, strove to exert their authority over and their access

2.9. Ceramic sherds from the Cuzco region, dating to the period prior to the consolidation of the Inca as a polity. (Image courtesy of Steven Kosiba)

to wealth-generating resources, most particularly land and water, and human labor. It was in this fragmented and highly contested political landscape that the Inca ethnic group and their charismatic leaders began to knit together the religiously inflected economic, social, military, and political forces that permitted them to consolidate self-identified communities into a multiethnic, plurilinguistic state and ultimately into the largest indigenous empire in the Western Hemisphere.

According to conventional historiography, Inca kings living before Pachakuti engaged in frequent military skirmishes with neighboring ethnic groups. Rather than concerted attempts at territorial annexation, these conflicts entailed mounting raiding parties to obtain booty, human captives, and political renown for the Inca warlords. Still, prior to the sudden imperial expansion that erupted under the aegis of Pachakuti, these Inca kings, their kinsmen, and allied nobles gradually assembled a territorially integrated, geopolitical heartland in the near-Cuzco region. This Cuzco heartland was characterized by significant projects of infrastructural development, particularly the creation of expansive irrigated agricultural terraces capable of sustained production of high-value crops such as maize (Bauer 1992, 2004; Covey 2006). Recent archaeological

2.10. The fortified site of Wat'a in the Cuzco region. First built before the Inca, this site underwent important physical and social transformations in the process of incorporation into the Inca state. (Image courtesy of Steven Kosiba)

research in the Cuzco area has documented dramatic transformations of village settlements during the nascent phases of Inca expansion in the fourteenth and early fifteenth centuries (Figure 2.10). Many villages in the greater Cuzco region associated with distinct non-Inca ethnic groups that had been founded in defensible locations well above valley floors were abandoned or significantly transformed during this time. New domestic settlements, as well as large agricultural estates, were established in previously unoccupied territory located in proximity to maize production zones on valley floors (Bauer 1992, 1998, 2004; Covey 2006; Dean 2005; Heffernan 1989, 1996; Kendall 1984, 1988). These developmental projects of the Inca nobility in the Cuzco heartland dramatically accelerated the accumulation of wealth that eventually underwrote the imperial ambitions of the last five Inca kings (Pachakuti, Thupa Inka Yupanki, Wayna Qhapaq, Waskhar, and Atawallpa), who, as we have seen, were the presumptive political authors of the Inca Empire. Parallel with this ambitious reconfiguration of geopolitical space, the Inca aristocracy in Cuzco began to intensify diplomatic overtures to the elites of neighboring polities by pursuing strategic marriage alliances, eventually forging a complicated, kin-based social network that crosscut enduring ethnic affiliations and territorial attachments (Covey 2006), initiating, in effect, a process of strategic viral hegemony. This territorial and social consolidation of the Cuzco heartland became the political and economic foundation for the subsequent lightning-like expansion of the Inca Empire.

Readers particularly interested in hypothetical historical reconstructions of Inca imperial expansion and military strategies can find them in a number of sources, all of which are based on close analysis and comparisons of Spanish chronicles, memoirs, legal disputes, and other primary documents (D'Altroy 2002; Julien 2000; Pärssinen 1992; Rostworowski 1999; Rowe 1946). For the remainder of this book, I will concentrate not on the reconstruction of Inca history, but on describing and analyzing the conceptual, organizational, and institutional instruments that undergirded and brought form to the phenomenon that we call the Inca Empire.

3　The Social Order: Kinship and Class in the Realm of the Four Quarters

All human societies have sets of beliefs and habitual practices that provide the framework for social order. These beliefs and practices constitute the social relations that regulate the rights and responsibilities of daily life. Ever since *Ancient Law*, Sir Henry Maine's (1982) seminal contribution to legal anthropology, scholars have debated his core concept that purported to distinguish between societies that based their social order on distinctions of kinship and communal social status ("tribal" and "traditional" societies) in contrast with those that regulated rights and responsibilities in terms of contractual agreements among autonomous individuals (modern state societies). Maine's notions on the evolutionary trajectory of legal systems were succinctly cast in terms of the phrase "from status to contract." Given the prevailing Victorian-era intellectual context in which he operated as a lecturer in jurisprudence at Cambridge and Oxford Universities and as an English colonial legal officer in India, not surprisingly Maine also perceived significant evolutionary differences between non-Western and Western societies in which the former structured social order around faith-based religious sentiments and practices, while the latter established rational, text-based legal codes and processes. Influenced by his experience of traditional villages in British colonial India, Maine created a model of the self-organized village community structured around natural bonds of kinship and locality rather than on "artificial" bonds of money and contract, along with communal ownership of productive resources, economic and political self-sufficiency, and customary, rather than text-based, law (Diamond 1991:122). Maine conceived this archetype of a village community as a relatively rudimentary form of social relationship that was ineluctably replaced in the modern world by the more complex social formation of capitalism, in which social relations were structured principally around contract and not status.

Still, Maine's evolutionary and teleological assumptions did not entirely blind him to the inherent complexity in his self-organized village community. In the real world, rather than in some ideal type, Maine astutely recognized that such village communities were not necessarily homogeneous and egalitarian, but rather were frequently structured in a hierarchy with dominant families taking leading roles in economic and political life. In the traditional village communities in India that were the subject of his analysis, Maine observed that on "close inspection" these communities were not "simple but composite bodies, including a number of classes with various rights and claims" (Maine 1895:123). In other words, the distinction between status and contract as distinct forms of the social regulation of rights and responsibilities does not necessarily recapitulate the distinction between simple and complex social orders.

If Maine had been familiar with the case of the Inca state, he would have realized just how much social complexity could be generated in a "traditional" society based on kinship, community status, and personal attachment to a leader, rather than on contractual relationships among autonomous individuals. The social order that structured the Inca Empire entailed a dynamic interplay of kinship, gender relations, class structures, occupational roles, religious sentiments, and various other forms of political alliances. Moreover, the Inca social order changed continually over time and space, incorporating new layers of complexity in the regulation of rights, resources, and social responsibilities as the empire rapidly expanded in the fifteenth and early sixteenth centuries. The role of kinship, and the structuring of social relations according to idioms of kinship, played an especially key role in the social order of the Inca Empire. Although most scholars, following Maine's original formulations, view societies operating at the geopolitical scale of the state as necessarily having replaced kinship with bureaucracy as a fundamental organizational principle, the Inca state, as we shall see, offers an intriguing counterexample.

The smallest scale of social production and reproduction in human societies is the nuclear family: a conjugal pair and their biological or adoptive children. To spread risk, ensure survival, and enjoy the cultural benefits of sociality, most traditional and indigenous societies incorporate extended families (married couples, their children, and various sets of consanguineal and affinal relatives) into the core activities of cohabitation, socialization of children, collective labor, shared meals, recreation, and common religious worship (Figure 3.1). Above the level of individual nuclear and extended families that represent the principal focus of daily sociality, such communities are often organized into even larger units of social interaction. These more inclusive communities may be defined in terms of kin-related descent groups, such as lineages, clans, and phratries, or in terms of common

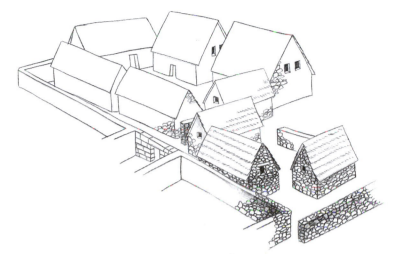

3.1. Artist's reconstruction of a *kancha* residential compound. The household compound was the site of daily activities for *ayllu* members and a residence for close kin members. (Adapted from Morris and Thompson 1985)

ownership and use of shared territories and natural resources, or in terms of both.

Multiple ethnic groups and *señorios* (independent kingdoms) competing for and defending territory and natural resources characterized the pre-Inca social landscape in the Andean highlands and *altiplano*. Many, if not all, of the *señorios* and political confederations that were eventually incorporated into the Inca Empire over the course of the fifteenth and early sixteenth centuries were organized into self-identified communities and ethnic groups living and working together in social groupings known as *ayllus*. We have substantial information on the structure, scale, and social meaning of the *ayllu* since this flexible and enduring social collectivity still exists in hundreds of indigenous communities throughout the highlands and *altiplano* of the Andes. The long-term continuity of *ayllus* as a fundamental, self-identifying social collective from at least the fifteenth century (and perhaps centuries prior to that) to the present is one of the principal reasons that many scholars have subscribed to the *lo andino* perspective that sees deep-seated sociostructural essences as particularly characteristic of the Andean region. But we must be careful not to assume that the organizing structure and characteristics of contemporary Andean *ayllus* are necessarily isomorphic with those we can identify in the pre-Hispanic past and in Inca society more specifically. Contemporary *ayllus* reflect an extremely plastic social concept of relatedness, sociality, and mutuality of interest. Ethnographically documented *ayllus* present multiple structural forms that embrace virtually any self-identifying social group, extending from individual families to tightly defined, highly localized patrilineal descent groups to larger social clusters of relatives or kindreds to *barrios* or neighborhoods in individual settlements to villages to an ethnic group not related by kin ties at all (Isbell 1978; Platt 1982). As Wernke (2006:180) remarks, "[C]ommonly translated as 'clan,' *ayllu* was actually emically conceived of as a multiscalar concept that could reference any segment along a continuum of biologically or socially related collectivities, from the consanguines of a patrilineage to clan-like groupings of patrilineages, moieties, and even an entire ethnic group." We must recall, however, that many of these descriptions of extraordinary flexibility in social and spatial scale and in the criteria of inclusion in an Andean *ayllu* stem from colonial period and more recent historical and ethnographic accounts that reflect the social structures of a deeply traumatized population, one that had undergone centuries of demographic collapse and rapid, deep-seated cultural transformations induced by its conquest and incorporation in the European colonial enterprise. The sociospatial flexibility that we see today may very well have been the result of indigenous adaptation to unprecedented historical circumstances of biological and cultural trauma perpetuated through ever-deepening structures of economic and social inequality from 1532 to the present. New, and more inclusive, forms of solidarity and of economic and social relations may have become essential for survival and self-defense in this sociohistorical context. That is, we cannot assume that this multiscalar and highly plastic concept of *ayllu* social relations necessarily typified the pre-Columbian Andean world. In particular, membership in the ancient Andean *ayllu* appears to have had a strong emphasis on kin relatedness, or at least on membership and social participation mediated through the idiom of kinship.

Synthesizing the best evidence from indigenous informants, as collected by early Spanish chroniclers, clerics, and colonial administrators, the ancient Andean *ayllu* can be defined as a group of related families that held land in common and traced their descent from a common ancestor. Stern (1982:6) defines the *ayllu* specifically as "an endogamous lineage" that "claimed (for social purposes) descent from the same ancestor." In a similar vein, Spalding (1984:48) describes the *ayllu* as "a group of people claiming access to productive resources, including the support and labor of one another, on the basis of the relationship established between them and defined by themselves and their culture as kinship"; further, she writes that "the traditions of the *ayllus* themselves described an *ayllu* as a group of lineages holding land conquered or occupied by their ancestors, heroes who were credited with originating all of the rules by which the group lived." John Rowe (1946:253) defined the Inca *ayllu* as "a kin group with theoretical endogamy, with descent in the male line" that owned, inhabited, and worked the lands of a defined territory. Common to these definitions of the *ayllu* is the quality of kin relatedness reckoned from an identified ancestral figure and a collective claim to a defined territory. The ancestor at the origin and apex of the *ayllu* may have been an actual progenitor of the patrilineage, or a more remote, even mythical ancestor socially recognized by *ayllu* members as the biological and spiritual source of their collective identity. Principles of common identity in the *ayllu* were mobilized around and deeply sedimented through interpersonal intimacy derived from shared history, shared labor, shared meals, and shared worship of a common ancestor.

In theory, and apparently often in practice, in the *ayllus* of highland Andean ethnic groups that were ultimately incorporated into the Inca Empire, there was no concentration of arable land or pasturage in the hands of a few wealthy private owners. Individuals as heads of households held the usufruct, or use right, to parcels of land, and the amount of land that could be exploited for the benefit of the household was not permanently fixed. The political leaders of the community, called *kurakas*, determined on a periodic basis the subsistence needs of each household and readjusted the size of the designated land allotment to conform to changes in the composition of these households. This system of communal disposition of productive lands reflected an age-old Andean ethic of mutual aid: no individuals were allowed to claim basic natural resources as their personal property, but at the same time, members of each household retained the right of assured access to sufficient community farmland, water sources, and pastures to support themselves and their family.

The system of communal land tenure also played a significant role in maintaining an ecological equilibrium in the fragile agricultural environment of the Andean highlands. Because individuals were not permitted to acquire land or water sources as personal property, they had no opportunity to enrich themselves in the short term by enclosing and continuously cultivating the greatest amount of land possible and then selling off surplus agricultural products at a profit. This built-in constraint on the potential for entrepreneurship and monopolization of natural resources by individuals ensured that the community as a whole would always have enough productive lands to guarantee its survival.

Communal rather than private ownership of land, water sources, and other natural resources characterized the vast majority of the rural populations in the Inca world. As we shall see, however, private ownership of wealth-generating resources, such as arable land, pastures, water sources, irrigation canals, fisheries, mines, *and* the labor to exploit them, did intensify as the Inca expanded and consolidated their political power. But principles of private ownership of such natural and social capital extended only to provincial aristocracy, Inca nobility, and especially to the royal families that occupied the apex of imperial authority and privilege, and not to the commoners.

For commoners, at least throughout the highlands of the Inca realm, the *ayllu,* with its ethic of mutual aid and communal resource use, was the most important suprahousehold association that empowered, structured, and regulated their social relations. *Ayllu* members gained access to corporately held land, water, and other essential natural resources by contributing household labor for the benefit of their own families and that of the larger collective. In these *ayllus,* collective work groups collaborated to build houses for newly married couples, cleared land for cultivation, opened new water sources for irrigation channels, constructed agricultural terraces, created and defended territorial boundary markers, and performed the labor-intensive tasks of maintaining the productive resources of their shared territory. Just as important as these physical tasks linked with social reproduction, the *ayllus* shared the essential tasks of worshipping their biological or socially conceived ancestor: the progenitor of the kindred. *Ayllu* members sacrificed the first fruits of their harvests to the ancestral figure and made periodic collective offerings of llama fat, *cuy* (guinea pig), birds, shells, aromatic wood, coca leaves, and other spiritually and energetically charged objects. Sacrifices and offerings were synchronized with the cycle of the agricultural seasons so that these acts of collective worship were conceived of and practiced directly as an essential component of the technology of production rather than simply as autonomous, inner-directed spiritual exercises. Individual households performed their own rituals of propitiation within the private sphere of the family, but the more public expressions of ancestor worship, accompanied by shared meals, competitive drinking bouts, dancing, singing, and recital of epic poetry that recounted the heroic acts of the ancestors, were among the most important collective expressions of *ayllu* identity.

The ancestors were ever present, not simply in the memory and oral histories of *ayllu* members but also physically embodied in elaborately preserved mummy bundles that were literally embedded in the landscape in shrines, crypts, and *chullpas,* or mortuary towers. These houses of the dead, built of masonry and adobe and decorated with stuccowork painted in primary colors, were highly visible to the community, a constant reminder of the proximity and accessibility of the ancestors. Apart from the ancestral relics housed in a necropolis, *ayllus* also recognized and regularly propitiated an array of prominent landscape features, such as caves, springs, lakes, cascades, trees, crevasses, unusual boulders, and mountain peaks. One of these features was believed to be the *pacarina* ("place of dawning"), or the physical point of ethnogenesis where the ancestors of the *ayllu*, or clusters of related *ayllus* that constituted an entire ethnic group, first emerged. The mummy bundles of the ancestors and these special landscape features were considered to be *wak'as*, a complex ontological category that can, for the moment, be glossed as any cultural object, feature, or quality of the landscape that held a particularly potent form of supernatural power. We will explore the concept, ontology, and significance of *wak'as* to the Inca in greater detail in Chapter 5.

Like many social dimensions of the *ayllu*, the network of the *wak'as* that were recognized and worshipped by the community was arranged in a hierarchy of potency and efficacy. The *wak'a* believed to be the *pacarina* occupied the highest rank in the network as the historical origin point of the entire *ayllu*. Mummies were venerated as the proximate, biological ancestors of the lineages and, as such, also held a prominent position in the hierarchy of worship, sacrifice, and offerings. The trees, springs, lakes, waterfalls, caves, boulders, and crevasses that animated the landscape and endowed it with vitality were immanent, but subordinate, nodes in this dense, physical network of the sacred.

The political leaders of the *ayllu*, the *kurakas*, asserted their status by virtue of their genealogy, claiming the most direct descent from the *wak'a* ancestors near the apex of this sacred hierarchy. Although their proximity to the ancestors endowed the *kurakas* with inherent prestige and the potential for leadership, they were required to constantly demonstrate their capacity in tangible acts that benefited the community at large. *Kurakas* were responsible for synchronizing the agricultural cycle of work and related festivals, for distributing usufruct rights to land and water to community members according to a principle of need, and for organizing the defense of community territory and resources from enemies and competitors. Just as important, the *kurakas* organized the cycle of sacrifices and offerings made in memory of the ancestors and consulted their lineages' mummy bundles in political feasts in which food, drink, and conversation were exchanged. Community worship of the *wak'as* was also the occasion for productive work. Religious festivals became the focus of communal labor projects, such as the construction of a new house, shrine, or temple, or the seasonal cleaning of irrigation canals that underwrote the agrarian economy of the *ayllu*. Worship and work were synchronized and, in a real sense, indistinguishable. The *kurakas* were the patrons of these religious festivals and the organizers of the collective work parties; in other words, they served simultaneously as priests and as politicians of the community. In focusing their collective worship on an apical ancestor figure and on the physical landscape of origins from which the *ayllu* was believed to have emerged, members of the *ayllu* were defining their unique social identity, validating their social history, and making strong moral claims to the territory in which they lived out their lives together with their kindred.

How can we bring these various strands together to understand the meaning and practices that constituted the ancient Andean *ayllu*? First, we must appreciate that life in an Andean *ayllu* was lived as a total social fact. That is, daily practices structured by the social reality of the *ayllu* touched virtually every aspect of an individual's experience. Life in the *ayllu* was all-embracing, multivalent, and constitutive of social reality. We can analytically break the *ayllu* into separate dimensions, but we must always keep in mind that we do this for purposes of clarity and understanding. All of these dimensions were lived and experienced by the members of the *ayllu* as seamless and inalienable realities. In sum, the Andean *ayllu* as a lived reality was simultaneously a physical phenomenon (a defined, inhabited territory; a shared placed of dwelling), a sociological phenomenon (a kindred, or a cluster of lineages that considered themselves biologically and/or socially related), an economic phenomenon (a group of individuals sharing labor, resources, production, exchange, and consumption), a political phenomenon (a group of individuals cooperating for common purposes of social reproduction, regulation of rights and responsibilities, and mutual protection), a psychological phenomenon (an affect-laden framework in which individuals shared a sense of emotional belonging), and a moral, or metaphysical phenomenon (a group of individuals who constituted a community of religious belief and practices focused on their own origins, history, and relationship to the nonhuman world).

The *ayllu* as an all-embracing social phenomenon was also flexible in its structural principles so that several *ayllus* might jointly recognize both a common ancestor (mythical, virtual, or real) and a large physical territory that they shared and subdivided. In this way, a single *ayllu* became the core organizational "cell" for larger political communities that consisted of multiple *ayllus* organized recursively as nested and ever more inclusive social groups. Drawing on an analogy from James Lockhart's (1992) analysis of Aztec *altepetl* or city-states, this "cellular-modular" organizational form of nested *ayllus* recognizing and living according to

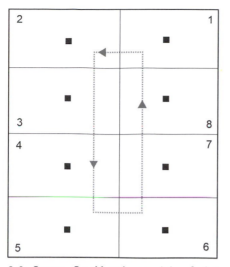

3.2. James Lockhart's model of Aztec "cellular-modular" social organization at the level of the *altepetl* group. (Adapted from Lockhart 1992)

similar social, political, and cultural principles characterized much of the late pre-Hispanic world in the Andean highlands (Lockhart 1992) (Figure 3.2). Entire ethnic groups and *señorios* inhabiting territories encompassing many hundreds of square kilometers were organized as recursive sets of *ayllus* that recognized and acted on mutual rights and obligations. At the local level, *ayllus* and their constituent households were the site of most quotidian activities, the daily acts of work, worship, shared meals, conversation, conflict, and recreation that concerned, at most, a few dozen people. At more inclusive scales, the principal events that would galvanize the larger political communities, polities, or ethnic groups to act in concert were large religious festivals and military campaigns of raiding or of self-defense that required mass mobilization of the population. As we shall see, these more inclusive political communities were often arranged in status hierarchies that stemmed from a principle (actual or asserted) of genealogical proximity to the founding ancestor of the community. That the *ayllu* was so broadly distributed in the Andean highlands on the eve of Inca imperial expansion implies that this social structure was a particularly effective, flexible, and sustainable form of social and community organization. The *ayllu*'s persistence in the Andes in the twenty-first century, even in the face of globalization with all of its attendant economic, political, and cultural transformations, attests to the efficacious and deeply rooted nature of this organizational form.

This brief analytical sketch of the Andean *ayllu* emphasizes its collective, corporate, and communal aspects. In many respects, shared experience and cooperative living arrangements do characterize the *ayllu*. But this does not mean that this kind of Andean *communitas* was not affected or even riven by conflict. *Ayllu* members often competed with each other for prestige and status and defended their individual claims to the shared resources of the *ayllu*. We know that today, for instance, disputes over land and water resources, even among siblings and other closely related family members, remain a principal source of conflict in Andean *ayllus*. These social tensions can erupt into violent, even deadly, encounters. Moreover, even though *ayllus* emphasize shared resources and shared experiences, they are not necessarily utopian and egalitarian in nature. In fact, most pre-Columbian *ayllus* were structured in various forms of hierarchical social arrangements that crosscut differences in gender roles, in class distinctions, and in political status. The *ayllu* was also a deeply *political* institution that internalized and regulated significant power differentials and social stratification. If we examine the social system specific to the Inca noble households in Cuzco, we can perceive just how these power differentials were understood and acted on in Inca society. We can then examine the highly elaborated class structure that emerged in Inca society during the Inca drive to empire, both within the aristocracy and between the aristocracy and different groups of commoners.

Panaqas and *Ayllus* in Cuzco: The Social Order of the Nobles

In the generation just prior to the Spanish conquest, the Inca royal family, high aristocracy, and subordinate nobility were organized in a system of twenty hierarchically ranked, kin-related groups inhabiting the imperial capital of Cuzco and its immediate hinterland. The Inca aristocracy itself constituted an internally differentiated class system that had a significant impact on the allocation, distribution, and circulation of wealth, status, marriage partners, social power, and prestige. The system consisted of four degrees of nobility: the emperor and his immediate royal household; nobles who were the direct descendants of Inca kings; nobles considered as distant or collateral relatives of Inca kings; and powerful non-Inca families and lineages who, in the course of imperial expansion and consolidation, were elevated to the status of "Incas by privilege." The first three classes of nobles lived in the innermost, exclusive core of the capital, organized into the system of twenty kindred; the Incas by privilege resided with their own kindred on a permanent basis outside the capital. Non-Inca nobility were incorporated in some, but not all, political and religious activities in Cuzco. As in many court societies globally, elaborate social rules of etiquette, residential patterns, marriage proscriptions, access to natural and human resources, and complex sumptuary laws materialized the nuances of class distinctions.

The pinnacle of social power and the ultimate reference point for this elaborate Inca class system was the king and his immediate royal family. Under the king's patronage, these members of the royal household controlled what was in contemporary economic terms a closely held corporation that succeeded in acquiring and exploiting resources for the benefit of its members. The royal households of the Inca kings were enormously wealthy, and the kin corporations of the later Inca kings during the fifteenth and early sixteenth centuries controlled vast private estates (Figure 3.3). The intrepid Spanish military man and chronicler of the Inca Empire, Pedro de Cieza de León, gives us a concise, but graphic, glimpse of the wealth held by the king and his family:

Accumulating such a fortune, and with their heir being obliged to leave the possessions of his predecessor untouched, that is to say, his house, his household, and his statue, the treasure piled up over many years, so that all the service of the king's house, even water jars and kitchen utensils, was of gold and silver; and not only in a single place, but in many, especially the capitals of the provinces, where there were many gold and silversmiths engaged in the manufacture of these objects. In their palaces and lodgings were bars of these metals, and their garments were covered with ornaments of silver, and emeralds and turquoise, and other precious stones of great value. And for their wives there was even greater luxury in their adornment and for their personal service, and their litters were all encrusted with silver and gold and jewels. Aside from this they had a vast quantity of ingots of gold, and unwrought silver, and tiny beads, and many other large vessels for their drinking feasts, and for their sacrifices still more of these treasures.... Even their drums and chairs and musical instruments and arms were of this metal. (Cieza de León 1976)

But the wealth of the Inca king and his immediate descendants was not limited to the hoards of precious metals and jewels so emphatically described by Cieza de León. The king and his family derived continuous streams of income from private agricultural estates worked by commoners attached to the royal house. In the Inca world, wealth was measured principally by the amount of human labor one could command, along with assured access to abundant fertile land and freshwater sources. The royal household enjoyed the most extensive social and political network of any social actors in the empire, and this network was predicated upon the rights and obligations of access to human labor. Labor in all its

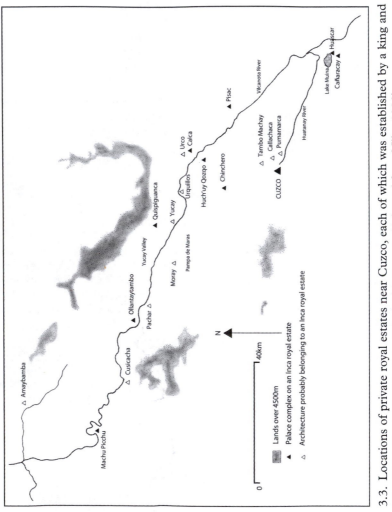

3.3. Locations of private royal estates near Cuzco, each of which was established by a king and inherited and managed in perpetuity by his *panaqa*. (Adapted from Niles 1999)

productive forms was the ultimate source of wealth and social power for the Inca king.

The royal households of descendants directly related to the Inca kings were also exceptionally large. For personal and political reasons, Inca kings, like many absolute monarchs, married multiple wives and fathered dozens of children with these wives and with numerous concubines. The enormous numbers of progeny, ranked hierarchically according to the status of their mothers, generated a complex, competitive social world within the confines of the royal household indexed in the acquisition and display of wealth objects. As a result, the status-based imperative to accumulate and display wealth in this uppermost stratum of Inca class society was a powerful motivating force that resulted in the concentration of truly staggering treasure troves that inspired both awe and profound concupiscence in the Spanish conquistadors who encountered and fought over the enormous riches of the realm.

Cieza's passage alludes to another fascinating dimension of the social organization of the Inca aristocracy: a specific pattern of dynastic residence and inheritance. We know from multiple sources, including Inca informants, that ten of the twenty principal kin-related groups inhabiting the Cuzco region were referred to as *panaqas*, or royal *ayllus*, each of which was said to descend directly from one of the Inca kings. Each of these descent groups was given a particular name that had historical and symbolic significance (Table 3.1). *Panaqas* were similar to *ayllus* in terms of their social, economic, and religious roles and activities, but they were also unique in that they were located only in and around the capital city of Cuzco and they enjoyed the differential opportunities, responsibilities, and prerogatives of the social group that possessed the highest social status in the realm. The *panaqa* incorporated all of a king's male and female descendants except for his royal successor, who formed his own *panaqa*. The seventeenth-century cleric Bernabé Cobo, working from mid-sixteenth-century accounts of Inca social organization, particularly the narrative of Sarmiento, observed that:

It was customary among all of these kings for each one to found his own lineage and family in the following way: Not counting the prince who succeeded his father as ruler, his [siblings] were considered to belong to a single lineage originated by their father the king; the crown prince did not belong to this group and family because, as the future king, he was to be the head and initiator of another new family, and every lineage of these had its own name. Furthermore, upon the death of the king, the prince did not inherit his house and treasure, but it was handed over along with the body of the deceased king to the family that he had founded. (Cobo 1979:111)

Table 3.1. Kings and their respective *panaqas* according to their Hanan and Hurin affiliation.

Upper	Atawallpa	
Cuzco (Hanan)	Waskhar	*Waskhar Ayllu*
	Wayna Qhapaq	*Tumipampa Panaqa*
	Thupa Inka Yupanki	*Qhapaq Ayllu*
	Pachakuti Inka Yupanki	*Hatun Ayllu Inaqa Panaqa*
	Wiraqocha Inka	*Zukzu Panaqa*
	Yawar Waqaq	*Awqaylli Panaqa*
	Inka Roq'a	*Wila K'iraw Panaqa*
Lower	Qhapaq Yupanki	*Apu Mayta Panaqa*
Cuzco (Hurin)	Mayta Qhaqap	*Uska Mayta Panaqa*
	Lloq'e Yupanki	*Awayni Panaqa*
	Zinchi Roq'a	*Rawra Panaqa*
	Manqo Qhapaq	*Chima Panaqa*

This brief passage encapsulates several insights into the sociological, political, economic, and religious qualities of the *panaqa*. According to Cobo's account, the *panaqa* was a descent group linked directly to a royal progenitor – one of the Inca kings. Implicitly, therefore, the *panaqa*, as descendants of kings, possessed the highest social status in the city of Cuzco and by extension in the empire. They were, in fact, the most aristocratic members of Inca society, constituting a class of related people who were not unlike Brahmins in the ancient caste system of India. This caste-like social quality was sustained and reinforced by the enormous concentration of wealth in the hands of the *panaqa* and the households allied with the royal dynasty. As Cobo noted, upon the death of their royal progenitor, the *panaqa* inherited the dead emperor's "house and treasure." In particular, the *panaqas* of the three emperors responsible for the major imperial conquests (Pachakuti, Thupa Inka Yupanki, and Wayna Qhapaq) were vastly wealthy since the "house and treasure" of their progenitors included expansive private estates, palaces and shrines, improved agricultural lands, water sources, extensive herds of camelids, forest preserves, numerous hunting and fishing grounds, mines of precious metals and gemstones, and, as important, legions of laborers attached to the patrimonial household of the king (Figures 3.4 and 3.5).

These ten royal *ayllus* were allocated (and, in a real sense, were socioeconomically defined by) exclusive rights to demarcated land and to water sources in and around Cuzco. The most productive and strategically located lands belonged to the ten *panaqas*, whereas lesser quality, less valued land devolved into the hands of the nonroyal and non-Inca

3.4. Machu Picchu is the most famous royal estate and was probably built by Pachakuti. (Image courtesy of L. Guengerich)

3.5. Tambo Machay is another well-known royal estate. Hydraulic features at this site reflect both aesthetic and cosmological principles intimately associated with Inca culture. (Image courtesy of author)

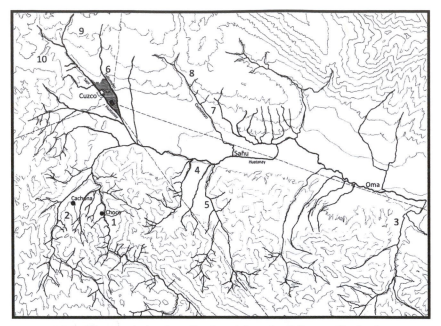

3.6. The ten irrigation districts (*chapas*) of Cuzco. Each *chapa* comprised primary and secondary water sources, and was associated with a royal *panaqa*. (Adapted from Zuidema 1990)

ayllus that were closely allied with the Inca royal family. The *panaqa* and the nonroyal *ayllu* landholdings in the metropolitan zone of Cuzco were demarcated into irrigation districts, or *chapas*, each of which consisted of a principal, high-elevation canal, branching secondary and tertiary channels, strategically located reservoirs, and all the land irrigated by these water sources (Sherbondy 1982, 1987:366; Zuidema 1990) (Figure 3.6). Each irrigation district radiated out from its principal water source to incorporate plots of land both in the nearby rural hinterland of Cuzco and within the city itself. City and countryside were intimately linked through these patrimonial estates that expanded in hydraulically defined, radial sectors from the surrounding mountain slopes that were the origin points of irrigation water down to the central plazas of Cuzco. The *panaqa* lands also contained numerous masonry *qollqas*, or warehouses, in which the crops and other valued commodities produced on these estates were stored for eventual distribution to members of the group or for consumption in political and religious festivals and military campaigns. Most of the uplands were significantly improved through massive labor investments in agricultural terraces that enhanced the yields of

3.7. The circular terraces at Moray demonstrate that aesthetic as well as infrastructural concerns were taken into account in this technique of agricultural engineering. (Photograph courtesy of L. Guengerich)

the most important cultigens, such as maize, quinoa, and various native Andean tubers. But these artfully contoured and exquisitely engineered terraces had more than instrumental significance; they were also aesthetically, symbolically, and religiously salient features on the land and constituted a kind of public, theatrical performance of the wealth and sociopolitical status of its owners (Figure 3.7). In other words, through original acts of royal concession, the physical landscape of Cuzco, together with all of its resources valued for their economically productive and religiously charged qualities, was organized into corporately managed estates under the exclusive jurisdiction of the twenty *panaqas* and *ayllus*. These irrigation districts became both critical, wealth-generating assets for the nobility and a social map that palpably inscribed on the land the political and ritual hierarchy of *panaqas* and *ayllus*. We will explore the complex hierarchical relationship among the *panaqas* and *ayllus* when we examine the social and religious organization of space and time in Cuzco in Chapter 5.

The highly skewed distribution of wealth between the *panaqas* and other sectors of Inca society (commoners and less highly placed nobility) generated intense economic inequalities that became the material signs of differential status and prestige, as well as the source of considerable social tension. *Panaqa* members held exalted political offices as provincial governors, tribute collectors, auditors, military chiefs of staff, judges, high priests, and counselors of state. In theory, they exerted their state-endowed authority on behalf of the reigning monarch, the Sapa Inca, but they also had multiple opportunities to advance their own interests and those of their immediate families in the process of governing a newly founded empire.

One feature of recruitment to *panaqa* membership emphasizes the strategic and fluid qualities of the group as a sociological phenomenon. Not every member of the *panaqa* was a biological descendant of the founding king. The nobility of Cuzco could choose the *panaqa* with which they wished to be affiliated, even if they were not direct descendants of that particular royal line. As long as they acknowledged and accepted the responsibility to serve the ancestor cult of the founding king, they were considered social, if not biological, descendants of that king and thereby incorporated as full members of the *panaqa* with all of its opportunities, privileges, and obligations. Even if this was not the most common method of recruitment, the possibility of voluntary *panaqa* membership opened up a socially sanctioned channel for personal ambition, strategic behavior, and potential social mobility within the ranks of the nobility. For instance, one young noble of Cuzco chose to become a high priest and therefore left his natal *ayllu* in order to affiliate himself with the *panaqa* of the king Viracocha Inca, who was considered to be the royal patron of the priesthood (Sherbondy 1982:20; Zuidema 1964). In the Inca social order, the possibility for personal choice and voluntary affiliation to a *panaqa* did not diminish the core kin realities and identities of this exclusive social group as some scholars have suggested.[1] On the contrary, all members of the *panaqa* considered themselves related to one another by blood or by social preference. All members referred to the other members in the idiom of kinship (as "brothers," "sisters," "uncles," "aunts," and so on), and all shared the same biological or virtual ancestor. For the Inca, the use of kin terminology was not merely notational or metaphorical; rather, it expressed a substantive acknowledgment of a social relationship that determined rights and obligations to tangible property, natural resources, and all the social, political, and emotional perquisites of group membership. A voluntary decision to affiliate with a particular *panaqa* was rewarded by the acknowledgment of full membership with all of its attendant entitlements.

[1] Cf. Sherbondy's (1982:19) claim that the *panaqa* was "not a real kinship group."

Yet, like the *ayllus*, *panaqas* were not seamlessly self-governing communities. Competition among the members of the *panaqas* contributed to the fluid, unstable political atmosphere of court life in the Inca Empire. One of the principal flash points for internecine rivalries, many of which turned violent, was competition over land, water, and access to the labor of commoners. There was continual social tension and litigation over what constituted the shared, corporately held lands of the *panaqa* as a descent group of a founding king charged with sustaining and managing his ancestral cult, and what was regarded as the personal inheritance of the king's descendants. Bitter disputes over land, water, and labor broke out frequently and may have occasioned more than one person to change their *panaqa* affiliation. Furthermore, the accelerated expansion of privately held, family property at the expense of corporate, collectively managed estates during the late Inca Empire destabilized the realm and weakened the bonds of kin-based solidarity that brought purpose and a sense of shared destiny to the nobility. The personal ambitions of noble families engendered a volatile ambiance of intrigue, envy, and anxiety in Inca court society. *Panaqa* members, as the most highly ranked aristocracy in the empire, played a particularly significant role in the critical, transitional moments of royal succession. As in many empires, nepotism, bribery, byzantine maneuvers, and strategic assassinations were among the repertoire of *panaqa* politics as various interest groups jockeyed to place their favorite on the throne. The intensely violent confrontation between Atawallpa and Waskhar on the eve of the Spanish conquest of the realm was as much a battle for wealth, prestige, and social cachet among competing *panaqas* as it was a power struggle between royal half-brothers. The high existential stakes of these internecine battles became abundantly clear in that confrontation between 1527 and 1533, which witnessed the utter destruction of whole lineages and their ancestral mummies; the public flaying, evisceration, and beheading of political envoys; the crucifixion of Waskhar's wives and the cold-blooded murder of his children and potential heirs; and the expropriation of the private estates, human retainers, and portable wealth in the possession of the vanquished *panaqa*.

The status of the *panaqa* was sustained not only by the group's inherited wealth but also by its possession of the mummified body of its royal progenitor. As Cobo commented, the body of the deceased king was "handed over to the family that he founded" (Cobo 1979:111). Possession of the royal mummy became the *panaqa*'s legal title to the dead king's accumulated wealth and to the continuing stream of income from his private estates, as well as to the social prestige generated by the mystique that enveloped the charisma-infused persona of the king. It was clearly in the political and economic self-interest of the *panaqas* to sustain a highly public cult around their royal ancestors that continually recounted their epic roles in the creation and governance of the realm. But we should also appreciate the less obviously instrumental quality of the relationship between the kings and the *panaqas* they founded. In addition to being highly political interest groups, the *panaqas* were also religious foundations endowed by their royal benefactors. As religious foundations, the *panaqas* worked to perpetuate the memory of their royal ancestors and to perform rituals of sacrifice and dedicatory offerings to the hundreds of *wak'as* in the Cuzco region that sacralized the capital city and its near hinterland. That is, the personal bonds between the dead king and his descendants were framed and understood as an explicitly religious relationship grounded in the belief that the Inca kings were divine. Belief in the divinity of the king as a direct descendant of the solar deity and possessed of intimate kin-based connections to a wide array of cosmogonic forces was widely circulated among his subjects. The principal ritual obligation of the *panaqa* members was to perpetuate the memory of the deceased king who had originally founded the *panaqa*. As we shall see, ancestor worship was the bedrock of indigenous Andean religion, the basis of ritual activity in the ancient social unit of the *ayllu*. Among Cuzco's nobles, ancestor worship took the form of an elaborate cult of the royal mummies, which both fascinated and repelled Spanish chroniclers who vividly recorded this key element of Inca spirituality (Figure 3.8).

The cult of the royal mummies was an intense expression of social and ritual solidarity within the Inca ruling caste, particularly among the ten *panaqas* that exploited and benefited materially from the patrimony of their kingly ancestors. The king's *panaqa* took responsibility for sustaining his public cult and the sacrality of the realm. Yet in the private context of the closely held family corporation that was the *panaqa,* the relationship of his descendants to the king, pre- and postmortem, was deeply affect laden and shaped by personal emotional bonds, as well as by calculated social and economic self-interest. One cannot gainsay the intense, genuine, religiously inflected emotion of the Inca king's relatives upon seeing, habitually interacting with, worshipping, and, in a real sense, making socially immortal his physically mortal remains. The outpouring of public grief upon the execution of Tupac Amaru in 1572, an entire generation after the Inca had lost their power to the Spanish conquistadors, poignantly illustrates the psychological intensity of these personal bonds of subjects and kinsmen to their king.

A final dimension of Cobo's passage needs consideration. He stated that the "crown prince" was excluded from the *panaqa* of the reigning

3.8. Bearing the mummy of a deceased king on a litter. The veneration of and personal engagement with deceased rulers and their queens was a vital part of Inca state ritual, politics, and religion. (Adapted from Poma de Ayala 1615)

king because the designated royal successor had the obligation to found his own distinct family line of which he was the political head and for whom he would ultimately become the subject of his own familial cult. By this logic, the ten *panaqas* in existence at the end of Wayna Qhapaq's reign ca. 1527 were the result of a gradual, incremental process of kingly succession. From this perspective, the specific number of ten *panaqas* encountered by the Spanish upon their conquest of the Inca Empire was a historical accident; that is, it was the number of royal *ayllus* that simply happened to be in existence at the time of the Spanish invasion. Presumably, if the Spanish conquest had not happened when it did in

1532, the number of *panaqas* would have kept expanding with further kingly accessions to the throne. But this scenario of the sequential emergence of *panaqas* through royal succession may not reflect historical reality. An alternative version based on accounts by Gutiérrez de Santa Clara (1905) and Juan de Betanzos (1996) claims that the *panaqas* were created simultaneously by a single king, and not successively as the result of royal succession. As Sherbondy (1996:181) summarizes this claim:

This organization was attributed to the king Pachakuti Inca. He is said to have divided the Inca population into ranked groups. The highest nobility formed Capac ayllu; these defined themselves as the descendants of Tupac Inca Yupanqui, Pachakuti Inca's successor and son. The members of Capac ayllu were the descendants of Pachakuti Inca's first wife (Zuidema 1986). This was the highest-ranking *panaca*. All the other nobility were called "Hatun ayllu Iñaca panaca" and were the descendants of Pachaquti Inca by his other wives.

By this account, the *panaqa* system was a unique administrative decision of King Pachakuti, who, by the conventional historical narratives, was responsible for originating the imperial expansion of the Inca and, in the process, for reorganizing the entire social, economic, political, legal, and religious fabric of Inca society. As extensively detailed by Betanzos (1996), the breathtaking scope of Pachakuti's putative root-and-branch remaking of the Inca world gives one pause. We know that like most absolute monarchs the Inca kings assiduously promoted their own hagiography by rewriting political history, in the process appropriating the accomplishments of royal predecessors and erasing the memories of inconvenient events such as humiliating defeats on the field of battle. A common aphorism, if overused, captures the point: it is the winners who write history. Although there is historical precedent for a single king who, possessed of overweening ambition, charisma, and a fortuitous concentration of political power, completely transformed his society, this is more likely the exception than the rule.[2] Whether Pachakuti represents the former rather than the latter is still uncertain, and so the actual origins of the *panaqa* system that Betanzos claimed Pachakuti invented remain obscure.

Yet another interpretation of the origins of the *panaqas* suggests that there were originally more than ten royal kindreds but in the process of succession struggles some were eliminated or purposely written out of the indigenous histories for political purposes (Rostworowski 1983). From this perspective, the social structure of the empire preserved in the accounts of Spanish chroniclers such as Sarmiento and Betanzos reflects merely the latest crystallization of a dynamic process of contestation among multiple noble kindreds competing for land, natural resources,

---

[2] E.g., Jayavarman VII of the royal dynasty of the Khmer Empire in Cambodia.

social status, political power, and historical legacy. Given inconsistencies and authorial bias in our sources, the effects of royal propaganda on social memory, repeated accounts of intense political competition among *panaqas*, and, especially, historical evidence for campaigns of extermination against *panaqas* that opposed the will of reigning monarchs (recall the fate of Waskhar's kindred), I find this interpretation to be the most historically plausible and sociologically convincing. During his reign, Pachakuti may very well have standardized the number and social relationships among the royal *ayllus* to fit a preconceived notion of an ideal civic order, but I find it less likely that he created this complex form of social organization out of whole cloth, entirely as a product of his unique administrative genius. Although the validity of either one of these alternative versions of *panaqa* historical origins may never be definitively established, all versions emphasize that the ten *panaqas* were royal kindreds that were ranked relative to each other, to the ten non-royal *ayllus* in Cuzco, and to all other social groups in the empire.

Hierarchy and Social Differentiation among the Nobility

What was the specific system of ranking that structured the Inca social order in Cuzco? Three intersecting principles, one genealogical, another generational, and a third sociospatial, generated the hierarchical system of the twenty *panaqas* and *ayllus*. Betanzos's claim that Pachakuti invented the *panaqa* system also reveals the fundamental genealogical principle that arranged these social groups into a specific status hierarchy. According to Betanzos's account, the most exalted Inca nobility were the direct descendants of King Pachakuti, the presumptive founder of the empire. These nobles were members of Qhapaq Ayllu, the *panaqa* of Pachakuti's heir and successor, King Thupa Inka Yupanki. Thupa Inka Yupanki dramatically increased the territorial reach and wealth of the empire both as the heir apparent spearheading aggressive campaigns of military conquest and, subsequently, as the reigning monarch. The members of Qhapaq Ayllu claimed direct descent from Pachakuti as the offspring of his principal wife, whereas lesser ranking nobles could trace their lineage only through his secondary wives or concubines. The "purity" and therefore relative rank of aristocratic bloodlines turned on the status of the emperors' wives. In the late Inca Empire (ca. 1470–1532), the king's principal wife, or *qoya*, was his full sister. Betanzos (1996:72) recounted that:

The Inca who is lord has a principal wife, and she has to be from his family and lineage, one of his sisters or first cousins. They call this woman *piuigurami* and by this other name *mamanguarme*. As the principal wife of their lord, the common people call her in their greetings *Paxxa yndi Usus çapaicoya guacchacoyac*, moon and daughter of the Sun, unique queen and friend of the poor. This lady has to be a direct relative of the Inca on both the paternal and maternal lines without the least trace of *guacchaconcha* [poor, or orphaned relatives, that is, of mixed royal and nonroyal bloodlines].

Thupa Inka Yupanki was said to have been the first emperor to marry his sister and to inaugurate the prerogative of and political mandate for royal incest. Nobility flowed in the blood. Brother-sister incest insured that the biological descendants of the royal couple were "doubly noble" in both the paternal and the maternal lines, and that the heir and successor to the throne would necessarily possess the "purest blood." This pattern of royal incest underscores, at the highest levels of social rank, the political importance of women as vessels of nobility and as active participants in the governance of the empire.

Direct male descendants of the king and his sister-queen were ensured of their status as the most noble in the realm and were eligible for the throne upon the death or abdication of their father. These candidates for kingly office were called *pihuichuri*, or legitimate, primary sons. All other descendants engendered by the king with his secondary wives were classified as *huaccha concha*, in effect the "poor relations" or secondary sons who did not possess a sufficient degree of noble blood to be eligible for the throne. The *huaccha concha* could, however, aspire to administrative positions in the empire, the power and importance of which were calibrated by the candidate's actual or asserted genealogical relationship to the reigning monarch. Given that the Inca kings married numerous women of various social statuses – full and half sisters, cousins, more distant female kin of Inca extraction, and non-Inca women from the imperial provinces – the number of aspirants and the degree of nobility of their bloodlines generated a vast pool of candidates for political office. Although the capacity to perform effectively in administrative positions played a significant role in Inca imperial administration, candidates for high office had to show how and to what degree they were related to the king in order to forward their case for appointment. Garcilaso de la Vega succinctly captured the Inca system of social ranking based on principles of descent and genealogical relationship to the living monarch, observing that the king's marriage preferences and practices generated three hierarchically ranked classes of royal offspring:

Apart from their legitimate wives, the kings had many concubines. Some were relatives within and beyond the fourth degree; others were foreign-born. Children by women related to the Inca were held legitimate because they had no taint of other blood. Purity of descent was highly venerated by the Incas,

not only among the kings but among all those of royal blood. Children of foreign concubines were considered bastards; and though respected as children of
the king, they did not receive the reverence and internal and external worship
which was reserved for those who were of legitimate blood [and were venerated
like gods, whereas the bastards were treated as human]. The Inca king thus had
three kinds of children – those by his wife who were legally entitled to inherit the
throne, those by his relatives who were of legitimate blood, and bastard children
by other women. (Garcilaso de la Vega 1961:208)

The Inca royalty's obsession with purity of bloodlines, degrees of relatedness to the reigning monarch, precise cultural definitions of legitimacy in paternal and maternal lines, and a continuum of differential
status defined by the pedigree of one's lineage will seem familiar to anyone with even a passing interest in the attitudes and practices of court
societies worldwide. These are commonly shared cultural ideas of what
constitutes nobility. By defining and in that respect constituting finely
nuanced gradations in noble bloodlines, such cultural concepts had dramatic pragmatic effects: they determined access to political office, social
networks, prestige, and ultimately wealth. They also engendered bitter
internecine rivalries and intense competition for the most advantageous
marriage partners who could ennoble a bloodline. Like courtiers everywhere, the Inca noble houses understood and assiduously practiced the
politics of blood (cf. D'Altroy 2002:chapter 5).

Complementing and complicating this genealogical system in which
degrees of relatedness to the king differentiate the nobility, the Inca
system also ranked the aristocratic *panaqas* by a generational principle focused on the reigning monarch. That is, members of the *panaqa*
founded by the king in any given generation held the highest social rank
in the empire. With the death of their founding patron and the accession of a new king, however, their status dropped relative to the new
king's *panaqa*. The newly crowned king and his immediate descendants
became the empire's center of social power and prestige. With each
new generation of the Inca dynasty, *panaqas* once at the pinnacle of
power sank in status, so that the descendants of the earliest Inca monarchs had the lowest status among the noble classes of Cuzco, whereas
descendants of more recent kings enjoyed higher status. The past, and
the past deeds of a royal ancestor, conveyed no special benefit. Rather,
rank revolved around the reigning monarch, and degrees of social status among the nobility were recalibrated upon the installation of each
new king. In some sense, when a new king acceded to the throne, often
amid an unstable political climate of contestation and internecine violence, the entire social fabric of the noble classes was torn asunder and
then quickly rewoven into a new pattern – one in which some social

actors rose in prominence while others, once among the most power-ful in the realm, lapsed into gradual but ineluctable decline. Although still considered nobility, they were no longer among the leading fami-lies of the realm. They no longer were "venerated like gods" or received the supreme deference accorded to the direct, lineal descendants of the reigning monarch. One can readily imagine that over time this structural pattern of sinking status, diminished prestige, and waning fortunes gen-erated endless social anxiety, bitter disputes, and palace intrigues among noble families as they struggled mightily to place their favorites on the throne and so to retain or enhance their prestige and social power.

The third principle of social differentiation among the aristocracy, this one conceptual and spatial in character, reflected the generational princi-ple of sinking status and materialized it into a tangible and publicly per-ceived physical space. The irrigation districts or *chapas* held by the ten *panaqas* as their patrimonial estates in and around Cuzco were geograph-ically divided into two segments termed *hanansaya* (upper sector) and *hurinsaya* (lower sector). The division of the social and spatial world into ranked, complementary halves, or moieties, was pervasive in the Andean world, and, like the *ayllu*, this form of dual organization still exists in many communities in the Andes. In Cuzco, moiety organization extended to vir-tually all aspects of public life, defining the segmentation of territory, social structure, political divisions, and religious practices. (We will explore fur-ther implications of this dual system of organization in Chapters 4, 5, and 6.) This form of social and spatial segmentation denoted status between the groups and individuals inhabiting each sector, so that citizens of the *hanan* (upper) sector held greater relative status than those of the *hurin* (lower) sector. Each moiety division of Cuzco incorporated five royal *ayl-lus* (*panaqas*) and five nonroyal *ayllus* such that ten social groups belonged to Hanan Cuzco and ten belonged to Hurin Cuzco (Table 3.1). Each nonroyal *ayllu* in Hanan and Hurin Cuzco was politically affiliated with and provided labor services for one of the *panaqas*, and so hierarchical pairing of social groups was a crosscutting and recursive phenomenon in which any given *panaqa* outranked any *ayllu*, and inhabitants of the *hanan* sector outranked those of the *hurin* sector.

The spatial organization of the city into upper and lower sectors was based on sociological, topographic, and hydrological grounds (Figure 3.9). The springs, streams, and mountain slopes of Hanan Cuzco included the irrigation districts of the *panaqas* that were affiliated with the last five kings in the standard dynastic accounts and, therefore, by the generational principle of social differentiation, were higher rank-ing than all other *panaqas* and *ayllus*. Hanan Cuzco was located in the upriver sector of the Cuzco Valley that was the source for the waters that

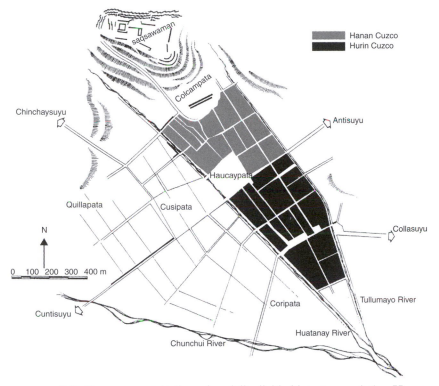

3.9. Cuzco was spatially and socially divided into two moieties, Hanan (upper) and Hurin (lower). (Adapted from Gasparini and Margolies 1980)

irrigated lower-lying lands. Apart from its kin affiliation with more recent dynasts, the symbolic and physical control of the Hanan Cuzco moiety over water sources that irrigated lands farther downslope also conveyed high status to the sector. Hurin Cuzco, in contrast, was located in the downriver sector of the valley, receiving irrigation water flowing through Hanan Cuzco, principally from the Saphi and Tullumayo streams that eventually converge to form the Huatanay River. Hurin Cuzco included the land, canals, and reservoirs of the *panaqas* affiliated with earlier Inca kings in the conventional dynastic narrative. These *panaqas* enjoyed lesser status than the *panaqas* of Hanan Cuzco, although, as nobility, they outranked all of the nonroyal *ayllus,* including those affiliated with the *hanan* sector.

This dual organization of social space was further partitioned into four *suyus,* or territorial segments, that together symbolically and

3.10. The four quarters of Tawantinsuyu: Chinchaysuyu, Antisuyu, Collasuyu, and Cuntisuyu

organizationally formed Tawantinsuyu, the Realm of the Four Quarters. The four socially and ritually demarcated quarters radiated out from the principal dual plazas in the heart of Cuzco along the four major roads that articulated Cuzco with the provinces of the realm (Figure 3.10). These four quarters were designated as Chinchaysuyu, Antisuyu, Collasuyu, and Cuntisuyu. Chinchaysuyu (geographically situated toward the northwest) and Antisuyu (southeast) were located in Hanan Cuzco, and Collasuyu (south) and Cuntisuyu (southwest) were located in Hurin Cuzco. As Sherbondy (1982:26) observes, this further partition of the moiety division into four parts also had a sociological, topographical, and hydrological rationale:

The most important quarters in each half are Chinchaysuyu and Collasuyu. Chinchaysuyu is the quarter that includes the headwaters of the Huatanay river, the drainage basin of the Saphi and Tullumayu rivers, and Collasuyu is the one that includes the lower part of the river. Chinchaysuyu includes the slopes above the city and Collasuyu the valley bottom. (Zuidema 1978a)

We can clearly identify a recursive logic of ranking operating in the social and spatial organization of Cuzco and its near hinterland: *hanan* (upper) outranked *hurin* (lower), and within the *hanan* sector Chinchaysuyu outranked Antisuyu, while within the *hurin* sector Collasuyu outranked Cuntisuyu. Although Betanzos again attributed the partition of Cuzco into ranked moieties and quadripartite sectors to the inspiration of King Pachakuti as part of the king's thoroughgoing reformation of Inca society in the mid-fifteenth century, moiety and quadripartite systems are deeply embedded and broadly distributed organizational structures in Andean society. Pachakuti may have reassigned lands, resources, and social ranks to various individuals and kin groups, but he did so within the broader preexisting institutional framework of the *ayllu* and moiety system. His was the invention of the historical content but not of the structural form.

The three principles of social differentiation among the Inca nobility (genealogical, generational, and sociospatial) together generated a spatially and temporally complex web of status, privilege, political power, and access to critical economic resources that was never static. Although classic structuralist analyses such as those of R.T. Zuidema (1964, 1990) have been roundly criticized for representing Inca society as an unchanging social formation encapsulated in a kind of sociological amber that ignores the impact of historical contingency, local politics, and individual agency, this is a caricature. We can perceive both long-term structural continuity and rapid social change in Inca society. *Ayllus*, dual corporate organization reflecting the logic of moiety systems, and recursive social hierarchies appear and reappear in Andean history, but they are never static structures that lock people into unchanging social roles and practices. We can think of the dialectic between structure and history in Inca society as a game of social power in which institutional constraint and individual choice continually interact and, in some sense, constantly press against each other. At times, this interaction can catalyze significant cultural change, such as Pachakuti's presumptive radical reorganization of Inca politics and social life. Yet institutional structures and social practices can also replicate themselves in similar forms over many generations because they are found to be flexible, efficacious, and well suited to particular social and physical landscapes.

Non-Inca Nobles and the Incas by Privilege

How did non-Inca people fit into the social order of the Inca Empire? What social roles and statuses did they have in the game of social power? We have seen that the Inca nobility itself was socially differentiated into three general classes of descending rank: the Inca king and his family, the members of the *panaqas* who shared in royal bloodlines by virtue of direct descent from Inca kings, and the members of nonroyal *ayllus* who were distant or collateral relatives of the royalty. Each of these noble classes had distinct rights, privileges, resources, and degrees of social status. In the process of expanding their political power outside of the Cuzco region, the Inca created a fourth elite class. These were certain non-Inca ethnic groups who were referred to as "Inca by privilege." The historical origins of this politically created class of nobles is not entirely clear, although the designation "Inca by privilege" indicates that this status was conferred on nonethnically Inca peoples at some point after the emergence of the Inca as the supreme political power in the basin of Cuzco and its immediate hinterlands. Initially, the Inca by privilege were the original, non-Inca ethnic groups inhabiting the Cuzco region whose political autonomy and control of natural resources had been usurped and appropriated by the emergent Inca elite. Local ethnic groups that did not resist the rising political power of the Inca, either because of military weakness or a calculated decision to cast their lot with the Inca, and that chose to pay tribute to the Inca nobility were granted the title of Inca by privilege. As a result of that status, they enjoyed some of the economic and social prerogatives of affiliation with the Inca nobility. They could exchange gifts, contract marriage alliances, share in some, though not all, of Cuzco's religious festivals and ceremonial feasts, and participate in the distribution of goods that flowed into Cuzco as a result of Inca success in wars of conquest and assimilation in surrounding territories. Local non-Inca groups and *kurakas* who distinguished themselves in service to the Inca lords by rendering tribute and participating in military campaigns were granted enhanced status. Although the Inca, mostly as a matter of political expediency, ennobled them, the Inca by privilege did not possess a permanent birthright to noble status. These groups and individuals could just as easily lose that status if the reigning monarch decided that they were politically untrustworthy or did not adequately fulfill their tributary obligations. So this was a contingent status, one that could be gained or lost at any time, and was dependent on loyalty to the Inca king and his powerful coterie of close kin.

But, at the same time, it was in the geopolitical interest of the Inca king to maintain close personal ties with the ethnic groups that lived all around Cuzco to reduce the ever-present threat of sedition and the potential for competition for ultimate power. For this reason, grants of noble title via the Inca by privilege category were an astute political move that bound local subject populations to their Inca overlords in intimate reciprocal ties of economic relations, shared religious practices, and interpersonal sentiment. Even though they were clearly marked as subaltern, junior partners – the archetypical *huaccha concha* – Incas by privilege came to believe and participate in a sense of shared destiny with the Inca elite. Here we see the subtle psychological effects of the Inca state's project to promote a viral form of hegemony that generated structures of political, social, and economic incentives – all the gifts of power – that created subjects willing to cede their own autonomy in order to gain a privileged position in the wealth-generating system of Inca imperialism. The Incas' initial, fragile form of laminar hegemony established in the Cuzco region through military conquest was rapidly transformed into a more pervasive and deeply rooted system of shared belief and practice – a viral hegemony – that bound subjects to the lords of Cuzco more completely and permanently than any form of coercion ever could.

The final class of nobles in the Inca social order was the non-Inca ethnic lords who, prior to their conquest by the Inca, ruled autonomously in their own *señoríos*. Depending on local political and strategic circumstances, the Inca kings would often confirm local lords in their positions as long as the lords acknowledged the authority of the Inca and complied with tributary demands. The lords of the most important conquered polities were obligated to travel periodically to Cuzco to render public homage to the reigning monarch and his *qoya* and to the principal *wak'as* of the state cults. In addition, powerful local lords sent their sons and presumptive heirs to Cuzco for education in the Quechua language and in Inca culture, social etiquette, philosophy, administrative practices, and religious beliefs. Through this multigenerational process of indoctrination, the Inca attempted to convert provincial nobility into loyal agents of their regime. For the postconquest, emerging generation of local elites, their experiences in Cuzco transformed their historical consciousness to the extent that their own sense of subjectivity was intimately and ineluctably bound up with their relationship to Cuzco and their Inca noble counterparts.

But this class of provincial nobility was also most at risk of losing status under the Inca imperial yoke. They could be relieved of their authority at will by the Inca king and replaced with an Inca noble or even a *yana* lord (see below). Their noble status depended exclusively on their political loyalties to the Inca king. This was a bitter pill for these once autonomous lords. Many violently resisted Inca usurpation of their authority. Some native lords of the most powerful competing polities, such the Aymara kingdoms of the Lake Titicaca basin, repeatedly contested Inca dominance of their homelands and, as a result of military defeats, were captured in the field of battle, humiliated publicly in the plazas of Cuzco, and then executed. When necessary to advance their political ambitions, the Inca were not loath to commit appalling acts of ethnocide, murdering the population of entire villages, destroying their *wak'as*, torturing and executing their leaders, and appropriating their women for themselves. Because of these tactical acts of extreme brutality, many other lords in what became the provinces of the Inca Empire practiced a kind of realpolitik once it became evident that they could not effectively resist Inca military prowess. They became collaborators in the Inca project of world building. For instance, the native lords of Chincha on the central coast of Peru, who controlled extensive, lucrative maritime and inland trade routes throughout the western Andes, became among the closest non-Inca political allies to the Inca monarchs. As a result of their fidelity and political allegiance to the lords of Cuzco, they were granted extraordinary privileges, including the right to be carried in a litter alongside the reigning monarch when he traveled through his realm. So, as with all Inca social categories, there was substantial nuance, with multiple degrees of status, privilege, and social power within and between categories.

Mitmaqkuna, Yanakuna, Kamayuqkuna, and *Aqllakuna*

Not all subjects of the Inca Empire were members of autonomous, self-sufficient *ayllus* or ethnic groups. The Inca also promoted identification with their social order through four potentially overlapping forms of specialized labor service: the *mitmaq, yana, kamayuq,* and *aqlla* institutions, which were, in essence, designations for special status relationships between individuals and Inca lords. The first institution, called the *mitmaq* (pl. *mitmaqkuna*) or *mitima* (pl. *mitimaes*), held special fascination for the Spaniards, possibly because the conquerors recognized certain elements that echoed their own traditions of statecraft. The contemporary Spanish chronicler and soldier Cieza de León left a detailed description of the *mitmaqkuna* that portrays the essence of the institution: "As soon as one of these large provinces was conquered," he wrote,

ten or twelve thousand of the men and their wives, or six thousand, or the number decided upon, were ordered to leave and remove themselves from it. These were transferred to another town or province of the same climate and nature as that which they left and these were called *mitimae,* which means Indians come from one land to another. They were given land to work and sites on which to build their houses. And these *mitimae*s were ordered by the Incas to be always obedient to what their governors and captains ordered, so that if the natives should rebel, and they supported the governor, the natives would be punished and reduced to the service of the Incas. Likewise if the *mitimae* stirred up disorder, they were put down by the natives. In this way these rulers had their empire assured against revolts and the provinces well supplied with food, for most of the people, as I have said, had been moved from one land to another. (Cieza de León 1976:56–57)

In a passage remarkable for its analytical perceptiveness, Cieza de León went on to distinguish three classes of *mitmaq* – military, political, and economic. The military *mitmaqkuna* served an important function as border guards, populating and commanding army garrisons on the fringes of the expanding Inca state. These were essentially groups of soldier-citizens who maintained a military profile on behalf of the Inca, as well as reclaiming and cultivating lands and herding llama and alpaca on the border zones of the empire. In many respects, these *mitmaqkuna* fulfilled roles similar to those of the army garrisons and civilian colonists who were established in frontier areas of the Roman Empire. Frequently, rudimentary army camps on the Roman frontier were transformed over time into colonial towns through the actions of the legionnaires who remained for many years, establishing farms, roads, markets, and smithies, and engaging in a host of other urban occupations.

The second class of transplanted colonists, the political *mitmaqkuna*, also served security functions. They were more numerous than the military *mitmaqkuna* and were found in every province of the empire. These *mitmaqkuna* had been forcibly removed from their homelands and resettled in other provinces, where they were required to retain their distinctive ethnic costume, headdress, customs, and forms of social organization. The strategic goal underlying the Inca's implantation of political *mitmaqkuna* was to reduce the chances for rebellion in conquered provinces by shattering traditional patterns of shared ethnic identity among large contiguous populations. By intermixing local inhabitants with pockets of foreigners in self-contained colonies, the Inca substantially inhibited the potential for subversive political coalitions. "In this way," observed Cieza de León, "all was quiet, and the *mitimae*s feared the natives, and the natives feared the *mitimae*s, and all occupied themselves only in obeying and serving" (Cieza de León 1976:60).

Cieza de León characterized the third use of *mitmaq* colonists as "stranger" than the others. He described these economic *mitmaqkuna* in the following terms:

[I]f, perchance, they had conquered territory in the highlands or plains or on a slope suitable for plowing and sowing, which was fertile and had a good climate ... they quickly ordered that from nearby provinces that had the same climate as these ... enough people come in to settle it, and to these lands were given, and flocks, and all the provisions they needed until they could harvest what they planted or a number of years no tribute was exacted of these new settlers, but on the contrary they were given women, coca, and food so that they would carry out the work of settlement with better will. (Cieza de León 1976:62)

To Cieza de León and other Spanish military men, the use of frontier garrisons and colonial outposts was entirely familiar. But the Inca principle of economic *mitmaq* was alien to these representatives of an essentially feudal, medieval European tradition. First, the institution incorporated the unfamiliar Andean ideal of reciprocity. In transplanting populations to reclaim productive lands in a new province, the state was initially obligated to provide the colonists with land, basic provisions, and gifts of valued commodities, such as textiles and women. Second, these *mitmaq* colonists were exempted from taxation until they could reclaim enough land to sustain themselves and produce a surplus for the state. Finally, and perhaps most importantly, few Spanish chroniclers or administrators grasped the significance of the economic *mitmaqkuna* as state expressions of the Andean archipelago economy. The principal intent of the economic *mitmaq* was to enhance the productive capacity of the Inca state by reclaiming marginal land and, in some cases, by focusing the labor of thousands of transplanted colonists on the production of a single prestige crop, maize.

One of the most remarkable and well-documented uses of economic *mitmaqkuna* occurred during the reign of Wayna Qhapaq (ca. 1493–1527). This last independent emperor of the Inca expelled the native populations of the Cochabamba Valley, one of the richest and most fertile in Bolivia, in order to install fourteen thousand new colonists from a variety of ethnic groups, who were placed there under the direct control of two Inca governors. These multiethnic colonists were brought to Cochabamba explicitly to produce maize for the state. The vast quantities of maize that flowed into the imperial storehouses in Cochabamba were eventually shipped to Cuzco for consumption by the Inca army. Wayna Qhapaq completely reorganized the system of land tenure in Cochabamba to accommodate this grand scheme of repopulation and intensive state maize production. He divided the entire valley into seventy-seven long strips, or *suyus*, and then assigned individual ethnic groups to work the *suyus* or fractional parts of *suyus*, depending on the topographic context of the designated strip and the population size of each colonizing ethnic group. Only seven of these strips of land, interspersed among the other seventy *suyus*, were allotted to the fourteen thousand colonists for their own subsistence. The remaining portion, more than ninety percent of the arable land in the valley, was given over to intensive production of maize for the state.

As was the case with other multiethnic *mitmaq* colonization schemes, the work assignments and other internal affairs of each ethnic group were governed by the group's own political leaders. These persons were then responsible to the two Inca governors who headed up the political hierarchy. In return for their service to the Inca, the various ethnic *kurakas* were rewarded with small plots of land within the valley, as well as with some Inca prestige goods, such as cotton mantles, and occasionally with women for secondary wives. By Inca governmental decree, each group maintained its own ethnic costume, headdress, and way of life. The economic *mitmaqkuna* served multiple purposes for the Inca state. Primarily, they became a tremendous engine of agrarian wealth, capable of producing massive quantities of maize for the state; in some environmental circumstances like the fertile, temperate Cochabamba Valley the colonists could produce two annual crops. More than two thousand preserved Inca stone storehouses on the hill slopes of the Cochabamba Valley attest to the productive capacity of these transplanted populations. Secondarily, of course, these colonists performed an important security function. A series of transplanted, fragmented ethnic groups working side by side in Cochabamba presented less of a threat to the Inca state than the potentially unified indigenous inhabitants of the valley deported by the Inca.

The three categories of Inca *mitmaq*, then, crosscut each other. Political *mitmaqkuna* frequently fulfilled economic functions; military *mitmaqkuna* were, almost by definition, also political *mitmaqkuna*; and, by their organization and multiethnic composition, large-scale economic *mitmaq* colonization schemes such as in the Cochabamba Valley became simultaneously effective security devices. Although the principal colonization projects organized by the Inca focused on agricultural development schemes, *mitmaq* colonists were also established to exploit specific concentrated natural resources such as salt, gold, silver, timber, clay for pottery, semiprecious stones for jewelry, hard stone for construction, and the like. The number of colonists relocated in these projects varied greatly, ranging from extended families to entire villages and ethnic groups reaching into the thousands, as in the case of Wayna Qhapaq's reorganization of the Cochabamba Valley.

We have no precise information on the total number of people removed from their homelands and resettled elsewhere. But all sources indicate that it was a substantial portion of the population. Betanzos reported that after a three-year campaign of conquest and assimilation in the

Ecuadorian highlands, the son and heir of King Pachakuti, Thupa Inka Yupanki, and his elder brother, Yamque Yupanki, who was the military commander of the campaign, "ordered the natives of Quito and the rest of the nearby inhabitants and provinces in the area and the Guancavilcas, Cañares, and Yungas to give him fifteen thousand Indians, who were to leave with him on the road he was taking. These Indians were young married men with their wives, their things, and seeds from their lands so they could be placed as *mitimaes* in the valleys and lands surrounding Cuzco" (Betanzos 1996:120). Similarly, King Wayna Qhapaq, the son and heir of Thupa Inka Yupanqui, after completing his early campaigns of conquest, massively redeveloped the temperate valley of Yucay, which is close to Cuzco, as his private estate, and "there Huayna Capac had many small towns of twenty, thirty, and fifty Indians built. In these towns he put many *mitimae* Indians from all the nations and provinces of the land. *Mitimae* means people, including them and their descendants, transplanted from their birthplace to reside permanently there where they were placed" (Betanzos 1996:170). These passages imply that large-scale, forced resettlement programs were a routine geopolitical strategy of Inca kings and their military commanders in the aftermath of conquest. Furthermore, the particular social identity of the *mitmaqkuna* as "young married men with their wives" reveals part of the deeper, strategic purpose of these population transfers on an imperial scale. Thus the Inca commandeered the most able-bodied families in the prime of their reproductive life from the conquered provinces. At one stroke, the Inca kings acquired an enormous pool of labor for their personal and state projects and, by expropriating the most productive members of the conquered ethnic groups, simultaneously undermined the demographic base of potential political competitors. Such massive transfers of entire *ayllus* and villages as *mitmaqkuna*, who thereby became directly dependent on the Inca state for their political security and for the enhancement of their social position and economic well-being, resulted in a gradual dissemination of Inca language, values, expectations, and cultural beliefs. Under the impact of this program of population mixing on an imperial scale, old ethnic identities, loyalties, and beliefs began slowly to transform themselves in conformity with the new Inca ideal, enhancing the unification of the empire itself. The ultimate cultural effect of this massive forced colonization scheme was to extend in viral fashion the hegemonic power of Inca cultural representations of social reality.

Like that of the *mitmaq* colonists, another form of labor status imposed by the Inca, that of the *yanakuna* (sing. *yana*), served to break down local identities, kin affiliations, and the capacity for autonomous political action by subject populations. The *yanakuna* have been interpreted as everything from a true slave class of the state responsible for the heaviest manual labor to domestic servants for the Inca elite. Perhaps the most satisfactory definition of the term *yana* is "personal retainer," or as Rostworowski (1999:149) styled them, "servants in waiting." In many respects, the *yanakuna* were much like vassals in a feudal state. They were attached to the households of individual Inca lords and owed personal fealty to them. In return for their personal service to their liege lords, the *yanakuna* were exempted from the tributary obligations assessed against the ordinary citizens of the realm. The nature of these obligations will be explored in detail in Chapter 5. The *yanakuna* did not reside in their own *ayllu*-based communities, nor did they possess or cultivate their own land. They sustained themselves and their families through usufruct rights granted by the lords they served to water sources, parcels of land, and other basic resources necessary for their social reproduction. Rather than forming their own autonomous households, they and their dependents became subordinate members of the extended patrimonial households of their lords.

The extensive variety of services that they performed for their Inca lords implies that there were several types of *yanakuna* situated within a complex hierarchy of status ranging from domestic servants who performed menial tasks to minor officials charged with certain administrative tasks. Many *yanakuna* cultivated the private estates of the king, the *qoya*, or other highly placed Inca nobles who had sufficient social power to amass their own patrimonial lands. Others gathered firewood, cooked meals, brewed alcohol, managed private llama herds, or worked as skilled artisans in the households of their lords. All of the agricultural estates of the *panaqa* kin corporations in and around Cuzco depended on the menial labor of the *yanakuna* who plowed the land and planted, harvested, and stored the produce in the estate's warehouses.

Some *yanakuna* were assigned to work on the temple lands of the state cults endowed by the king, or as custodians of specific shrines. The principal oracle centers consulted by the king and his court, such as Pachacamac on the central Peruvian coast, Catequil in the northern highlands of Huamachuco, and Vilcashuaman in the central highlands, as well as the most sacred temple complexes of the state, such as those on the Copacabana Peninsula and the Islands of the Sun and Moon in Lake Titicaca, were permanently endowed with numerous *yana* laborers and their families. Proximity to and intimacy with the numinous qualities of these sacred sites conveyed a measure of prestige to the *yanakuna* who labored in the service of the state cults.

Like some officials of pharaonic Egypt who were originally of commoner status, *yanakuna* could rise in the social hierarchy of the empire to hold privileged and responsible positions in the state's governance. They became, in effect, *yana* lords, serving as officials on the staffs of Inca provincial governors and frequently overseeing the labor of forcibly transplanted colonists on state plantations and in pasturelands, fishing and hunting grounds, and mines. In return for faithful service and personal loyalty, these *yana* lords were rewarded with gifts of land, women, food, and clothing, and with emblems of their special status in the eyes of the Inca state, such as a particularly fine cotton mantle, or perhaps a copper cup, armband, ring, or other adornment. Since the *yanakuna*, particularly those who served in the royal households of the Inca, owed their relatively high status to direct personal relationships with the Inca elite, their bond of traditional loyalty to ethnic groups or villages of origin was weakened in favor of their service to the Inca government.

The Inca kings readily grasped the strategic advantage of amassing a labor force that owed their well-being and the possibility of social mobility to their personal relationship with the Inca nobility and not to their own autonomous communities. Resistance to Inca hegemony congealed around local lands, local *wak'as*, and local political solidarities among the numerous ethnic groups that the Inca subjugated. By initiating and expanding the *yana* institution among subjugated populations, the Inca kings were gradually breaking down the deeply entrenched sociological, economic, and spiritual ties of Andean populations to their natal ethnic groups and lands. Replacing a native lord of a recalcitrant ethnic group with a loyal *yana* lord attached to the royal household was another powerful demonstration that declared, in effect, "submit to the Inca, or risk losing your title, your prerogatives and perhaps even your head." *Yanakuna* themselves exchanged their autonomy and self-sufficiency for political and economic security, and for the chance, however slight, that they might rise in the empire's social hierarchy to become lords, albeit subaltern lords, in their own circumscribed domains. If they ever attained the status of a petty lord in the Inca system of social hierarchy, the *yanakuna* could even aspire to passing their newly gained title to their heirs, who would then constitute a new line of hereditary lords. This was a powerful incentive for the *yanakuna* to cut ties with their natal communities and to cast their lot with the powerful Inca kings and the new imperial world they were creating. From the perspective of the Inca kings, as Rostworowski (1999:149) astutely observes, the *yana* institution held its own political attraction:

The advantage of appointing a *yana* as lord consisted in finding himself, by his very condition, separated from his origins, with no ties of kinship or reciprocity with his birthplace. With the *yana* [as lord], the Inca had no need to recur to the mechanism of reciprocity, and could give orders directly.

Because of this mutually beneficial dynamic that constituted a kind of political symbiosis, the *yanakuna* became essential players in the daily administration of the empire and pivotal actors in the Inca strategy of domination and governance in their conquered territories. The Inca political creation of a new class of *yanakuna* and *yana* lords illustrates one of the social processes that generated what I have termed strategic viral hegemony. In this process, state elite create political and cultural conditions that so thoroughly transform the historical consciousness of subjects that the subjugated populations come to broadly share the ruling class's ideology of hierarchical social relations and governance. In such a circumstance, the Inca had little need to repress or to maintain close surveillance of their "servants in waiting" because the *yanakuna* (or at least a substantial portion of them) believed that they benefited from their social position in the hierarchy, even if that position was subordinated to the Inca lords. Of course, we must also acknowledge that in some cases one of the inducements to move into *yana* status presented by the Inca may have been less benign – the threat to liquidate entire lineages who resisted the invitation to accept the Inca as their lords.

The special civic status of the *kamayuq* (pl. *kamayuqkuna*) was similar to that of the *yana*. They labored full-time on behalf of individual Inca lords in the noble households in Cuzco and in the provinces; they were exempt from the otherwise universal labor tribute; and, as with the *yanakuna*, their status was inherited, handed down from generation to generation. Documents of the early sixteenth century preserve for us an expansive list of specialized occupations of people identified as *kamayuqkuna*. They were miners of precious metals; stonemasons; carpenters; weavers of fine textiles; sandal makers; potters; dye makers; leather, wood, bone, and shell workers; goldsmiths; hunters; herders; honey gatherers; herbalists; porters; litter bearers; bodyguards; and accountants, among other productive activities. Sons and daughters of *kamayuqkuna* were apprenticed to their parents and other close relatives. They began to work in the particular trade as soon as they had the physical capacity to contribute. In this way, *kamayuq* households and *ayllus* became the focal point for particular craft and occupational specialties, developing their own styles and recognized workshops. Often, entire villages containing one or two hundred people specialized in a particular craft occupation, such as weaving, woodworking, or potting. These villages of *kamayuqkuna* supported their daily subsistence needs by cultivating land given to them by the Inca state for that purpose, or

3.11. Ceramic plate with painted images of fish and *ají*. Exquisite objects such as this were crafted by specialized *kamayuq* artisans. (Inca, south coast or southern highlands, Peru, Ceremonial Vessel (Aryballos), AD 1450/1532, ceramic and pigment, 20.6 x 17.8 cm [8 1/8 x 7 in.], Kate S. Buckingham Endowment, 1955.2219, The Art Institute of Chicago. Photography © The Art Institute of Chicago)

by exchanging their craft products for food. Certain *kamakyuq* groups such as salt miners and silversmiths exploited, or depended upon, concentrated natural resources for their products. Frequently, these groups were moved from their villages of origin by the Inca state to new sources of essential raw materials. Like the more numerous transplanted colonists engaged in agrarian and pastoral pursuits described earlier, these craft-specialized *kamayuqkuna* became a strategic part of the state-managed economy by providing a constant flow of desired commodities to the Inca elite. Many of the products of the craft *kamayuqkuna* were essential for the Inca kings' massive public demonstrations of generosity and for the private gifts given by the kings to assure the loyalty of local *kurakas* who were the key to Inca political patronage and control of newly conquered provinces. Some of the finest artisans of the craft *kamayuqkuna* achieved wide repute, honor, and prestige within the royal households of Cuzco, and were materially rewarded for their virtuosity in creating exquisite objects of display (Figures 3.11, 3.12, and 3.13). Unlike the highest-status *yanakuna*, however, who could hold positions of trust and moderate power as petty managers and enjoy some upward social mobility in the Inca state, the *kamayuqkuna* held specific, fixed occupations that they discharged for the Inca elite throughout their life-

3.12. Ceramic *aríbalo*-type vessels, used for storing and transporting liquids. (Inca, probably vicinity of Cuzco, Peru, Plate Depicting Suche Fish and Peppers, AD 1450/1532, ceramic and pigment, 7.6 x 23.7 cm (3 x 9 5/16 in.), Kate S. Buckingham Endowment, 1955.2223, The Art Institute of Chicago. Photography © The Art Institute of Chicago)

time. In the Inca state, vertical movement in the hierarchy of power was strictly controlled.

Perhaps a partial exception to the permanent, nonnoble status of the *kamayuq* was the *khipu kamayuq* and the *llacta kamayuq*, both of whom performed particularly strategic functions for the administration of the Inca state. The *khipu kamayuqkuna* specialized in keeping historical and numerical accounts on the unique Andean mnemonic device of the *khipu*, a complex artifact of knotted, multicolored cords (Ascher and Ascher 1981; Salomon 2004; Urton 2003) (Figure 3.14). Cieza de León recounted his skepticism that such an artifact, in the absence of alphabetic writing, could record detailed narrations and economic accounts, but then describes this accounting system in some detail based on a demonstration given to him by a *kuraka* named Huacarapora in the central Andean highland province of Xauxa. The Inca, Cieza de León said:

3.13. Anthropomorphic *k'ero*, a drinking vessel used for serving *chicha* beer in political and religious rituals. (Image © The Field Museum of Natural History, #A78539)

3.14. A *khipu*, a recording device made of knotted, multicolored strings. (Image courtesy of author)

[H]as a method of knowing how the tributes of food supplies should be levied on the provinces when the Lord-Inca came through with his army, or was visiting the kingdom; or, when nothing of this sort was taking place, what came into the storehouses and what was issued to the subjects, so nobody could be duly burdened, that was so good and clever that it surpasses ... the Mexicans for their accounts and dealings. This involved the *khipus*, which are long strands of knotted strings, and those who were the accountants and understood the meaning of these knots could reckon by them expenditures or other things that had taken place many years before. By these knots they counted from one to ten and from ten to a hundred, and from a hundred to a thousand. On one of these strands there is the account of one thing, and on the other of another, in such a way that what to us is a strange, meaningless account is clear to them. In the capital of each province there were accountants whom they called *khipu-camayocs*, and by these knots they kept account of the tribute to be paid by the natives of that district in silver, gold, clothing, flocks, down to wood and other more insignificant things, and by these same *khipus* at the end of a year, or ten, or twenty years, they gave a report to the one whose duty it was to check the account so exact that not even a pair of sandals was missing. (Cieza de León 1976:173–174)

The complex, esoteric knowledge required of a *khipu kamayuq* demanded a substantial period of training to master the creation and reading of the *khipu*. Physical dexterity, abstract reasoning, exceptional mathematical skill, and an eidetic memory must have been required to achieve full competency as a *khipu kamayuq*.

Like the *khipu kamayuqkuna*, the *llacta kamayuqkuna* performed accounting services for the Inca state, but they operated in a more comprehensive and more explicitly political and administrative context than that in which the *khipu kamayuqkuna*, who were in the individual service of the various ethnic lords in the Inca realm, functioned. Betanzos described this critical administrative position created by the Inca in great detail:

The Inca ordained that in each town a man be identified who was the most able and diligent of the town and of good judgment. If the town were large, one man from each *parcialidad* [section or moiety] of the town would be selected. This man or men would be in charge of keeping track of male and female children born each year as well as those who died. Each one would keep track of the people of their town. He should know about the lives of everyone and how they made their living, what livestock they were raising. Those who raised livestock were to have an insignia of it hanging on their door, such as the sheep's [i.e., llama or alpaca] leg or jawbone. If they had birds, they should have its feathers and eggs hanging from the door of the house where they lived. If the man were a hunter, a fisherman, or a farmer or had any other trade, he should hang on the door of his house some insignia of it. The designated man should take care to know what each person harvested from their fields and the livestock that each one had as well as the increase of it. And each one should keep track of increases and what was acquired.... The Inca ordered that the man who had these responsibilities be named *llacta camayo*, which means "town official." (Betanzos 1996:109)

Given that a sophisticated system of accountancy capable of producing and storing huge databases of narrative and numerical information was essential to the logistics of empire, we can reasonably assume that the *khipu kamayuqkuna* and the *llacta kamayuqkuna* were held in great esteem, and that some of them may have been granted minor noble status in the same manner as the *yana* lords. The *kamayuqkuna*, then, formed another distinct category of individuals and communities who rendered specialized, highly skilled or technically sophisticated services to the Inca elite. *Kamayuq* individuals and communities may or may not have been relocated to facilitate their specialized occupations, but given the corporate nature of many of the craft and technical skills they performed, unlike the *yanakuna* who were attached as retainers to the households, *ayllus,* and *panaqas* of the Inca lords, the *kamayuqkuna* likely remained affiliated with their *ayllus* and communities of origin.

To the modern mind, perhaps the most exotic of the specialized forms of labor relations created by the Inca was the institution of the *aqllakuna* (sing. *aqlla*) and *mamakuna* or "chosen women" (Figure 3.15). Betanzos succinctly captured the key features of this institution, which, like the *yanakuna*, established a special service relationship between individuals (in this instance, young women) who were purposely removed from their communities of origin and Inca state agents:

The Inca ordained that there be certain designated houses in the provinces and principal towns. In them a certain number of young virgins would be placed. These would be the wives of the Sun who faithfully fed the Sun and made sacrifices to him every day. This lord also sent to the provinces many idols which the people of these provinces could worship and honor with sacrifices just as he had done in the city of Cuzco. These sacrifices would be made in these provinces to the idols in the same way as was done in Cuzco before the idols. He ordered that the statues of the Sun which he sent to these provinces be placed in those houses where the *mamaconas* were, that storehouses of food and garments be made and fields be designated for this service of the Sun and sustenance of these *mamaconas*. All of this was to be put in the name of the Sun. In addition, other houses should be made where there were placed other *mamaconas*, virgins, daughters of lords. These would be called the wives of the Inca. They should also be given lands and storehouses made for all their provisions. In order to provide for all this and be its collectors, certain men of the town were designated. And those who had dealings with these *mamaconas*, both these and the others, and the guardians who looked after them were castrated Indians. (Betanzos 1996:110)

The *aqllakuna* and *mamakuna* were divided between those who served the state cults (wives of the Sun) and those who served the royal family and individuals favored by the king (wives of the Inca). The Inca rulers selected young females as chosen women from the provinces, reputedly

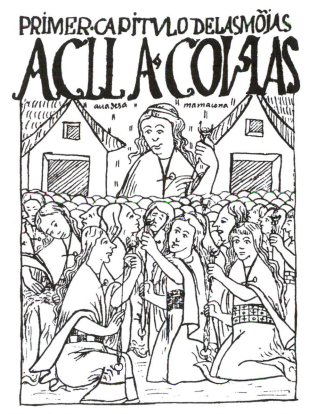

PRIMER·CAPITVLO DELASMÖIAS
ACLLA·COYAS

3.15. *Aqllakuna* weaving at an *aqllawasi*, supervised by a female over-seer. (Adapted from Poma de Ayala 1609)

for their beauty and physical perfection, when they were approximately eight to ten years old. As Betanzos related, these chosen women lived communally in special residential compounds, referred to as the *aqlla-wasi* (house of the chosen women), in the larger cities, towns, and temple precincts of the empire (Figures 3.16 and 3.17). The king endowed the *aqllawasis* with lands and *yana* servants to sustain the community of chosen women and thereby free them from the ordinary labor of working the fields so that they could concentrate full-time on their more specialized tasks on behalf of the state cults or the royal family. There the women performed a variety of services for the state, spinning cotton and wool for the clothing of the Inca elite; weaving particularly luxurious textiles; cooking delicacies; brewing *chicha*, or maize beer, in great quantities for public ceremonies; and tending to the daily chores for maintaining the

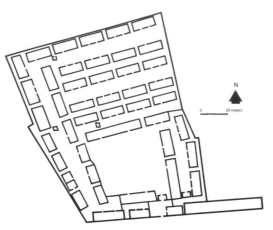

3.16. Plan of an *aqllawasi* from Huánuco Pampa. The building's function is indicated by evidence of large ceramic vessels for brewing *chicha* and by numerous spindle whorls for large-scale weaving. (Adapted from Morris and Thompson 1985)

3.17. Reconstructed *aqllawasi* built of adobe bricks from the Inca component of the site of Pachacamac, central coast of Peru. (Image courtesy of A. Guengerich)

principal shrines of the state cults. Some of the *aqllakuna* were drawn from the families of the highest nobility, the daughters of lords, and were called the "wives of the Inca." These particularly high-status *aqllakuna* frequently served as concubines to the emperor himself. Other *aqllakuna* of similar high pedigree were distributed by the Inca ruler and his generals as secondary wives to warriors who had distinguished themselves in battle or to local regents and *kurakas* who had demonstrated loyalty to the Inca cause. On the occasion of his marriage to his principal wife, the Inca king Pachakuti assigned one hundred *aqllakuna* for her personal service, and the steward of the state cult of the Sun gave her an additional fifty.

In essence, then, the *aqllakuna* provided concentrated skilled labor for the state cults and for the Inca monarchs and their royal families, as well as precious commodities for the conduct of diplomacy. Like most monarchies throughout the world, the Inca relied on strategic marriages to strengthen political ties with the provincial nobility. Of course, females who were direct descendants of the royal household in Cuzco were the most desirable marriage partners for the highest-status native lords of the provinces. Their marriages constituted true dynastic alliances and resulted frequently in heirs with aspirations to high positions in the central governmental bureaucracy, or even with pretensions to the throne itself. But the genius of Inca statecraft was to apply this somewhat circumscribed notion of dynastic alliances among the princes and princesses of royal households to virtually every rung in the social hierarchy of control. The tremendous concentration of unencumbered *aqllakuna* in the provincial capitals of the Inca state was the key to this institutionalization of strategic marriages. Because of their elevated status as "chosen women" of the Inca, the *aqllakuna* were seen as desirable marriage partners, endowed with the prestige of the state and promising the provincial nobility identification with the power and authority of the central government. It is not surprising that the *aqllawasis* in the principal cities of the empire were jealously guarded by the Inca and that the violation of a "chosen woman" was designated a capital crime in the state's criminal code. As was true for the Inca nobility, the Incas by privilege, the *yanakuna,* and the *kamayuqkuna,* the social status, privileges, and labor obligations of the *aqllakuna* varied considerably, depending on the young women's "social origins, beauty and aptitudes" (Rostworowski 1999:176). These ranked gradations of *aqlla* social identities included the *yurac aqllakuna,* who were of the purest noble bloodlines, serving as wives of the Inca monarch and in the precincts of the solar cult; the *huayrur aqllakuna,* who could become secondary wives of the king; the *paco aqllakuna,* who were given as gifts by the Inca to nobles and favored military captains; and the *yana aqllakuna,* who were not of "exceptional rank or beauty" and so were placed in service to the other *aqllakuna* (Rostworowski 1999:176).

A final social category deserves brief mention: captives of war. Betanzos (1996:94) mentions that men and women taken captive in war were referred to as *piñas.* In the same passage, Betanzos refers to these war captives as "slaves" and then as "male and female Indian servants." We do not know if the *piñas* were actually treated as slaves, or to what extent they were analogous to the *yanakuna,* incorporated relatively benignly into the elite households of their captors as domestic servants. The actual social status and conditions of treatment of the *piñas* by their masters may have depended on the individual circumstances of the *piñas'* capture, the disposition of their captors, and the personal relationships that the warriors had with their captives, rather than having been a result of formal legal and institutional practices. In general, the Andean social practice of framing all social relations in the idiom of kinship suggests that a true slave status in which people are treated as chattel, as commodities to be bought, sold, and exchanged, was rare, if not entirely absent, in the Inca world.

As with virtually all Inca social categories explored here, principles of hierarchy and ranking, expressed through the idiom of genealogical pedigree, crosscut all classes and social relations and were one of the most important defining characteristics of the Inca social order. When we examine the political order of the Inca Empire and its strategies of statecraft, we will come to realize just how critical genealogical realities and the idiom of kinship were in creating, extending, and legitimizing the Inca social order. We will see that Sir Henry Maine's famous dictum expressing the transition from "tribal" to state society as necessarily representing a movement in social and juridical relationships from status to contract does not apply so easily or so clearly to the Inca Empire.

4   The Economic Order: Land, Labor, and the Social Relations of Production

> The face of the country was shagged over with forests of gigantic growth, and occasionally traversed by ridges of barren land, that seemed like shoots of the adjacent Andes, breaking up the region into little sequestered valleys of singular loveliness. The soil, though rarely watered by the rains of heaven, was naturally rich, and wherever it was refreshed with moisture, as on the margins of the streams, it was enameled with the brightest verdure. The industry of the inhabitants, moreover, had turned these streams to the best account, and canals and aqueducts were seen crossing the low lands in all directions, and spreading over the country, like a vast network, diffusing fertility and beauty around them. The air was scented with the sweet odors of flowers, and everywhere the eye was refreshed by the sight of orchards laden with unknown fruits, and of fields waving with yellow grain, and rich in luscious vegetables of every description that teem in the sunny clime of the equator.
>
> W. H. Prescott, *History of the Conquest of Peru*

W. H. Prescott's magisterial nineteenth-century work *History of the Conquest of Peru* resonates with poetic descriptions of the people and landscapes of the ancient Andes, some of which sound, to the contemporary ear, extravagant and rather precious. Yet his evocation of the exceptional fertility, diversity, abundance, and beauty of the Andean environment, assiduously worked and cultivated "to the best account" by its inhabitants, rings true for anyone who has experienced harvesttime in the Andes. Witnessing seemingly endless expanses of crimson-tinged quinoa growing on the windswept high plateau or massive terraces carved into impossibly steep mountain slopes covered in orderly rows of maize or potatoes elicits precisely the kind of deeply sensory experience Prescott portrayed. At harvesttime, the senses are engaged, sight and sound, smell and touch. Water threaded through fields and across mountain slopes can be heard in different intensities flowing and pooling. From all directions, the wind brings the smells of soil, vegetation, animals, wood fire. Nature, shaped and reshaped by human hands in an endless cycle of the agricultural seasons, seems visibly animate, alive with possibility, and, indeed, beautiful.

Given the intimate, sensual relationship of humans to their environment in agrarian societies like that of the Inca, we should not be surprised that both the land and the everyday practices of the farming that
produced the annual harvests of grains, tubers, vegetables, fruits, spices,
and medicinal plants were considered to be sacred and were subjects
of elaborate ritual and worship. To these agrarian societies, spirits were
immanent, embedded in the land, and humans communicated with
them on a daily basis in the everyday acts of tilling the soil and planting,
watering, weeding, harvesting, and processing the crops that sustained
life. Labor in the fields was inflected with moral sentiments and experienced as a collective, social enterprise. These realities must be taken
into account when we analyze how societies like the Inca thought of
and organized their systems of production and their state economies.
Understanding how the Inca structured the means and relations of production in their empire will entail exploration of the complex interrela-
tionships among land tenure; labor relations; access to natural resources;
environmental constraints; the technologies, logistics, and social organization of production; and, not trivially, religious beliefs. In other words,
to grasp and appreciate the internal logic of the Inca economic order,
we must again move readily across the analytical boundaries of Western
social categories.

The economic pediment of premodern states such as the Inca was
surplus labor extracted from rural populations. As Garnsey (1988:271)
aptly comments in the context of the Mediterranean world in classical
antiquity:

The unique urban civilizations of antiquity were supported, when all is told, by
the common labour of peasants. The survival of the peasantry hinged on the
nature of their response to environmental constraints and to the demands of
those wielding political and economic power. Peasants followed a production
strategy designed to minimise risk, endeavoring to reduce their vulnerability by
dispersing their land holdings, diversifying their crops and storing their surplus.
It was also essential for them to cultivate reciprocal relationships with their social
equals, kin, friends and neighbors, and superiors who could act as patrons.

Rural commoners in the Inca state worked out similar tactics for survival:
diversifying landholdings and crops, propagating an ingrained ethic of
sociability and mutual aid, and seeking well-elaborated reciprocal bonds
with political superiors. As we have seen, the pervasive social organization of *ayllu* and moiety systems reflects just this kind of risk-reduction
strategy, one eminently suited to the rigorous physical environment of
the Andean highlands, as well as to the considerable political instability
and intense competition for resources that characterized the centuries
immediately prior to Inca emergence.

Before proceeding to that analysis, I want to reemphasize that the Inca themselves did not conceive of "the economy" as a social phenomenon separate from other human activities, with autonomous behavioral rules, beliefs, and practices. In the contemporary world, many people who subscribe to religious beliefs set aside a specific day for rest and worship; they make a marked distinction between sacred and secular activities. We do not routinely think that our quotidian jobs, the daily nine-to-five tasks that earn our living, have an intimate, necessary relationship with our personal philosophies, values, and religious beliefs. Even those of us who make such a connection can conceive of and describe "sacred" and "secular" concepts and practices as distinct domains of life. This was not the case in the indigenous Andean world. From the frame of reference of the *ayllu*, work was worship and worship was work. The social world of *ayllu* members, the rhythms of their everyday life, conjoined the activities and practices that contemporary Western societies treat as separate domains. Plowing fields and conversing with *wak'as*, sharing meals and exchanging gifts, doing politics and expressing moral sentiments were all framed in terms of similar understandings of the reciprocal social relationships among humans, and between humans and their physical environment.

So this inquiry into the economic order of the Inca Empire will require a broad definition of what constitutes "economics," inflected by native Andean concepts, as nearly as we can understand them. Rather than strictly an exploration of the Inca's economic order, we will explore the political economy of the Inca state writ large. By political economy here I mean the aggregate processes of production, distribution, and consumption by which populations reproduce the biological and cultural bases of their society. The core elements of this meaning of political economy are the mechanisms of resource production and resource allocation; the stress, in effect, is on the production and flow of energy through the interaction of human labor, technological capacity, and the given physical environment. But these generically economic mechanisms entail a variety of social processes that do not necessarily partake directly in the technology of production. Thus the emergence and promotion of class stratification, the pursuit of economic self-interest by individuals and groups, and the generation of religious and cult behavior to modulate group action are trenchant examples of fundamentally social processes that work through this notion of political economy. Simply put, ideology and political economy substantially interrelate in most societies. By ideology, I follow the pragmatic meaning formulated by Paul Friedrich, which, as he suggests, is consonant with "scientific realism":

Ideology is a system, or at least an amalgam, of ideas, strategies, tactics, and practical symbols for promoting, perpetuating, or changing a social and cultural order; in brief, it is political ideas in action.... Such sets of ideas for action arise from the creative engagement of individuals with practical problems and necessarily reflect or express the will and interests for control or change of some social group or class – notably its economic interests. (Friedrich 1989:301)

Friedrich extends this definition of ideology by recapitulating the "analytically priceless, mainly Marxist notion of ideology as a set, or at least an amalgam of ideas, rationalizations, and interpretations that mask or gloss over a struggle to hold onto or get power, particularly economic power, with the result that the actors and ideologues are themselves unaware of what is going on. In this second, critical meaning, ideology arises from the interests of a class, usually an economic class or an economically defined class, and it is thus historically embedded.... [I]deology is ... simply the projection of group interest" (Friedrich 1989:302). Here, again, in the analytical definition of ideology we find an ineluctable intermingling of ideas, political strategies, belief systems, and the promotion of group economic and social interests. So we will examine here not only Inca concepts of wealth and the technologies and logistics of production but also how these economic concepts and practices were deeply embedded in the total social fabric of indigenous Andean life, including its ideological precepts and practices.

Land Tenure, Labor Relations, and Tribute

The role of labor and its relationship to land tenure resides at the core of native Andean economies, and the Inca economy in particular. Most of the Inca subjects in the Andean highlands, the commoners or *hatun runa*, worked lands and herded llama and alpaca as members of the collective social community of their *ayllus*. As we have seen, the *kurakas* or ethnic lords prior to Inca conquest were responsible for organizing the agricultural cycle of the seasons in their communities, as well as the religious festivals that were integral to the process of production. In return for their administrative work, the ethnic lords received the labor of community members, who cultivated *kurakas'* fields and provided other personal services necessary for them to fulfill their political and managerial roles. This same kind of exchange of labor for political services operated in the Inca state, but the pattern of labor extraction intensified over time. What was once a reciprocal exchange of labor services in form and in content, often became reciprocal in form alone.

The most detailed information we have on tributary relationships framed in terms of labor exchange comes from our sources on Inca culture at the time of the Spanish conquest. Understanding the tributary relationships perceivable in the early sixteenth century will aid us in reconstructing the potential forms of surplus labor extraction that powered the Inca Empire. The key to Inca extraction in their imperial provinces was in their tapping into two fundamental rural resources: land and labor. According to our sources, one of the first steps the Inca took after absorbing a new territory was to reorganize the prevailing system of land tenure to suit the economic needs of the empire. Bernabé Cobo provides a thorough account of how this reorganization of productive lands was undertaken. He noted that when an Inca king

> settled a town, or reduced one to obedience, he set up markers in its boundaries and divided the fields and arable land within its territory into three parts.... One part he assigned to religion and the cult of his false gods, another he took for himself, and the third he left for the common use of the people.... In some provinces the part assigned to religion was greater; in others that belonging to the Inca; and in some regions there were entire towns which, with their territory and all that it produced, belonged to the Sun and the other gods.... [I]n other provinces (and this was more usual), the king's share was the largest.... In the lands assigned to religion and to the crown, the Inca kept overseers and administrators who took great care in supervising their cultivation, harvesting the products and putting them in the storehouses. (Cobo 1979:211)

Cobo was fascinated by the manner of disposition of the third division of arable land that was to be allocated to the local inhabitants in the nature of commons. "These lands," he remarked, "were distributed each year among the subjects by the chief [the local ethnic lord], not in equal parts, but proportionate to the number of children and relatives that each man had; and, as the family grew or decreased, its share was enlarged or restricted. No man was granted more than just enough to support him, be he noble or citizen, even though a great deal of land was left over to lie fallow." Furthermore,

> When the *chacaras* [*chakras*, Quechua term for agricultural fields] of Religion were finished, the fields of the Inca were immediately sown, and, in their cultivation and harvest, the same order was followed. All members of the people who were present came in a group, and with them the lords up to the most important caciques and governors, dressed in their best and singing appropriate songs. When they cultivated the fields of Religion, their songs were in praise of their gods, and, when they cultivated the king's fields, in his praise. The third part of the land according to the division above was in the manner of commons, it being understood that the land was the property of the Inca, and the community only had the usufruct of it. It cannot be determined whether this share was equal to the others or greater, although it is true that each province and town was given sufficient lands to support its population. Every year the caciques distributed these lands among their subjects, but proportionate to the number of children

and relatives that each man had; as the family grew or decreased, its share was enlarged or restricted. No one was granted more than just enough to support himself, be he noble or plebeian, even though a great deal of land was left over to lie fallow and uncultivated; and this method of dividing the fields is practiced to this day in the provinces of Collao and elsewhere; and I have been present when it was done in the Province of Chucuito.... When it was time to sow or cultivate the fields, all other tasks stopped, so that all taxpayers together, without anyone absent, took part, and, if it was necessary to perform some job in an emergency, like a war or some other urgent matter, the other Indians of the community themselves worked the fields of the absent men without requesting or receiving any compensation beyond their food, and, this done, each one worked his own fields. This assistance which the community rendered to its absent members caused each man to return home willingly when he had finished his job; for it happened that when the Indian returned to his house after a long absence he might find that a harvest that he had neither sown nor reaped would be gathered into his house. (Cobo 1979:212–213)[1]

At least in their initial conquest of an ethnic group or *señorío*, the Inca grasped the strategic importance of respecting native notions of community autonomy and relative self-determination. Although Inca kings expropriated substantial tracts of land for purposes of the state, they made certain at the same time that sufficient land was allotted for the support of the local communities. More importantly, in many instances they shrewdly chose not to usurp the traditional prerogative of the local *kurakas* to decide how this land would be allocated among community members. Once land was redistributed, the Inca also imposed a labor tax on their new subjects. This agricultural labor tax was not an invention of the Inca, but was an ancient feature of the Andean social landscape (Moseley 1992). Throughout the Andes, local political leaders and ethnic lords had extracted surplus labor in community-owned fields from their subjects for generations before the coming of the Inca. The Inca, operating within an idiom familiar to any pre-Colombian Andean farmer for whom work rather than money was the essential means of discharging economic and social debts, simply assessed additional labor obligations on the local communities. Although Inca provincial administrators set quotas for the labor tax in each village and province and supervised the accounting of the agricultural goods that flowed into the state storehouses, it was generally the responsibility of the local *kurakas* to give individual work assignments to the heads of households, who then distributed the tasks among household members, including all able-bodied men, women, and children.

[1] See also Falcón 1918:152; Garcilaso 1961:part 1, book 5, chapter 15.

With the onset of the highland planting season in August and September, the two classes of fields that belonged to the state – those reserved for the support of the state religious cults and those of the king – were worked first, followed by the fields that remained for the support of the local populations. The fields were divided into long strips or sections, called *suyus* by the Inca, and each section became the responsibility of an individual household, or group of related households. By incorporating the local leaders into the supervision of the agricultural labor tax, the Inca reduced their own administrative costs. More importantly, however, this also minimized Inca intrusion into the daily life of the provincial villages and towns, permitting these communities to maintain the politically valuable illusion that they retained local autonomy. This pattern of indirect rule meant that the newly subordinate lord was incorporated into the kin-based idiom of governance emanating from Cuzco. Important local lords exchanged gifts with the Inca kings and his royal representatives. These exchanges were framed publicly as reciprocal, kin-based prestations, further drawing the provincial lords into a posture of collaboration.

But this technique of ruling through the native lords of conquered groups did not apply in all provinces, or in all geopolitical contexts. In areas of obdurate resistance, such as among the native Aymara lords of the Lake Titicaca basin, or where powerful kingdoms represented a potential political threat to Inca domination, such as the coastal kingdom of Chimor, Inca kings summarily executed or simply replaced native lords with compliant *kurakas* and loyal, kin-related nobles from Cuzco. The level of wealth extraction in the provinces, moreover, did not remain static. Over time, on repeated tours of their conquered provinces, Inca kings increased their landholdings by expropriating additional land for their personal estates, for military operations, and for the state cults. The dynamic of imperial expansion required increasing the extraction of both land and labor to fund state activities. That is, the imperial budget inevitably expanded along with the empire, requiring Inca kings to acquire additional landholdings and to increase the tributary burdens on the provinces. Rostworowski provides a particularly clear example of this incremental process from the Chincha Valley, citing the *Relación de Chincha* by Castro and Ortega Morejón [1558] in which:

General Capac Yupanqui is named as the first Cusqueño [inhabitant of Cuzco] to appear in the *señorío* in question. As a result of his visit, reciprocity was established between Cusco and Chincha. Year later, Tupac Yupanqui arrived with his army; among his impositions was the requirement of state lands. Later Huayna Capac did the same, drawing new boundaries that increased the landholdings of the ruler. (Rostworowski 1999:187)

For these native Andean societies grounded in an intense attachment to the soil, the Inca kings' continually expanding need to expropriate patrimonial lands in their conquered territories must have generated substantial political tension and most likely was one of the principal factors in the eruption of frequent rebellions in the provinces. The burdens of empire were onerous for both subjects and kings; the former suffered from loss of political autonomy and increasingly heavy tribute quotas, whereas the latter had to continually sustain costly armies in the field to maintain their supreme authority.

Elsewhere in his commentary, Cobo hit upon the key to the tremendous productive capacity of the Inca state. After the Inca expropriated a certain portion of arable lands in newly conquered provinces for the support of the state cults, the king, and the nobility, "the labor of sowing and cultivating these lands and harvesting their products formed a large part of the tribute which the taxpayer paid to the king." In addition to carving out lands from the conquered provinces for themselves, the Inca also exacted an annual contribution from villagers and townspeople in the form of agricultural labor. The local inhabitants were required to prepare, plant, weed, and harvest the state fields (Figure 4.1). As Cobo described it, the products of these fields were then processed, tallied, and stored under the watchful eyes of Inca overseers in immense state granaries. In other words, in a precapitalist world, where money was not a principal feature of economic transactions, taxation took the form of labor service for the state. Although payments in kind, such as designated quantities of tropical forest bird feathers, honey, salt, dried fish, mollusks, and other raw products, were assessed by Inca administrators in some provinces, the principal source of revenue for the Inca state was the labor tax, rather than the direct expropriation of goods.

Apart from the labor tax to work the lands of the state assessed at the community level, the Inca also demanded a second form of annual labor service from taxpayers. This obligation, called the *mit'a*, varied greatly in kind and length of service. The Inca used the *mit'a* to provide temporary work gangs for the construction of huge public monuments, for filling the ranks of the Inca army during its frequent campaigns in the provinces, for cultivating the private estates of the Inca elite, for extracting precious metals from state mines, and for many other services for the state that required manual labor. The scale of some *mit'a* operations was truly astonishing. Spanish chroniclers related that more than thirty thousand men were simultaneously mobilized for the construction of Saqsawaman, the great fortress-shrine of the Inca that perched on the mountain slopes above the imperial capital of Cuzco. Similarly, according to Betanzos, King Wayna Qhapaq assembled one

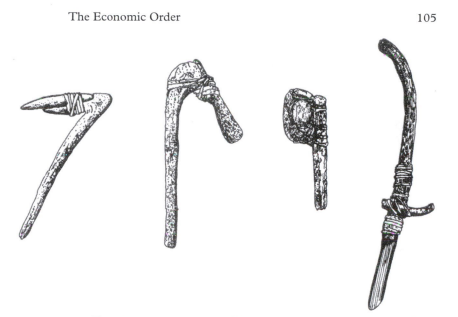

4.1. Farming implements used by modern Aymara, similar to those that would have been used by Inca farmers. *From left to right:* two kinds of *liukana*, a *kupana* (all three are kinds of mattocks), and a *hyuso* (digging stick or foot plow). (Image courtesy of author)

hundred fifty thousand subjects under the command of their hereditary lords from several subject provinces to labor on the redevelopment of the Yucay Valley as his personal retreat (Betanzos 1996:170). Although the Spanish sources may have exaggerated these numbers for dramatic effect, the magnitude of labor mobilization on behalf of the state and the private projects of the royal family was clearly enormous and without precedent in the ancient Andean world. The "tax rate" of the *mit'a* varied depending on the political needs of the king and his court. According to Cobo, "[T]here was no other rate or limit, either of the people that the provinces gave for the *mita* labor service or in the other requirements, except the will of the Inca. The people were never asked to make a fixed contribution of anything, but all of the people needed were called for the aforementioned jobs, sometimes in larger numbers, other times in lesser numbers, according to the Inca's desires, and the result of those labors was the royal tribute and income" (Cobo 1979:234).

The *mit'a* labor tax system possessed a number of uniquely Andean features that distinguished it from corvée or other forms of forced labor routinely employed by empires elsewhere in the ancient world. Much like the agricultural labor tax, the *mit'a* system was administered principally through local officials of the various ethnic groups subject to the Inca. When a draft of men was required for a military campaign, or to construct a bridge or an irrigation canal, the Inca governor in the affected province would call upon the heads of the various villages, towns, and ethnic groups, who would each be obliged to supply a designated number of taxpayers to complete the task. These local officials would then select from among the pool of eligible taxpayers (married heads of households) in their community on a rotational basis to supply their quota. In this way, the labor obligation was distributed equitably both among the different local ethnic groups in the province and within the groups themselves. No individual taxpayer was forced to serve the *mit'a* more frequently than another, and, apart from some special exemptions, all communities and ethnic groups participated in the system, contributing labor service according to the size of their population.

Local autonomy in implementing the *mit'a* labor tax was one of the special characteristics of the system that enhanced its efficiency and flexibility. But there was another principle in this system of taxation that reveals its character as a quintessential native Andean institution. To the indigenous peoples of the Andes, the *mit'a* was not perceived as a simple, one-sided tax debt assessed by their political superiors. Rather, they viewed the *mit'a* as a complex skein of reciprocal obligations. If the Inca compelled them to contribute labor on public projects, or on the private estates of the ruling elite, the state, in turn, had the obligation to provide the taxpayers with food, drink, clothing, tools, and housing if the project was distant from the home community. To the *hatun runa*, the Inca *mit'a* was a variant of an ancient pattern of reciprocity among family, kin, and neighbors that, even today, remains a vital principle of social relations in rural Andean communities. In this system, for instance, a newly married couple, with the aid of local officials, may call on their relatives and friends to help them build their first house. In return for this donated labor, the couple, and perhaps their immediate family, provides food, drink, and hospitality while the job is completed. They also incur a future obligation to contribute some equivalent service to those who participated in the house raising. This mix of mutual labor service and hospitality permits individuals to mobilize labor beyond that available in their households and contributes to community solidarity.

When the Inca assessed the *mit'a* labor tax, they acknowledged the reciprocal nature of the social obligation by holding large ceremonial banquets in the principal administrative centers of the province. Both local political leaders and commoners were feted with great quantities of food and maize beer drawn from the imperial warehouses. At times on these occasions, the Inca administrators would also distribute clothing and sandals to the *mit'a* work gangs. Of course, if one compared the relative economic value of the labor service contributed by commoners with that of the hospitality and occasional suit of clothes contributed by the central government, there was no equivalency. The purpose of the system, however, was not to exchange work for an equivalent value in goods, but to reaffirm symbolically the fundamental social principle of reciprocity. That symbolism was projected vividly by a telling ritual convention. Theoretically, the Inca king and his political avatars were obliged to "request" *mit'a* work crews from the local *kurakas*; they could not compel the labor service directly by fiat. In practice, this convention was little more than a fiction. At any time the Inca had sufficient coercive power to force subject communities into compliance. By engaging in this symbolic gesture of reciprocity and ritualized state generosity, the Inca confirmed, in at least a fictive sense, the authority and autonomy of local leaders and their communities, achieving in the process an enormous propaganda coup. The Inca, like any imperial state, held the power to rule by intimidation and coercion and did so when local political conditions demanded the application of force. Yet, whenever possible, they chose to govern by persuasion and positive incentives through the local chain of command, at least giving the appearance that they respected the basic institutions of traditional Andean societies. In analytical terms, we can understand this choice as a conscious strategy of the Inca nobility to transform costly physical coercion and assimilation of subject populations (laminar hegemony) into more durable, associational regimes in which subjects willingly accede their effective political autonomy and thereby hope to gain the added value of sustained social relationships with the Inca (the intended outcome of viral hegemony).

The Inca request for *mit'a* labor service involved a variety of tasks necessary for the expansion and consolidation of their empire. We can think of the *mit'a* as an institutionalized periodic, rotational labor tax on the subjects of the empire, the precise tasks of which depended on the shifting desires and needs of the king. Although substantial *mit'a* labor was invested in ongoing agricultural work on state- and cult-owned fields, the *mit'a* was also deployed in specific contingent circumstances, such as episodic warfare, to provide soldiers, porters, drovers, cooks, healers, and all the other services needed to sustain an army on the move. Most public projects commissioned by the king and noble lineages, such as the construction and maintenance of palaces, temples, roads, bridges, storehouses, irrigation networks, and agricultural terraces, were accomplished with the input of large numbers of *mit'a* laborers drawn from the subject communities.

Apart from the ongoing work on state fields, a second form of universal *mit'a* obligation imposed on all subject communities centered on the production of the most important object of wealth in the native Andean world after that of human labor itself: cloth. Scholars have long recognized the complex instrumental, symbolic, semiotic, social, religious, and political role of textiles in the Andes. The Inca were not the only Andean people to focus almost obsessively on the production and circulation of wool, cotton, spun yarn, weaving tools, and finished textiles. Some of the finest and most technically complex tapestries in the world were designed and woven in the court societies of the ancient Andes, predating the Inca Empire by at least two thousand years. But the Inca seem to have taken the production of utilitarian, ceremonial, and luxury cloth to a virtually industrial scale. In addition to the obligation to work the lands of the king, the Inca nobility, and the state cults, subject communities were required to weave cloth for the state, using wool and cotton fibers drawn from imperial warehouses. Like the obligation to work designated plots of land, the textile *mit'a* imposed by the Inca Empire was an intensification of the traditional labor obligations that local communities owed to their own *kurakas,* who provided the raw materials for community members to produce a designated amount of commissioned textile products: tunics, sashes, hats, belts, loincloths, blankets, coca bags, wall hangings, burial shrouds, and ritual bundles. Fiber production, carding, spinning, and weaving were core cultural activities shared by men and women, involving the work of the entire household on a virtually continuous basis to satisfy their own consumption needs as well as the requirements of local *kurakas* and the Inca state. According to Cieza de León, annually each subject household was obligated to produce one blanket and each person in the household one shirt to discharge their cloth *mit'a* to the state (Cieza de León 1976). But this precise production quota applied across all the subjects of the realm seems improbable since most other forms of Inca labor extraction were context specific and relative rather than fixed. It is more likely, as other sources claim, that subjects "simply wove what they were ordered to weave and were always at it" (cited in Murra 1962:716).

Whatever the rate of textile taxation, the enormous scale of production generated by this universal textile *mit'a* stunned the Spanish. Early participants in the Spanish invasion of the Andes, such as Pedro Pizarro, describe with evident astonishment thousands of warehouses of the royal family, Inca nobility, and the state cults filled to the ceiling with every conceivable garment and other items fabricated from cloth tied in bundles. *Khipu kamayuqkuna* assiduously tracked the flow of textiles that poured into the state warehouses, keeping close accounts on this

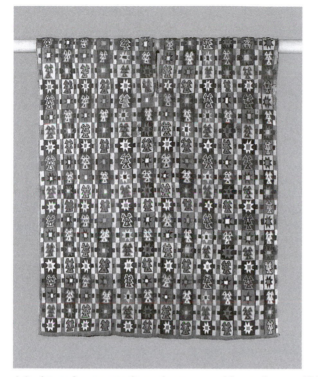

4.2. An *unku*, or man's tunic woven without sleeves. (© The Metropolitan Museum of Art/Art Resource, NY)

exceptionally valuable wealth item. Cloth entered into every domain of daily life in the Inca Empire. Clothing and other textiles marked transitions in the life cycles of children. They were exchanged in marriage ceremonies, bartered for other valued goods, and distributed as gifts to establish or consolidate social relations among peers or between subjects and their lords. They were intended as emblems of social identity and commissioned by nobles for luxury wear in order to ostentatiously display their status (Figure 4.2). Interred with the dead as funerary clothing, burial shrouds, and mummy bundles, textiles became a medium to express this most profound ontological passage for commoners and elites alike, although, of course, vast differences in the quantity and quality of cloth that accompanied the dead clearly indexed these status distinctions. Textiles were among the most precious and numerous items consumed in offerings to household and state cults. Not least, the finest textiles were objects of consummate beauty, among the principal cultural vehicles for expressing the subtle aesthetic sensibilities of their creators. In the Andes, and certainly for the Inca, cloth can be understood as the exemplary artifact of desire, the single material object that indexed and, in some sense, was endowed with and mimetically reproduced the social and political qualities of humans. John Murra (1962:722) aptly summed up the comprehensive cultural role of cloth in the Inca world:

> A primary source of state revenues, an annual chore among peasant obligations, a common sacrificial offering, cloth could serve at different times and occasions as a status symbol or a token of enforced citizenship, as burial furniture, bride-wealth, or armistice sealer. No political, military, social, or religious event was complete without textiles being volunteered or bestowed, burned, exchanged, or sacrificed. In time, weaving became a growing state burden of the peasant household, a major occupational specialty, and eventually a factor in the emergence of retainer craft groups like the *aclla*, the weaving women, a social category inconsistent with the prevailing Cuzco claim that services to the state were no more than peasant reciprocity writ large.

Murra's comments on the emergence of the specialized social category of the *aqlla* as a product of the Inca obsession with producing and accumulating cloth in enormous quantities emphasizes the primary role of labor obligations, both general and specialized, in the Inca economic order. Although the agricultural tax and the *mit'a* labor service were the two principal sources of generalized revenue for the Inca, specialized institutions such as the *mitmaq*, *aqlla*, *kamayuq*, and *yana* forms of labor that emerged in the empire contributed substantially to the productive energy of the Inca state. The general *mit'a* obligation together with these specialized forms of political and labor relations generated an enormous flow of goods and services for the Inca Empire. In addition to their function as tools of production, these institutions performed strategic roles in Inca statecraft, emphasizing the intimate nexus between economic and political behavior in the Inca regime.

We do not have accurate census records from the late Inca Empire that reveal the actual size of the labor force that the kings commanded. Unfortunately for historians of the empire, the Inca kept their census records of subject households encoded in the *khipus*. This presents scholars with two virtually insuperable problems: first, the vast majority of *khipus* were destroyed in the aftermath of the Spanish conquest (and, to a lesser extent, by Inca kings prior to the conquest who desired to rewrite history to accord with their own political interests); second, we still cannot definitively decipher the numerical and narrative information encoded in the few *khipu* artifacts that have survived intact, despite significant recent advances (Ascher and Ascher 1981; Salomon 2004;

Urton 2003). In short, our primary data source on the demographics of the Inca Empire has been irretrievably lost. So we must rely on estimates of population size derived from early Spanish colonial period administrative documents adjusted by approximations of the extreme mortality rates of the early conquest years (Cook 2004), substantiated in a few cases by archaeological research on pre-Hispanic settlement size and distributions. At most, this suboptimal methodology can generate an order-of-magnitude approximation for the empire's population, but, for the moment, this is our sole alternative. Using this approach, plausible population estimates for the Inca Empire as a whole range from 9 million to 16 million people. If we take this range as a reasonable approximation, the number of male heads of household of the *hatun runa* subject to the tribute in labor would have been on the order of 1.8 to 3.2 million, together with an equivalent number of females who actively participated in the *mit'a* labor system as members of the household. The labor tribute owed to the state was calculated on the basis of households, not on individual members of the household. Therefore, a couple with many children and other dependent relatives residing with them could discharge their labor obligation more quickly by sharing labor among all able-bodied household members. As Cobo described the system, commoners "divided the work they had to do by lines, each section being called a *suyu* [a division of any kind], and, after the division, each man put into his section his children and wives and all the people of his house to help him. In this way, the man who had the most workers finished his *suyu* first, and he was considered a rich man; the poor man was he who had no one to help him in his work, and had to work that much longer" (Cobo 1979:212).

In this sense, their labor was a key form of wealth for the commoners, as well as for the nobility. We cannot be certain how many people, male and female, would have rendered their labor service through the general *mit'a*, or as *mitmaqkuna, yanakuna, kamayuqkuna,* or *aqllakuna* instead. We can assume with some confidence that the number of people engaged in the latter four specialized categories of labor service grew as the empire expanded. Assuming that the Spanish chroniclers and subsequent administrative documents were reasonably correct about the numbers of laborers involved in Inca state projects, the *mitmaq* and *yana* labor statuses, in particular, constituted a significant percentage of the working population, perhaps reaching as much as one-third of the total. Such a significant proportion of the population in the status of state colonists (*mitmaqkuna*) and personal retainers (*yanakuna*) appears plausible given the trajectory in the late Inca Empire of expanding claims to private property by the royal family, the aristocracy, and the priests of the state cults. The accelerating privatization of land, natural resources, and labor subtly transformed and destabilized the traditional principles of common property regimes, the ethic of mutual aid, and the practice of generalized reciprocity among native Andean communities. Personal identification with the *ayllu* of birth, particularly for the *yanakuna* and *aqllakuna*, was replaced by affiliation with and loyalty to the Inca noble houses and state institutions to which these retainers were attached. In other words, the domestic economy of the *mitmaq*, *yana*, *kamayuq*, and *aqlla* became directly dependent on the political economy of the aristocracy.

The Agricultural Economy

What were the principal sources of wealth and the related systems of production that generated wealth in the late Inca Empire? In broadest terms, as a fundamentally agrarian society, the Inca depended on farming for both subsistence and surplus. Agricultural crops as both political commodities and food for primary consumption circulated through state redistribution networks and constituted a main source of wealth in the Inca Empire. Inca kings consistently invested in huge land reclamation projects to intensify the production of a wide variety of staple food crops such as maize, potatoes, quinoa, and beans; condiments such as *aji* (chili peppers); specialty crops, such as coca, used for ritual and medicinal purposes; and industrial crops such as cotton and bottle gourds. In the Andean highlands, the Inca state created or expanded agricultural terraces and their related irrigation networks of canals, reservoirs, dams, and sluice gates. These massive enterprises consumed the labor of thousands of commoners mobilized through the *mit'a*, *mitmaq*, and *yana* systems and resulted in the extraordinary feats of agricultural engineering that transformed great stretches of the Andean mountain chain into a substantially anthropogenic landscape (Figures 4.3, 4.4, and 4.5). The Inca kings' investments in this kind of landscape capital represent a facet of imperial political economy that receives relatively little attention. Most analyses of the Inca Empire emphasize its attempts to expropriate land, extract labor, and alienate the natural resources of subject communities; they focus, in other words, on the empire's extractive and coercive dimensions. But in many contexts, particularly in that of land reclamation projects, the Inca Empire was also a developmental state, creating an entirely new infrastructure and implementing management techniques that increased agricultural resources, not simply extracted them (Chepstow-Lusty et al. 2009). Given the fragmented, topographically complex landscape of the Andes, these royal reclamation projects were among the most technically complex and labor-intensive undertakings ever realized in the empire. A dramatic though essentially accurate portrait of the region's agroecology emphasizes the exceptional environmental challenges and opportunities encountered by native farmers in the Andean highlands and implicitly explains the rationale for the royal reclamation projects that were designed to increase the agricultural productivity of the empire:

The Andean region was quite unlike the other regions where clusters of crops were domesticated. Here were no vast, unending plains of uniformly fertile, well-watered land as in Asia, Europe, or the Middle East. Instead, there was an almost total lack of flat, fertile, well-watered soil. Andean peoples grew their crops on millions of tiny plots scattered over a length of thousands of kilometers and perched one above another up mountainsides rising thousands of meters. This complicated ecological mosaic created countless microclimates – including some of the driest and wettest, coldest and hottest, and lowest and highest found anywhere in the world. Perhaps no other contiguous region has such a broad range of environments as in the ancient Inca Empire. And the region is so fragmented that rainfall, frost, sunlight, and soil type can vary over distances as short as a few meters. For instance, a valley floor may have thick soils, abundant sunshine in the daytime, and severe frost at night, whereas immediately adjacent slopes may be thin soiled, shaded, and frost free. To protect themselves against crop failure, ancient Andean farmers utilized all the microenvironments they could. Conditions causing poor harvests in one could produce bumper crops at another. Farmers deliberately maintained fields at different elevations, and this vertically diversified farming fostered the development of a cornucopia of crop varieties, each with slightly different tolerances to soil type, moisture, temperature, insolation, and other factors. The resulting diversity of crops served as a form of farm insurance, but the differing growth cycles of different elevations also permitted work to be staggered and therefore more area to be cultivated. (National Research Council 1989:16)

This passage succinctly conveys the unique, highly diversified environmental setting that confronted indigenous farmers, as well as some of the farm management techniques they used to maximize production and minimize vulnerability to meteorological and climatic conditions. In a kind of farming version of stock portfolio theory, one common technique was to diversify landholdings so that their physical properties had the widest variety possible of topographic, soil, water, and sunlight characteristics (Figure 4.6). Most of the peoples incorporated by the Inca into Tawantinsuyu were relatively self-sufficient agriculturalists, generally capable of producing enough food to satisfy their basic caloric

4.3. Inca terraces drastically transformed the Andean landscape, rendering steep slopes cultivable and vastly increasing their productive potential. Here, Ollantaytambo. (Image courtesy of author)

4.4. Terrace at Pisac. (Image courtesy of L. Guengerich)

Table 4.1. Ancient Andeans domesticated and grew a wide variety of cultivars. This table includes some of the lesser-known native crops, which were
grown along with more familiar species first domesticated elsewhere, such as
maize and *aji*, or hot peppers.

Roots and tubers:	*Achira* *Ahipa* *Arracacha* *Maca* *Mashua* *Mauka* *Oca* *Potatoes* *Ulluco* *Yacon*	Vegetables:	*Peppers* *Squashes*
		Fruits:	*Native berries* *Capuli cherry* *Cherimoya* *Goldenberry* *Highland papayas* *Lucuma* *Naranjilla (lulo)* *Pacay (ice-cream beans)* *Passion fruit* *Pepino* *Tamarillo (tree tomato)*
Grains:	*Kaniwa* *Kiwicha* *Quinoa*		
Legumes:	*Basul* *Nuñas (popping beans)* *Tarwi*	Nuts:	*Quito palm* *Walnuts*

Adapted from National Research Council 1989.

4.5. Terrace at Colca Canyon. (Image courtesy of A. Guengerich)

4.6. Like that of many settlements in the Inca period, the landscape surrounding the modern town of Chuquibamba is a complex patchwork of plots of land used to raise different crops at a variety of altitudes and microenvironments. Chachapoyas, Peru. (Image courtesy of A. Guengerich)

requirements. The inhabitants of the highland basins above 3,000 meters in elevation, however, were more constrained by the kinds of food crops they could cultivate. Agriculture at high altitudes in the Andes is inherently risky, prone to debilitating frosts, hail, wind, droughts, and floods. Only the hardy, high-altitude-adapted tubers such as potatoes, oca, ullucu, and mashwa and the unique chenopod grains, quinoa, *kiwicha*, and *kañawa*, grow well in that environment (Figure 4.7). In starkest numerical terms, approximately 95 percent of the principal Andean food crops can be cultivated below 1,500 meters, but only 20 percent reproduce readily above 3,000 meters. The implication of this contrasting resource distribution is clear. In order to enlarge the variety and quantity of their foodstuffs and reduce the risk of subsistence agriculture, people living at high altitudes sought access to the products of lower, warmer climatic zones. But the desire of highland inhabitants to gain access to lower-altitude lands was not exclusively, or even principally, an environmentally driven imperative to produce subsistence crops. Protein-rich highland grains (*kiwicha, kañawa,* and quinoa), tubers (potatoes, *oca,*

4.7. Major cultivars of the contemporary *altiplano*. *Clockwise from far right*: *jank'o luk'i* potato (*Solanum juzepezukii*, tuber and plant), *sani imilla* potato (*Solanum andiginum*), *huaycha* potato (*Solanum andigenum*), and quinoa (*Chenopodium quinoa*). (Image courtesy of author)

achira, and *mashwa*), and legumes (*tarwi*), along with fresh and preserved llama meat, provided a substantial daily diet.

Politics, sociality, and ritual played into the diversified agricultural system of Andean natives as much as did the desire for culinary variety or the need for subsistence goods. Significantly in this respect, the most highly prized of the temperate-land crops were maize and coca. As Murra (1960) demonstrated, maize and coca were highly valued as ceremonial and prestige crops in the Andes: under the Inca, they were state crops par excellence, produced in many areas under the centralized control of the government through the labor of forcibly resettled colonists. Maize was important as a bulk food product, but even more so as the principal ingredient of *chicha*, or maize beer, an essential component of the political feasts that *kurakas* hosted throughout the ancient Andean world. Coca was the preeminent ritual plant of the Andes, and it was indispensable for the entire panoply of formal communal ceremonies related to agriculture, animal fertility, and transitions in the human life cycle, and for a multiplicity of informal rites performed by individuals and households. In the highlands, the desire to obtain access to these essential crops produced only in more temperate zones often meant that communities and households held land at multiple elevations. These landholdings ranged from the highest, windswept pasturelands of the *puna* over 4,000 meters, suitable for herding, tuber cultivation, and grain production, to the high and middle altitudes of the *suni* (~3,500–4,000 meters) and the *quechua* (~3,000–3,500 meters), ecological zones in which a wider variety of grains, tubers, and legumes could be produced, to the even lower-lying, subtropical *chaupiyungas* and *selva* zones that yielded many of the temperate-zone crops as well as a wide variety of vegetables (peppers, squashes, tomatoes), fruits (berries, *cherimoya*, papayas, *lucuma*, *pacay*, beans, passion fruit, *pepino*, *tamarillo*), and nuts, among other warm-land products such as honey, aromatic wood, and tropical bird feathers.

The strategy of *ayllus* and ethnic groups with landholdings dispersed across the terrain, often sharing the land and resources of particular microclimates with other *ayllus* and ethnic groups, has been aptly called discontinuous territoriality. That is, the recognized and defended territory of many *ayllus* consisted not of large, contiguous blocks of land, but of many relatively small and diversified landholdings intercalated in a mosaic, pixel-like pattern with the landholdings of other ethnic groups. After the conquest of the Inca, Spanish viceroys and colonial administrators were confused by this pattern of discontinuous landholdings, a kind of land tenure system that did not have any real precedent in Iberia. They attempted to resettle inhabitants into centrally located towns and villages within a bounded, contiguous territory for ease of taxation, surveillance, and religious instruction.

Because the principal axis of environmental and natural resource variation in the Andes derives from altitudinal change, the indigenous strategy of direct access to a maximum number of ecological zones by a single group has been called "verticality," or vertical economic complementarity (Murra 1972; Salomon 1985). Even today, some rural communities, particularly along the eastern slopes of the great Andean cordillera, maintain use rights simultaneously to pasturelands for llama and alpaca in the high, cold meadows of the mountains above 4,000 meters, to potato, *oca*, and quinoa fields in the mountainous basins above 2,800 meters, and to plots of maize, coca, and other warm-land crops in regions well below 2,000 meters.

The exploitation of resources stratified by elevation takes many specialized forms in the Andes, but we can identify two principal variations that capture the essence of this remarkable economic practice. The first is what may be referred to as compressed verticality, in which a single village or ethnic group resides in a physical setting that permits the community easy access to contiguous or closely located ecological zones. Different crop zones, pasturelands, or other localized resources, such as sources of salt, honey, or fruit trees, are within one or two days' walk of the parent community. Generally, the parent community is situated in an agriculturally productive mountain basin above 2,000 meters, although individual members of the community or, at times, the entire village may reside temporarily in one of the lower ecological zones to manage the extraction of products unavailable in the high-altitude homeland. The village maintains temporary dwellings on a number of ecological "floors" and rotates residence among them in accordance with the agricultural and pastoral cycle of the seasons. The efficiency of this system relies heavily on group solidarity and the sharing of reciprocal obligations. Communities engaged in this form of verticality are characterized by strong bonds of kinship and by an ethic of self-help.

The second variation resembles compressed verticality in that a single group maintains residences in multiple stratified environmental zones. But in this stratagem, which has been called the vertical archipelago, the ethnic group or village exploits resources in zones that are noncontiguous and widely dispersed, constituting a series of independent "islands" of production. In some villages engaged in this strategy, community members must trek for ten to fourteen days from their home base in the mountains to reach distant fields in the tropical lowlands. This form of land use was most highly developed in the late pre-Hispanic period by complex societies such as the indigenous Aymara kingdoms of the Titicaca Basin. In these kingdoms, the vertical archipelago was transformed into a formal, specialized system of production in which satellite communities from the home territory were sent to reside permanently as colonists in distant tropical forest and Pacific coastal locations. There, the colonists grew crops and extracted products for their own consumption and for transshipment back to their high-altitude compatriots. In establishing this policy of permanent colonization, these polities enhanced the efficiency of their economic system by producing crops and other goods in multiple ecological zones. In this system, food crops, raw products, and other commodities, rather than people, circulated through the archipelago. The colonists from the highlands frequently shared with the indigenous inhabitants the resources of the foreign territories in which they were resettled, at times adopting the dress and customs of the local people. The colonists, however, maintained basic rights to marriage, residence, familial lands, and property in their communities of origin in the distant highlands. The number and kind of colonists maintained by the *altiplano* kingdoms in the various islands of production were highly variable and could range from single extended families of a few people to entire villages.

Rather than completely dismantle the native tradition of discontinuous territoriality and local archipelago economies when they began to reorganize populations and production in their nascent empire, the Inca expanded and intensified this economic strategy in some geopolitical contexts. This trait of co-opting and adapting local institutions, beliefs, and patterns of economic and political behavior to the needs of their empire distinguished the Inca. The success of Inca imperial expansion owed as much to the elite's perceptive manipulation of preexisting values, economic strategies, and political concepts concerning the reciprocal relationship of rights and obligations between community leaders and their people as it did to brute superiority in force of arms. The Inca adoption and further development of discontinuous territoriality and archipelago economies is one example. We will see other aspects of this geopolitical strategy when we examine the religious and political institutions and practices promoted by the Inca in their imperial reorganization of the ancient Andean world.

At the same time, however, in several areas strategically distributed across the empire, Inca kings completely transformed local land tenure arrangements to create large-scale state farms and personal estates (Figure. 4.8). In these cases, the state farms consisted of large, uninterrupted blocks of land that were worked by *mitmaq* colonists and *yanakuna* resettled on lands expropriated from local communities and ethnic groups. King Wayna Qhapaq's expulsion of the local population, reorganization of the land tenure regime, and resettling of fourteen thousand foreign-born *mitmaqkuna* to produce maize in the fertile Cochabamba Valley in Bolivia represents an archetypical instance of this geopolitical strategy, which owes more to the audacity of force than to the niceties of diplomacy. Wayna Qhapaq's grandfather, King Pachakuti, exercised the same power of coercion when he expelled autochthonous inhabitants around Cuzco to create the *chapas* irrigation districts for the royal *ayllus* of the Inca aristocracy.

The Inca's technology and social organization of agricultural production generated an enormous flow of diverse crops and processed foodstuffs that underwrote the economy of this agrarian empire. According to one assessment, at "the time of the Spanish conquest, the Inca cultivated almost as many species of plants as the farmers of all of Asia or Europe. On mountainsides up to four kilometers high along the spine of a whole continent and in climates varying from tropical to polar, they grew a wealth of roots, grains, legumes, vegetables, fruits, and nuts" (National Research Council 1989:1). The Inca taxed commoners for labor to work state-owned fields and appropriated vast amounts of land

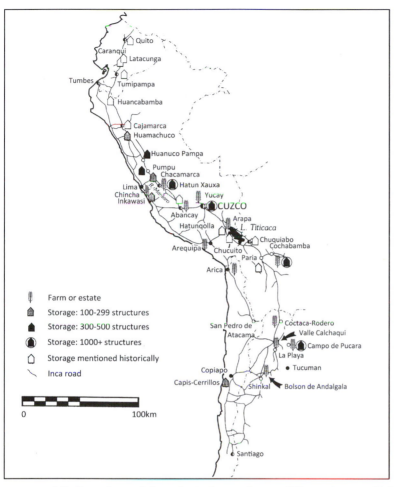

4.8. Locations of the principal state farms of Tawantinsuyu. (Adapted from D'Altroy 2002)

for state farms, private estates, and the religious cults. Many of these agricultural estates were dedicated to the production of maize as the principal prestige crop of the empire.

The Pastoral Economy

Although farming was the cornerstone of the imperial economy, and the principal occupation of most of the empire's population, another critical sector contributed heavily to the wealth of the Inca state: the raising, care, and management of livestock. Unique to the pre-Hispanic Americas, the

4.9. A llama grazes at Machu Picchu. Llamas and alpacas were the most important domesticated animals in the Andes. (Image courtesy of L. Guengerich)

Andes was home to vast herds of domesticated and wild camelids: the llama, alpaca, guanaco, and vicuña. These animals yielded wool, leather, milk, and meat. The llama served as a pack animal in trade and military operations to transport bulk commodities, agricultural crops, processed food, wood, minerals, textiles, ceramics, and many other goods over the rugged, tortuous terrain of the Andes (Figure 4.9). But the economic uses of the camelids speak only superficially to the complementary social, ritual, and emotional roles played by these animals in the minds of the Andean people. The relationship between humans and camelids in the Andean *altiplano*, or high plateau, was ancient and pervasive, and entailed a peculiarly intense form of symbiosis. The llama was a source of food and tools, clothing and transport; it was also an avatar of the supernatural, an animate creature both sacred and profane. Llama hearts, livers, and lungs were extracted and examined to interpret auguries and prognosticate the future. Llama sacrifices marked critical episodes of the human life cycle and may have punctuated and defined temporal transitions in a sidereal-lunar agricultural calendar (Zuidema 1983c). Llama husbandry, rituals of llama sacrifice, and agricultural fertility were intimately associated with this calendrical system, reflecting social, symbolic, and ecological relationships between pastoralism and agriculture in the high plateau. As Zuidema (1983c:16) notes: "while the crops are growing, the animals are

4.10. Although never domesticated, herds of vicuñas still roam the
puna at high altitudes and are a source of extremely high-quality wool.
(Image courtesy of A. Guengerich)

kept away from the fields, but after harvest they are led into them [to permit llamas to graze on the remaining stubble and thereby regenerate the
fertility of the fields with dung].... [T]hus, crops and animals alternate
in the same fields." The social and physical ecologies of agriculture and
pastoralism, although in and of themselves potentially antagonistic, were
integrated by the ritual calendar: the rhythms of rite, crop, and herd were
brought into productive synchrony.

As early as seven thousand years ago, the Andean peoples domesticated two of the four native camelids that originated in the high, rolling
plains of the *altiplano*: the llama and the alpaca. The llama was raised
for many purposes, and all parts of an animal's body in life and death
were integrated into the daily life of the owner. The smaller alpaca was
raised principally for its wool, which is less coarse than that of the llama
and more suitable for weaving into fine garments. Two other camelids,
the guanaco and vicuña, remained in the wild. The guanaco was hunted
for sport and for its strongly flavored, gamey meat. Although never truly
domesticated, wild vicuña herds were carefully managed by Andean
peoples in order to obtain the animals' coveted soft, silken wool. In
the Inca imperium, vicuña wool was reserved for royalty, to be woven
into extraordinarily precious ceremonial tunics (Figure 4.10). Although
vicuña are a protected species today, their wool remains an almost mythical symbol of luxury in the realm of *haute couture*, vastly more valuable
than cashmere, the commonplace wool of the Himalayan goat.

In the Andean high plateau, the domesticated herds of llama and alpaca were a principal source of wealth, and their exceptional abundance over the millennia was a testament to their central role in native livelihood (Figure 4.11). The size of the herds during the height of the Inca Empire, and quite likely for centuries before that, was truly staggering. A full generation after the Spanish conquest that had induced a massive demographic collapse among native populations, census records from the mid-sixteenth century report that commoners along the western shores of Lake Titicaca owned as many as one thousand animals. Don Juan Alanoca, an ethnic Aymara *kuraka* in 1567, owned fifty thousand animals. The same document recording these exceptional numbers of herd animals in the early colonial period present tallies of animals in the possession of natives resident in the indigenous settlements around Lake Titicaca, including the townships of Juli, Pomata, and Zepita, which were the former capitals of Aymara polities prior to their incorporation by the Inca. These Aymara *marka*, or principal towns, still controlled herds in the tens of thousands even after the trauma of conquest, disease, and depopulation. In the first years of the Spanish conquest, ethnic lords of the Wanka, bitter rivals of the Inca allied with the Europeans, furnished enormous trains of llama to transport supplies and as meat on the hoof for the invading armies. Again, contemporary records refer to tens of thousands of animals serving these critical strategic purposes for the conquistadors. One can only imagine that the pre-Hispanic camelid herds must have been even larger and that the total population of camelids at any given time in the Inca realm totaled conservatively in the millions. The llama, although not the alpaca, which is more sensitive to habitat changes and prefers the high altitudes and climate of the *altiplano*, was also bred and maintained on the desert Pacific coast, even if not in the enormous herd sizes evident in the high plateau. Coastal llama herds grazed the specific microenvironment of the *lomas*, a narrow, seasonally humid band of vegetation on the margins between the coastal plain and the foothills of the Andes. This special microenvironment was a point of convergence for highland and coastal populations with their herds of llama serving a critical transport function in moving goods up and down the vertical landscape of the Andean massif.

Given the deep antiquity of camelid exploitation, their substantial economic, social, and religious significance to native populations, and their mutualism with human populations, we should not be surprised to discover that the Inca developed elaborate management techniques and cultural protocols for their relationship with camelids. Bernabé Cobo's extended account of herd management under the Inca offers some key

4.11. The frequency with which camelids were depicted in works of art, and the valuable materials invested in portraying them, attest to the camelids' social, ritual, and economic value to the Andean people. This picture demonstrates *conopa*-type stone votives of alpacas. (Image ©The Field Museum of Natural History, #A114468_30d)

insights into the logistics and cultural rules of camelid breeding and exploitation in the empire:

The Inca had the same division made of all the domesticated livestock [llama and alpaca], assigning one part to religion, another to himself, and another to the community; and not only did he divide and separate each one of these parts, but he did the same with the grazing land and pastures in which the livestock was pastured, so that the herds were in different pastures and could not be mixed. The Inca divided these pastures and had them marked in each province. The pastures of religion and the Inca were called *moyas*. And it was unlawful to put the livestock of religion in the *moyas* of the Inca, nor could the opposite be done, for each herd or flock had its own specified district. The borders between provinces were also divided; the pasturelands of different provinces were not common even for the livestock of the same owner. For example, there were pastures in the province of Chucuito [in the northern *altiplano*] where the Inca's livestock were raised in that province; and the animals that the Inca himself had in the bordering province of Pacajes [around the southern shores of Lake Titicaca] could not cross over there to graze. In keeping these animals, great care was taken to assign herdsmen and foremen to count the increase in the flocks and animals that died; and in contributing the people necessary for this purpose, the towns paid a considerable amount of their tribute. The part of the livestock that belonged to the common people was much smaller than either of the other two parts, as can be noticed by the names that were given to each one. The herds belonging to religion and to the Inca were named *capac llama*, and the herds owned by either the community or privately were named *huacchac llama*, which means "rich herds" and "poor herds." Moreover, the king took animals from the part belonging to the community; these were given to caciques and persons who served him as a favor to them; the king also ordered that the residents be allotted the number of animals that they needed. None of the animals that the king gave as a favor to develop and start herds could be divided or transferred, any more than the lands; thus, the heirs of the first owner possessed his herds in common. This domesticated livestock of llamas was one of the greatest riches that the Indians had. In order to conserve it so that it would always be on the increase, the Inca had ordered two very important things. First, any animal that got *caracha* (a certain illness like mange or scab which these animals often catch, and many die of it) was to be immediately buried alive and very deep, and no one was to try to cure the sick animal or kill it for food, and this was done in order to prevent the disease from spreading, for it is extremely contagious; second, the females were not to be killed for sacrifices or for any other reason. Owing to these measures, the vast number of these animals in their kingdom was incredible. (Cobo 1979:215–216)

This passage eloquently conveys the Inca elite's obsession with the reproductive success and health of their llama herds, and explicitly describes some of the mechanisms and sociology of herd management. Much as they did with the agricultural landscape, the Inca divided camelid herds into three broad categories of possession, control, and use: state and private property of the king and royal family, property of religion, and property of the local community. These three principal categories of herds were rigidly segregated spatially as an accounting technique to keep track of the animals and their annual fluctuations in population and, most likely, also as a reaction to localized scarcity of good pastureland. Color coding of the herds facilitated the accountancy system that tracked the numbers of animals in the various status categories. Llamas were separated into white, black, brown, and mixed color herds that were then keyed to the same colors on the record-keeping cords maintained by the *khipu kamayuqkuna*. As in the case of agricultural lands, the other critical resource of the indigenous economy, dedicated herds were distributed to the local ethnic groups, local lords, provincial Inca officials, and the royal family for their personal use. Both local *kurakas* and the Inca monarch also endowed the *wak'as* and religious cults with herd animals for the support of the priestly class and the retainers responsible for maintaining the cults. There were, in short, parallel systems of allocation, redistribution, and accountancy for agricultural land and camelid herds, reflecting the deep social and ritual interdependency of farming and herding. As Cobo recounted, similar to the system of labor taxation to cultivate state fields, many subject towns, particularly in the Andean high plateau, discharged their tribute obligations by providing herdsmen for the empire's elites and for the state religious cults.

The Inca reciprocated tributary labor provided by subject towns by periodically redistributing llamas to local *kurakas* and their communities. In other words, Inca taxation of the pastoral economy did not entail direct expropriation of a certain number or percentage of animals in subject towns and polities. Just as in community agricultural production, tribute was not framed in specific amounts of a given commodity, in this case, animals or animal by-products such as wool, meat, and leather. Rather, the Inca demanded only manual labor from subject communities, who worked dedicated pasturelands expropriated from the local polity during its incorporation in the Inca Empire. In this respect, Inca tributary strategies and protocols were astute. Once the initial expropriation of subject polities' resources had been accomplished, subsequent extraction from the community did not entail further alienation of critical natural resources, even though the additional burden of working the lands and pastures of the state was clearly onerous. The psychological burden of taxation was lessened in the sense that products produced on the lands of individual community members were not taken and shipped back to Cuzco. Community members kept what was their own production, but of course the amount of what they could have produced for their own benefit was substantially reduced by the original Inca expropriation of their lands. Still, over the generations, the memories of autonomy and of the original possession of more land and resources may have receded and a "new normal" of production established that already factored in the labor owed to the Inca. Subject communities at least did not have to witness Inca governors forcibly seizing crops, herds, and other community products, bundling them up and shipping them off to the distant lords of Cuzco. In this process of memory recalibration, we can again see the subtle transformation of historical consciousness induced by the Inca elite's application of a strategy of viral hegemony. Cloth, livestock, and access to land were three principal sources of portable and fixed wealth that sustained social power in the Inca Empire. But, in the end, access to labor, deployed in many forms and mobilized through several distinct institutions, was the coin of the realm. Labor that was accumulated and managed locally was the key to the success of Inca imperial ambitions and ultimately the true source of the empire's wealth.

The Logistics of Empire

How did the Inca manage this economy? How did they coordinate the production, maintenance, circulation, and consumption of goods and services on an imperial scale? Again, the words of Cieza de León, written in frank admiration of the audacity of Inca imperial organization, offer us vital clues:

> In more than 1,200 leagues of coast they ruled they have their representatives and governors, and many lodgings and great storehouses filled with all necessary supplies. This was to provide for their soldiers, for in one of these storehouses there were lances, and in another, darts, and in others, sandals, and in others, the different arms they employed. Likewise certain buildings were filled with fine clothing, others with coarser garments, and others with food and every kind of victuals. When the lord was lodged in his dwellings and his soldiers garrisoned there, nothing, from the most important to the most trifling, but could be provided. (Cieza de León 1976:68)

Perhaps more than any other native state of the ancient Americas, the Inca were justly renowned for the scale and efficiency of their elaborate commodity warehousing system. The progress of the Spanish conquest of the Andes, in fact, would have been slowed substantially had it not been for the endless ranks of Inca storehouses, known in the Quechua language as *qollqas*, filled with food, clothing, arms, and supplies, that the conquistadors found arrayed on the outskirts of Inca towns (Figure 4.12).

Bernabé Cobo, like Cieza de León, described the Inca storage system, and he provides us with intriguing insights into its internal organization. "The storehouses of the Crown and of Religion were different," he wrote, "although they were always together, like the owners of what was stored in them and the uses to which it was put. The storehouses of the Incas were much bigger and longer than those of Religion; this implies that the Incas' share of lands and animals was greater than that which was given to the gods" (Cobo 1979:218). This perceptive passage suggests that when the Inca incorporated a new province into their empire they linked the construction of massive storehouses with the reorganization of the land-tenure system, which, as we have seen, partitioned territories into three principal divisions – central government, state cult, and autochthonous landholdings. Products from the state's two territorial partitions flowed into spatially segregated *qollqas*. One set of storerooms was designated for the state cults and another for the use of the central government. If Cobo was right, the governmental *qollqas* were larger and more numerous and contained a wider variety of raw and manufactured goods than those designated for the support of the religious cults.

4.12. *Qollqas*, such as these at Ollantaytambo, did not merely contain goods, but by prominently displaying them, also demonstrated the wealth of the state. (Image courtesy of L. Guengerich)

The *qollqas* were substantial circular or rectangular structures built of fieldstone, wood, and thatch, and they were frequently provided with elaborate ventilation systems to assist the preservation of bulk food supplies like potatoes and maize. Special processing of potatoes, other tubers, and llama meat extended the capacity of the storehouses to meet the long-term dietary needs of the population. One technique, still widely used in indigenous communities in the Andes, was to freeze-dry root crops such as potatoes into a product called *chuño*. After harvest, potatoes and other tubers are laid outside in the open during the cold nights and dry days characteristic of the Andean highlands and high plateau. Farmers trample on the exposed tubers during the day to eliminate water released by the previous night's freezing. The process results in a lightweight, freeze-dried product that has exceptional storage properties, retaining nutritive value for years without refrigeration. Similarly, fresh llama meat was dried in strips and processed into *charki*, a product like beef jerky, which could be easily transported over long distances. *Chuño* and *charki* were critical to the logistics of empire because they were the Inca armies' ready-to-eat meals while on the march. In times of drought, flooding, killing frosts, or other natural catastrophes, these processed foods became an insurance policy that enabled the empire to withstand regional famine, and the political disturbances that accompanied hungry, desperate populations. Today, *chuño* still serves as a famine food, comprising a substantial portion of the natives' diet in the Andean highlands during times of crop failure.

At the Inca provincial capital of Huánuco Pampa in the north-central highlands of Peru, systematic archaeological investigation has documented more than two thousand storehouses with distinct architectural characteristics related to their warehousing functions. Here, circular *qollqas* were used for maize storage. Ceramic remains discovered in the storehouses indicate that the maize was stored in the form of kernels in large, sealable storage jars. Rectangular *qollqas* seem to have been assigned to tuber storage. Tubers in these storehouses were laid out on straw matting and tied up into individual bundles bound with cords. The Huánuco storehouses possessed specialized structural features such as raised thresholds, double gravel and stone floors, and stone-lined conduits aligned with prevailing air currents that facilitated ventilation (Morris 1992a). These features enhanced the capacity of the structures to minimize the impact of mold, fungus, insect, and rodent damage to stored commodities. The spatial and architectural distinctions between circular and rectangular warehouses may also have been designed to facilitate rapid *khipu*-based accounting for the stored commodities.

As in the case of the great camelid herds, keeping like with like eased the tedious, time-consuming task of annual inventories mandated by the Inca kings. To control the flow of bulk foodstuffs and manufactured products through the warehousing system, the Inca maintained a corps of civil servants, the "representatives" and "governors" mentioned by Cieza de León, who accounted for the collection and transshipment of these valued goods. In terms of the logistics of empire, the class of civil servant that was particularly important was the *khipu kamayuq*. As we have seen, *khipus* were ingenious mnemonic devices that encoded, through a series of complex recursive patterns of knotted and colored cords, a wide array of economic, political, social, ritual, and narrative information critical to the smooth functioning of the state bureaucracy. The *khipu kamayuqkuna* were a hereditary, occupationally specialized (*kamayuq*) class of men in the Inca state who recorded on the knotted cords essential information regarding the amount of goods circulating into and out of state storehouses, and who performed tasks analogous to those of scribes in other archaic states. The *khipu kamayuqkuna* reported directly to the higher echelons of state functionaries, to the *kurakas*, to provincial or territorial governors, and ultimately to the Inca emperor himself.

The scale of storage capacity commanded by the Inca state was extraordinary and did not fail to impress the Spanish conquistadors. Two brief passages, one from an eyewitness to the Spanish conquest and the other from a chronicler, convey the exceptional diversity and quantity of commodities stored throughout the realm, as well as one of their principal functions. Around Cuzco there were "storehouses full of blankets, wool, weapons, metals and clothes – and of everything that is grown and made in this realm ... and there is a house in which are kept more than 100,000 dried birds, for from their feathers articles of clothing are made.... There are shields, beams for supporting tents, knives, and other tools; sandals and armor for the people of war in such quantity that it is not possible to comprehend how they had been able to tribute so many and different things" (Sancho de la Hoz 1917, cited in Morris 1992b:ix–x). Likewise, "The Inca ordained that the captain who took the soldiers have large storehouses made by the *tambos* [inns, or way stations] every forty leagues from the city of Cuzco to the last place he reached. These storehouses should have all types of food, including maize, *chuño*, papas [potatoes], quinoa, *ají* peppers, salted dried meat, fish and livestock. This food was for the soldiers who arrived on a conquest campaign or who were pacifying some province that had rebelled. Each of these soldiers should be given as much of this food as he needed to make it to the next *tambo*, forty leagues from there, where he would be given more food" (Betanzos 1996:108). These two passages reveal not only something of the quantity and diversity of commodities stored by the Inca but also the systematic emplacement of warehouse facilities along the empire's roads to facilitate military campaigns, as well as the movement of the king and his court.

Archaeological evidence substantiates the Spanish descriptions of the Inca's vast warehousing capacity. Many of the state's provincial centers, such as the Mantaro (Figure. 4.13), Huánuco, Huamachuco, and Cajamarca basins, contained thousands of storehouses built in linear arrays on hill slopes surrounding important towns. The Mantaro Valley alone has approximately 2,750 archaeologically recorded storehouses (D'Altroy 2002:281). Warehousing facilities of similar scale were constructed near state farms, royal estates, and religious shrines. For instance, D'Altroy notes that the settlement of Cotopachi, adjacent to the imperial farm in Bolivia's Cochabamba Valley developed by King Wayna Qhapaq, included 2,400 storehouses, and that the number of storehouses at Campo de Pucará in Argentina reached 1,717 (D'Altroy 2002:281). These bare numbers give us only a glimpse of the magnitude of the empire's ability to produce, store, and circulate staple foods, luxury commodities, and strategic goods necessary for military campaigns.

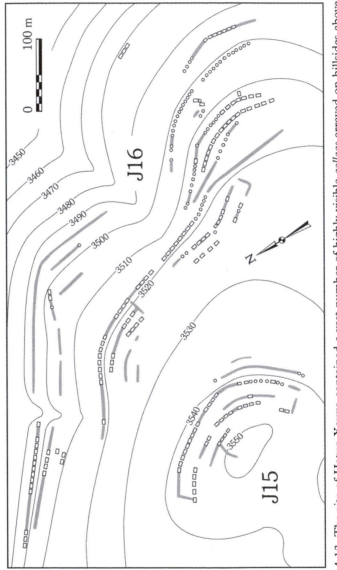

4.13. The site of Hatun Xauxa contained a vast number of highly visible *qollqas* arrayed on hillsides above the city center. (Image courtesy of T. D'Altroy)

The regular, strategic emplacement of warehousing facilities reveals that the maintenance of vast quantities of readily deployable commodities was a key element of Inca statecraft, a theme we will explore in greater detail later.

The vast bulk of state storage facilities was constructed in the imperial capital of Cuzco and near important towns, provincial capitals, state farms, royal estates, and religious shrines of particular renown along the Qhapaq Ñan, or royal road of the Inca (Figure. 4.14). The Qhapaq Ñan was formed by two north–south routes, one in the highlands and the other along the Pacific coast, bound together by a series of east–west lateral linkages through the principal mountain passes of the western mountain chain of the Andes, the Cordillera Negra. The highland route of the Qhapaq Ñan extended more than 4,800 kilometers, from Chile to Ecuador, while the entire road system may have covered as much as 41,000 kilometers, integrating disparate, intractable landscapes including the deserts of the Pacific coast; the highland pocket basins of Peru and Ecuador; the vertiginous, dissected mountain slopes of the great Cordillera Blanca's eastern flanks; and the trackless high plains of Bolivia and Chile. Radiating out from the central plazas of Cuzco, the various branches of the Qhapaq Ñan united the four principal geographic segments of the Inca realm: Chinchaysuyu, Antisuyu, Collasuyu, and Contisuyu.

An extended passage from Cieza de León brilliantly conveys the visual majesty, military importance, and political, social, and symbolic significance of the Inca road network:

There are many of these highways all over the kingdom, both in the highlands and the plains. Of all, four are considered the main highways, and they are which start from the city of Cuzco, at the square, like a crossroads, and go to the different provinces of the kingdom. As these monarchs held such a high opinion of themselves, when they set out on one of these roads, the royal person with the necessary guard took one, and the rest of the people another. So great was their pride that when one of them died, his heir, if he had to travel to a distant place, built his road larger and broader than that of his predecessor, but this was only if this Lord-Inca set out on some conquest, or [performed] some act so noteworthy that it could be said the road built for him was longer. This can be clearly seen for there are three or four roads near Vilcas.... One of these is called the road of Pachakuti, the other that of Topa Inca, and the one now in use and which will always be used is the one ordered built by Huayna Capac, which runs near the Angasmayo River to the north, and to the south well beyond what we now call Chile, which roads are so long that there is a distance of more than 1,200 leagues from one end to the other. Huayna Capac ordered this highway built, larger and wider than that his father had made, as far as Quito, where he planned to go, and that the regular lodgings and storehouses and posts be transferred to it. So that all these lands might know that this was his will, messengers

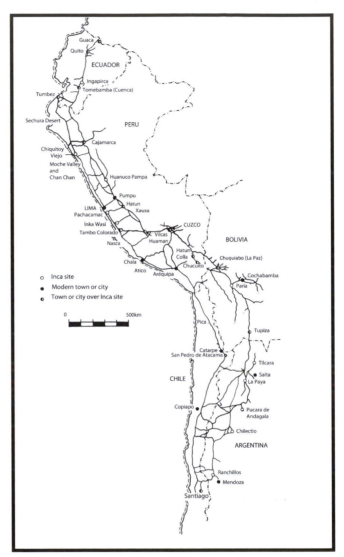

4.14. The Qhapaq Ñan, the Inca road system, crisscrossed the Andes running north to south from Ecuador to Chile, while transverse segments ran from east to west. (Adapted from Hyslop 1990)

were sent out to notify them, and then *Orejones* [Inca nobles] to see that it was fulfilled, and the finest road in the world was built, and the longest, for it started in Cuzco and went to Quito, and joined that which led to Chile. In the memory of the people I doubt that there is record of another highway comparable to this, running through deep valleys and over high mountains, through piles of snow, quagmires, living rock, along turbulent rivers; in others over sierras, cut through the rock, with walls skirting the rivers, and steps and rests through the snow; everywhere it was clean-swept and kept free of rubbish, with lodgings, storehouses, temples to the sun, and posts along the way. Oh, can anything comparable be said of Alexander, or of any of the mighty kings who ruled the world, that they built such a road, or provided the supplies to be found on this one! The road built by the Romans that runs through Spain and the others we read of were as nothing in comparison to this. (Cieza de León 1976:137–138)

The Inca road system, particularly in the tortuous terrain of the Andean highlands, was an audacious engineering achievement and, quite likely, the largest single construction project ever attempted in the ancient Americas. The Qhapaq Ñan, together with its lateral feeders, was a powerful tool of political integration for the Inca state. Messages could be sent along the royal road between Cuzco and its far-flung provincial capitals with incredible speed, using a system of relay runners called *chaski*, who were stationed along designated segments of the road. In addition to speeding the transmission of critical information, the extensive and technically sophisticated road system greatly facilitated the efficient movement of bulk and manufactured goods, *mitmaq* colonists, provincial officials, and, of course, Inca armies throughout the empire. The highways also functioned as symbolic representations of Inca rule and of the majesty of the individual kings who competed to enlarge and make more magnificent the roads of their predecessors. Cieza's commentary on the construction of separate roads and bridges reserved for the exclusive use of the Inca king and his court emphasizes the intensifying class distinctions among royals, nobles, and commoners that emerged in the late Inca Empire. So, their road system, like virtually every other physical artifact of the Inca imperial infrastructure, served multiple purposes, from the most economically instrumental to the deeply political and symbolic. In a real sense, we can consider the infrastructure itself, imbued with social, political, and religious qualities, as an active agent in the extension and consolidation of Inca power (Figure 4.15).

Provincial temple and government precincts, such as those in Xauxa, Cajamarca, and Pachacamac, were established along the length of both the highland and the coastal routes of the Qhapaq Ñan to coordinate local administration and the economic exploitation of natural and human resources. In regions where there was no local settlement that could serve as an appropriate provincial capital, the Inca created cities such as Huánuco Pampa, frequently building them on a symmetrical grid plan, or modeling large sections of them on the core area of the imperial capital of Cuzco (Figure 4.16). In conquered territories that already possessed substantial urban centers, the Inca simply absorbed the native town into the network of cities that were the focus of Inca

4.15. Inca roads traversed steep mountain terrain. (Image ©Ricardo Espinosa)

administration. As at the ancient coastal settlement of Pachacamac near modern Lima (Figure. 4.17), Inca rulers often constructed a few important administrative buildings, such as a temple for the state's solar cult, storerooms, residential compounds for the Inca elite, and perhaps an *aqllawasi*, placing them in prominent locations within the towns to mark and symbolize their incorporation into the Inca Empire.

Along the royal road in the provinces between these principal cities, towns, and capitals, the Inca state maintained a series of inns, or way stations, called *tampus* (Figure 4.18). Each *tampu* offered temporary accommodations and meals for traveling Inca officials and could provide food for the army during military campaigns. *Tampus* usually consisted of a series of large rectangular structures that were intended as residence

4.16. Symmetrical principles of organization are apparent at the site of Huánuco Pampa, a major provincial center and archaeological source of significant knowledge concerning Inca settlement planning. (Adapted from Morris and Thompson 1985)

4.17. The temple to the solar cult of Inti was one of several buildings that the Inca constructed at the ancient pilgrimage site of Pachacamac on the central coast of Peru near the modern city of Lima. (Image courtesy of A. Guengerich)

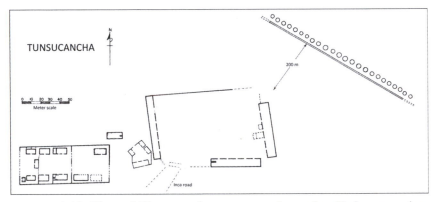

4.18. Plan of Tunsucancha, a *tampu* from the Huánuco region. (Adapted from Morris and Thompson 1985)

halls for travelers and were arrayed around a central plaza, communal kitchens, and banks of storehouses that were stocked with food. More elaborate *tampus* close to the provincial capitals frequently included stone baths. The *tampus* also often included shrines for the state cults. These way stations along the royal road were constructed, maintained, provisioned, and most likely staffed by local *mit'a* labor from the surrounding region. The *tampus* were essential links in the chain of command and communication that bound the Inca provinces with the imperial capital of Cuzco. Thus the network of provincial cities, towns, temple precincts, and *tampus*, the centralized clusters of state storehouses, and the highly developed road system, all constructed and maintained through the coordinated efforts of local *mit'a* labor forces, constituted an effective physical infrastructure for the Inca imperial enterprise. But the organizational system that the Inca devised for administering their empire was no less impressive than these more visible physical artifacts. This political infrastructure of the Inca state will be the subject of Chapter 6.

Merchants, Markets, and the Inca Economic Model

When we analyze the economic order of the Inca state, we cannot help but notice that a fundamental institution of economic integration, a common tool for the exchange and circulation of goods and services shared by virtually every state society, ancient and modern, appears absent. That institution is the market. All of our sources on the Inca concur that the exchange of goods and services in the empire did not take place in formal markets, even though markets and marketing behavior did apparently exist in the northern provinces of the late Inca Empire in what is now Ecuador (Salomon 1986). Markets in preindustrial societies were both designated spaces and a social process in which interested sellers of a particular good or service could interact with buyers for the purpose of completing a transaction that was presumably mutually satisfactory. In theory, forces of supply and demand set the price of goods and services being exchanged in the market. Prices send "signals" to the sellers concerning what buyers desire and about the buyers' capacity or willingness to pay a designated price. If people want more of something than is available for purchase, prices will rise, stimulating sellers to produce or procure more of the desired good. The preferences of sellers and buyers are reflected in supply-and-demand curves of various markets and set the price of goods and services. This, of course, is the theory of an entirely "free" market. No such markets ever existed in the premodern world, nor, for that matter, exist today. There are always some "distortions" in the market in the form of collusion, monopolies, price manipulation, and government regulations. Even the purest capitalist economies set constraints on the exchange of commodities. Nevertheless, the theory of the free market still refers with some reverence to Adam Smith's famous "invisible hand" driving the market by virtue of "rational" individuals acting in their self-interest and thereby promoting their own well-being as well as that of society as a whole. That is the theory, but the reality is rather different. Certainly in the premodern world, Smith's invisible hand never truly existed. Buyers and sellers never acted entirely independently in the marketplace. Most premodern states established tight controls over markets and marketplaces, converting them into administered markets rather than free markets. These types of administered markets existed throughout ancient Mesoamerica, among the Aztecs (Berdan 1985; Hassig 1985; Hodge and Smith 1994; Smith 1980, 2004), Maya (Coe 2005; Demarest 2004), and Zapotecs (Joyce 2010), among others. The eyewitness account of the market in the Aztec capital of Tenochtitlan-Tlatelolco by the Spanish conquistador Bernal Díaz conveys the vitality and complexity of this social institution in the Mexica-Aztec civilization and is most likely representative of the goods, services, and administrative organization of markets in the ancient Americas:

The moment we arrived in this immense market, we were perfectly astonished at the vast numbers of people, the profusion of merchandise, which was there exposed for sale, and at the good police and order that reigned throughout.... Every species of merchandise had a separate spot for its sale. We first of all visited those divisions of the market appropriated for the sale of gold and silver wares, of jewels, of cloths interwoven with feathers, and of other manufactured goods; beside slaves of both sexes. This slave market was upon as great a scale as the Portuguese market for negro slaves at Guinea. To prevent these from running away, they were fastened with halters about their neck, though some were allowed to walk at large. Next to these came the dealers in coarser wares – cotton, twisted, thread, and cacao. In short, every species of goods which New Spain produces were here to be found.... If I had to enumerate everything singly, I should not so easily get to the end. And yet I have not mentioned the paper, which in this country is called amatl; the tubes filled with liquid amber and tobacco, the various sweet-scented salves, and similar things; nor the various seeds that were exposed for sale in the porticoes of this market, nor the medicinal herbs. In this market-place there were also courts of justice, to which three judges and several constables were appointed, who inspected the goods exposed for sale. I had almost forgotten to mention the salt, and those who made the flint knives; also the fish, and a species of bread made of a kind of mud or slime collected from the surface of this lake and eaten in that form, and has a similar taste to our cheese. Further, instruments of brass, copper, and tin; cups, and painted pitches of wood; indeed I wish I had completed the enumeration of all this profusion of merchandise. The variety was so great that it would occupy more space than I can well spare to note them down; besides which the market was so crowded with people, and the thronging so excessive in the porticoes, that it was quite impossible to see all in one day. (Díaz del Castillo 1844:235–237)

Exchange in the great marketplace of Tenochtitlan occurred in the form of barter – one commodity traded for another in accord with the inclinations of buyers and sellers – but also through monetized exchange using standardized currency that took several forms: cacao beans and turkey quills filled with gold dust being two of the most prominent forms of currency. As noted by Díaz, appointed judges and "constables" policed the market to maintain order among the thousands of buyers and sellers present, to adjudicate disputes, to ensure that sellers were adhering to fixed prices for commodities, and to enforce sumptuary laws that prohibited commoners and lower-ranking nobility from acquiring prestige goods, such as quetzal feathers, jade, and other luxury commodities emblematic of political office and nobility.

Spanish accounts relate that up to sixty thousand people bought and sold this "profusion of merchandise" in the market of Tenochtitlan every day. Since the Aztecs did not possess draft animals, the logistics of marketing at this scale must have occupied the labor of thousands of porters carrying the goods on their backs, or in the case of the canal-crossed city of Tenochtitlan, conveying them in small boats. Market exchange in ancient Mesoamerica was closely associated with a wealthy and politically powerful class of merchants called *pochteca,* who specialized in the long-distance trade of luxury commodities. The *pochteca* were as much agents of the state as they were independent merchants trading on their own accounts. They were affiliated with and worked as traders on behalf of the Aztec noble houses, but they also worked as agents provocateurs, departing on their trading expeditions in heavily armed convoys to survey the land, resources, and defenses of neighboring polities as potential targets for Aztec military expansion. This dual role, as traders and as spies, illustrates that politics as much as economics shaped both the *pochteca*'s social role and status and the markets they served.

The Inca had no markets such as that in Tenochtitlan, nor did they use a standardized currency. Moreover, no such endogenous class of merchants such as the *pochteca* existed within the Inca social order. Merchants similar in function to the *pochteca* worked on behalf of local noble houses in the northern Andes, where they were called *mindalá,* but there were no equivalents in most of the Inca Empire. Another possible exception concerns the wealthy Peruvian coastal polity of Chincha. María Rostworowski has published extensively on a document referred to as the *Relación de Chincha* (or the *Aviso*) that describes this complex polity as divided into thirty thousand tributaries specialized by distinct occupations in agriculture, fishing, and long-distance trading. Some six thousand tributaries to the lords of Chincha engaged in trading (Rostworowski 1970, 1989). The document describes them as "very daring, intelligent, of good breeding" and, according to Rostworowski, "the only ones in the Inca realm who used 'money,' since they bought and sold with copper" (Rostworowski 1999:209). This money may refer to the small, size-standardized "axes" made of thin copper sheets (and

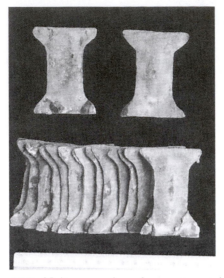

4.19. *Naipes*, axe-shaped monetary tokens from the Sicán culture, northern Peru. (Image courtesy of I. Shimada)

therefore nonutilitarian, at least as true axes) found in various archaeological contexts throughout the northern coast of Peru and coastal Ecuador, including in large-scale foundries in the Lambayeque Valley (Shimada 1985a, 1985b) (Figure 4.19). The extent to which this copper-axe money was a widely circulated, generalized currency rather than a more specialized medium of exchange in which its value was calibrated by its symbolic and ritual efficacy is unclear. But the fact that many wrapped packets of axe money are encountered in elite tombs suggests that this currency may have been restricted to certain social persona and deployed in class-specific political and ritual contexts.

We do know from the *Aviso* that the Chincha traders operated a geographically expansive trade network that radiated overland from Peru's central coast to the Andean highlands and *altiplano*, linked with sea-going vessels venturing northward to the southern coast of Ecuador. The overland highland trade seems to have concentrated on procuring copper, silver, gold, and other minerals in exchange for prestige goods. The logistics of this articulated land and sea trade route demanded both terrestrial caravans of thousands of llamas and their drovers, and sea-worthy vessels technologically capable of tacking and sailing with and against prevailing ocean currents. A sophisticated balsa-wood raft equipped with rudder, tiller, and sail was captured by the Spanish sea captain

Bartolomé Ruiz in 1528 during Francisco Pizarro's second, exploratory voyage along the coast of Ecuador. The description of the encounter indicates that the indigenous vessel carried as many as twenty people and a substantial cargo of luxury goods: *qompi* cloth of delicate, spun wool and cotton; tapestries; gold and silver objects; jewelry crafted from emeralds and other precious and semiprecious gemstones; fine ceramic vessels; and many *Spondylus* shells, or *mullu*, the warm-water bivalve found in the coastal waters of Ecuador (Rostworowski 1999:211). The beautiful, ritually charged *mullu* was coveted by Andean elites for millennia as an emblem of social authority, as a symbol of the life-giving forces of nature, and as a medium of political exchange.

The cargo of this trading expedition, which likely originated in Chincha, is highly revelatory. Even taking into account the particular interests of the Spanish in describing those commodities that had value within their own political economy, the cargo appears to have been dominated by luxury goods that, in the native Andean context, were never widely circulated among all social classes. Although dried fish and other basic subsistence goods, such as potatoes, quinoa, and maize, apparently were part of the cargo of coastal trading vessels, most of the trade objects were not destined for barter in town marketplaces. That is, the merchants of Chincha clearly did not serve a universal market of consumers, of all classes and social statuses, nor did they bring their goods to a central marketplace for sale in a disinterested, anonymous transaction with any willing buyer. They were not part of a monetized, merchant-market institution. Rather, like the northern *mindalá*, they served the interests of particular lords who commissioned them to procure goods valued by the political elite. These goods subsequently became important sources of political capital as items of status display and gift exchange. When the Inca incorporated the Chincha polity into their realm, most likely in the late fifteenth century, rather than disarticulate this well-developed system of long-distance exchange, they negotiated with the Chincha lords to continue procuring and exchanging desired objects, particularly the precious *Spondylus* shells found only in the distant waters of Ecuador. As part of this negotiation, Inca kings extended to the paramount lords of Chincha the exclusive privilege of riding in litters in full royal regalia next to the Inca king himself during military campaigns or when the Inca king and his court circulated through the realm on tours of inspection and visitation. As long as the Chincha lords rendered homage and tribute to the Inca king, they were free to carry on their lucrative trade. As a result, even as tributary subjects they may have become considerably wealthier after their incorporation into the broader geopolitical world of the empire. In this respect, the Inca Empire was not simply an engine of economic extraction, but, in some contexts, was also a pole of development and wealth creation. Military intimidation was certainly one technique in the political repertoire of the Inca kings, but so too was the far more subtle inducement of avarice, the potential for elite subjects to secure new sources of wealth and power.

What, then, can we conclude about the economic order of the Inca state? As we have seen, the Inca operated within a political economy that differed in considerable degree if not completely in kind from that of other premodern empires in the Americas and elsewhere. It is extremely rare to find a society as complexly organized as the Inca Empire was without a significant monetary economy or not deeply enmeshed in a web of merchant-market transactions. Moreover, many states and empires emphasize tribute in the form of commodities. An intense focus on discharging obligations to the state by labor service rather than by payment of currency, of standardized manufactured goods, or of other sorts of primitive money distinguishes the Andes. The politics of premodern states such as the Inca required a steady flow of surplus labor channeled toward elite classes residing permanently in urban centers. The organizational structure of the extractive process varied in degree and in kind according to local social context and historical circumstance. One fundamental distinction turns on the nature of this extraction: the kind of formal exchanges (tribute, coerced or voluntary) that occurred between urban elites and rural commoners. For instance, whereas this exchange relationship in the Andes relied more heavily on direct labor service, in ancient Mesoamerica tribute exchanges between commoner and elite frequently were of commodities (tribute in kind). This was certainly the case in the Aztec Empire, in which designated quantities of tribute goods flowed back to the capital of Tenochtitlan from thirty-eight tributary provinces on a periodic, often semiannual or annual, basis. Subjects produced or procured tribute items on their own lands and rendered tribute to both local and imperial officials in the form of sacks of maize, chile peppers, *amaranth* grain, and other bulk and processed goods. The Aztec also assessed tribute in labor for public works, but this was not the principal form of taxation, as it was in the Inca state. In one sense, of course, the argument could be made that this distinction is not terribly significant since tribute in kind is simply a product of labor: a portable objectification of surplus work. However, the potentially deeper social significance of direct labor service from commoner to elite in the ancient Andean world deserves closer scrutiny.

Tribute in labor form represents a more subtle and, at the same time, more forceful incorporation of colonial subjects into a hegemonic regime than does tribute in commodity form. To be involuntarily dispossessed of a commodity may be to experience an unwelcome, oppressive act of extraction. Moreover, the labor that was invested in producing the commodity is expropriated along with the objectified product itself. The social relations surrounding the organization of this labor, however, are internalized within the community from which the commodities are being extracted. In contrast, a requirement to labor directly on behalf of an exogenous dominant person or community is a more thoroughgoing, externalized expression of social, economic, and political subordination. Repeated acts of labor service create and reify hierarchical social bonds. A household's labor changes social properties from self-managed and inalienable to externally controlled and alienable. The structure of the social relations of labor extraction are externalized and shaped in great part by social actors and forces outside the tributary community. Generations of labor service extracted from colonial subjects by their overlords may, in itself, serve to transform the historical consciousness of both subjects and lords, until the coerced relationship becomes subtly "naturalized." In other words, tribute in commodity form, although conceivably even more economically disadvantageous than tribute in labor, does not have the same capacity to transform the consciousness of subject populations so that they perceive tributary obligations as a natural, constitutive element of their social relations with elites, both local and foreign. In this respect, the obligation to perform labor service on behalf of the empire became not only an instrumental source of concentrated wealth for the Inca royal household and its state agents but also an effective cultural mechanism of political and moral indoctrination. Habituated to laboring for king, *kuraka,* and community, subjects became enmeshed in an Inca economic order that was simultaneously and indivisibly a social, political, and moral order. That is, the Inca economic order intersected with and, in a real sense, was constituted by fundamental social and political relations and core cultural values. The principal cultural value that provided the logic for economic, political, and ritual transactions was that of mutual obligation and reciprocity – reciprocity between kin and kith, subjects and lords, humans and their physical environment, people and their gods.

5   The Moral Order: Religion and Spirituality among the Inca

The Inca people lived in a complex moral and spiritual world that interpenetrated virtually all aspects of their daily life. To understand the nature of religious belief and practices among the Inca, we must recognize the importance of social realities that emerged from the continual engagement of people, landscapes, and material culture. We must grasp how these social realities were enmeshed in a broader field of signifiers imbued with a shared cultural understanding of the immanence of the spiritual in the quotidian.

Just as land and labor were at the core of the Inca economic order, so too were they the principal focus of Inca moral order and religious practices. The Inca people possessed a deep and abiding attachment to the land that was the source of their intense spirituality. In a real sense, the daily, collective tasks of farming and herding, of working the land and tending the fields, were acts of worship. Inca religious experience turned on highly elaborated conceptual and affective ties to the inhabited landscape. Many of the abstract philosophical and eschatological notions held by the Inca were ultimately grounded in the concrete acts of tilling the soil, building a terrace, cleaning a canal, fertilizing the fields, harvesting the crops, culling the herds, and expressing reverence for all acts of procreation – human, animal, and vegetal. Work and worship were not separate realities or distinct activities. No special day of the week was formally set aside from quotidian labors for the purpose of prayer, contemplation, or conversation with the deities. To paraphrase Hocart (1970:256), there was no religion in the Andes, only a system that in Europe had split up into religion and business. To the Inca, making a living and worshipping the gods were, in essence, indistinguishable acts of daily life. Even the most esoteric state cults and religious practices of Inca royalty were grounded in the bedrock of productive activity, whether that was the production of wealth in the form of agricultural crops, camelid herds, fisheries, or the extraction of minerals and forest products, or was the social reproduction of people.

Inca religious thought codified a set of abstract beliefs about ultimate reality and the roles, social responsibilities, and fate of humans. But, just as importantly, Inca religion entailed a set of concrete, material practices focused on the sacral qualities of the natural world and designed to channel the propitious (and ward off the inauspicious) forces of nature for the benefit of humans. In this system of beliefs and practices, the physical landscape itself possessed certain human qualities and the power to affect human destiny. The dramatic Andean landscape of ice-clad mountain peaks, remote high plains, vertiginous gorges, surging cascades, turbulent rivers, and violent, roiling thunderstorms evoked in the minds of its indigenous inhabitants a sense of the uncanny, latent power in the earth. In this animist mentality, nature was believed to possess something like a soul – an invisible substance that literally animated material reality, including all those elements of the landscape such as rocks, earth, caves, springs, rivers, lakes, and oceans that contemporary Western thought considers inert. By virtue of this soul-like quality, nature had the capacity to communicate directly with humans, particularly through the mediating capacities of shamans, healers, priests, and kings who served as conduits to the deep, underlying forces of the universe that were considered both dangerous and potentially beneficial.

To the Inca, worship required establishing communication between the natural and social worlds, and certain objects and places in the landscape were believed to be privileged points of access in making this communicative intersection between these parallel worlds. This point of access was known to and named by the Inca as *wak'a*. The concept of *wak'a,* together with the complex beliefs and material practices focused on the worship of *wak'as*, permeated Inca religious experience among both commoners and elites. A closely related concept, that of *camay*, which we can gloss as a kind of *élan vital*, the vitalizing, creative power imbued in all material reality, was critical to Inca religious philosophy. Understanding Inca religion begins with exploring the meaning and social power of *wak'a* and *camay*. These two concepts appear to have had ancient roots in indigenous Andean mentality, predating any ideological systematization under the Inca political regime. They provided the deep structure, the material and metaphysical *raison d'être*, for both folk and state religious cults. The mutually implicated notions of *wak'a* and *camay* also served to articulate the social relationship between humans and nature upon which Andean peoples depended for their livelihood and their cultural reproduction.

Wak'a and *Camay*

What exactly, then, was a *wak'a*?[1] The first mention of the term *wak'a* in documents published by the Spanish occurs in Juan de Betanzos's recording of one of the origin myths of the Inca. This myth describes the terrible creative and destructive powers of Contiti Viracocha Pacha-yachachic, "God, Maker of the World." As the Lord of Creation, Viracocha emerged from Lake Titicaca near the ancient archaeological site of Tiwanaku in the Inca province of Collasuyu, and proceeded to make all of the people of Peru, "forming them of stones" and giving them names. As Betanzos recounts the story, Viracocha pointed to the stones he created and said: "[T]hese will be called the so and so and will come out of such and such a spring in such and such a province and will settle there and be increased, and the others will come out of such and such a cave and will be called the thus and so and will settle in such and such a province. Just the way I have painted them and made them of stone thus they must come out of the springs and rivers and caves and mountains in the provinces which I have told you and named" (Betanzos 1996:8). The Lord of Creation then set off to call out the people he had created from their *pacarina*, their ethnic origin point. When he came to the province of the Cacha, the people, heavily armed, confronted Viracocha in order to kill him and defend their territory. But Viracocha, perceiving their murderous intent, "caused fire to fall from heaven, burning a range of mountains near the Indians" prompting them to prostrate themselves in abject terror before him. Viracocha tells the Cacha that he is their creator, and, as Betanzos relates, in commemoration of this epochal revelation, the Cacha "built a sumptuous *guaca* [*wak'a*], which means a shrine or idol, at the place where he stood when he called fire from heaven and from which he went to put it out. In this *guaca* they and their descendants offered a great quantity of gold and silver. They set up a stone statue carved from a great stone almost five *varas* [about 15 feet] in length and one *vara* in width, more or less, in the *guaca* in memory of Viracocha and of what had taken place there. The *guaca* has stood there from ancient times until today, and I have seen the burned mountain and the burned stones" (Betanzos 1996:10).

Betanzos's extraordinary narrative reveals many interlocking dimensions of the meaning and social significance of the term *wak'a*. Materially, the *wak'a* is a physical place, a shrine that is the site of worship for all

---

[1] Van de Guchte (1990:ch. 9) provides an excellent summary of various meanings of the term *wak'a*, and how the term was understood by Europeans in the sixteenth and seventeenth centuries.

5.1. The carved "Intiwatana" stone, an example of a well-known *wak'a* at the site of Machu Picchu. (Image courtesy of L. Guengerich)

those people who recognize its special quality (Figure 5.1). In this case, the *wak'a* as a material object was fabricated by the Cacha to commemorate an event that revealed the deity who created them. As a result, the shrine becomes a material emblem of their origin place and implicitly a cultural claim to the surrounding territory. Here the Cacha also create an "idol" for the worship of Viracocha. They install this image of the Lord of Creation within the shrine, making an even more explicit, divinely sanctioned claim to their original territorial rights. The *wak'a* becomes the equivalent of a title to land, authorizing the Cacha to legitimately possess, use, and defend the land as their property. Acts of worship to Viracocha's idol within the *wak'a* require rich offerings of gold and silver, thus emphasizing the social and economic power of the shrine. The *wak'a* as a concrete, fixed place in the landscape and the idol installed within become a composite religious artifact that references a specific time (the moment of origin), place (the land of the burned mountains), and people (the Cacha, who first confront, then recognize Viracocha as the divine power of creation).

Betanzos's text refers to the structure that the Cacha built in memory of this epochal event of ethnic creation and recognition as an *adoratorio*.

This term can be translated as a physical shrine, but also in a more active sense as an oratory, a place of prayer (Pizarro 1921:202; Van de Guchte 1990:243). The latter translation conveys more of the dynamic, transactional quality of an Andean *wak'a*. An ancient *wak'a* was an identifiable material entity most often, though as we shall see, not always one fixed concretely in the landscape. But the significance of a *wak'a* exceeds mere materiality. A *wak'a* was also a place or an object of worship that served as a conduit of communication between people and the divine forces of nature. In a real sense, the power latent in the materiality of the *wak'a* as a shrine becomes activated only when the *wak'a* is used as an oratory in the moments of communicative worship – of the placing of offerings, of the sharing of food and drink by the community of believers. The power of the *wak'a* to affect the destiny of its owners and believers can only be realized in moments of contact, communication, and exchange between the community and the deified forces of nature. That is, to be efficacious, the *wak'a* must be activated as a *social* entity, as a communicative object; it cannot remain in a mute, material state of latent power.

This realization opens up even richer veins of significance of the term *wak'a* for the Inca people. In the Andean world, *wak'as* were (and to a significant extent continue to be) integral parts of a sacred landscape around which ethnic groups organized their spiritual and ceremonial life. The *wak'a* is the ultimate point of meeting and of communication between humans and the natural world, a locus of convergence between heaven and earth, the material and the immaterial, nature and culture, the sacred and the profane. In order to achieve that privileged state of communicative efficacy, the *wak'a* and the idols and objects within must be capable of speech. To the Inca, prayer was not a monologue of human supplication addressed to a distant, unresponsive deity. *Wak'as* were entities defined by their capacity for communicative exchange. They were privileged vehicles for the community of believers to engage in dialogues with their gods. These dialogues between the Inca people and their gods were not passive affairs. Gods and humans actively negotiated with each other. Intermediaries acting on behalf of the Inca kings posed questions of particularly prominent *wak'as* to elicit oracular utterances that could guide the kings at critical junctures in their careers, such as before military encounters or in the celebration of religious feasts (Figure 5.2). At times, if the king did not like the outcome of the oracle, he berated, refused to render obligatory offerings, or even threatened to destroy the *wak'a*. The most famous instance of an Inca king's awe-inspiring fury with an oracle not to his liking occurred during the war-plagued reign of the last emperor, Atawallpa. During his dynastic struggle with his half-brother, Waskhar, Atawallpa sent two noble emissaries to the prominent

5.2. The king convenes the *wak'as* and converses with them in order to make demands and elicit oracular pronouncements. (Adapted from Guaman Poma de Ayala 1609)

wak'a oracle of Catequil in the mountains of Huamachuco. As recounted by Betanzos (1996:231), "this *guaca* was on a hill on top of a very high mountain. The idol in it was made of stone about the size of a man. There was also a very old man who spoke with this idol and it with him." Atawallpa ordered his royal ambassadors to make sacrifices on his behalf so that "from it his great success and good fortune might be known" (Betanzos 1996:231). The answer from Catequil was not what Atawallpa anticipated. The old man who gave the idol-oracle's response berated Atawallpa for his murderous acts against Waskhar's allies and armies, and predicted a grim future for the emperor. Atawallpa was enraged and declared that "this *guaca* is also as much an enemy *auca* [a traitor, enemy] as Huascar." In response, Atawallpa ordered his army to surround Catequil in battle array "so that the idol would not escape," and the king "himself, in person, climbed to the *guaca* where the idol was ... and gave the idol such a blow in the neck with a battle-ax he carried that he cut off the head. They then brought there the old man, who was held as a saint and who had given the idol's reply to the messengers. Atawallpa also beheaded him with his battle-ax" (Betanzos 1996:232). Not content with just beheading both the idol of Catequil and its religious attendant, Atawallpa proceeded to burn the idol and the corpse of the old priest, to ground the remains of both into dust, and then to set fire to the entire hill on which the *wak'a* idol-oracle had been placed.

Though perhaps an extreme instance of the tense, potentially conflict-ridden relationship between *wak'as* and kings, this story underscores the simultaneous power and vulnerability of *wak'as* as entities with humanlike qualities and propensities, as well as with a human-like capacity for communicative intercourse. People did not merely pray to or passively supplicate the *wak'as*. Rather, for better or worse, they talked, negotiated, argued, and engaged in active social relationships with the *wak'as*. In a discussion of the most important temples of the Inca, Pedro de Cieza de León emphasized this dialogic capacity of the *wak'as* by referring to them explicitly as oracles: "The third oracle and temple of the Incas was the temple of Vilcanota famous throughout these kingdoms, [that] ... spoke through the mouth of the false priests who were at the services of the idols.... The fourth temple of the Incas and natives of the provinces esteemed and frequented was that of Ancocagua, where, too, there was an ancient oracle held in high regard. It lies along the province of Hatuncana, and at times they came devoutly from many regions to listen [to] the vain replies of this devil" (Cieza de León 1976:151). Cieza de León mentions another shrine, Coropuna, in the province of Cuntisuyu, frequented by Inca nobility who endowed the temple with enormous quantities of gold, silver, and other precious objects and supported its priests, *aqllakuna,* and servants (of which he relates "there were many"). He goes on to remark that there "were always people from many places in it, and the devil [the oracle] talked here more freely than in the aforementioned shrines, because he continually gave a thousand answers, not periodically, as in others" (Cieza de León 1976:151).

Cieza's commentary indicates that some *wak'as* had greater powers of oracular speech than did others and therefore had greater social efficacy. Just as did the most effective Inca kings, these *wak'as* exuded a kind of charisma. They attracted more adherents to their cult and, as a result, received even richer endowments that further enhanced their perceived spiritual capacity to bestow health, well-being, and power on their worshippers. Not all *wak'as* were alike. As were all acts of social exchange in the Inca world, the *wak'as* were arrayed in a hierarchy of power and prestige: some ranked higher than did others, perhaps analogous to the hierarchy of chapels, churches, basilicas, and cathedrals of the Roman Catholic Church.

Augustín de Zárate confirms the oracular character of Andean *wak'as* and describes priestly intermediaries who communicated with the *wak'a*: "[The priests] are always dressed in white. When they go up to the *huacas*, they carry white linen or cloths in their hands, and prostrate themselves, crawling on the ground. In addressing these idols, they use a language that the Indians do not understand" (Zárate 1968:50). This passage contributes another facet of meaning to our understanding of *wak'as* by describing the actual process of communication between the *wak'as* and their adherents. Clearly, *wak'as* were addressed not in common, vernacular speech, but rather through a form of ritualized speech performed by specialists who, like the ill-fated old priest of Catequil, acted on behalf of the community of worshippers. This ritual speech was accompanied by the priests' elaborate gestures (prostration) and wearing of special, symbolic clothing. Apparently in this instance, communication with and through the *wak'a* to divine forces was channeled through intermediaries. Common folk understood neither the specialized discourse of the priests nor the corresponding replies of the *wak'a*-oracle. This capacity to speak with the *wak'as* and receive oracles from them became another significant source of social power for the kinds of people (shamans, curers, priests, and kings) who could serve as such specialized intermediaries in the Andean world.

Physically, *wak'as* could be purpose built, as were the shrines of the Cacha or the various temples commissioned by Inca kings and nobility to commemorate a mythical or historical event that revealed the intercession of the divine or the memorable actions of humans. But they could also be sanctified natural objects: ravines, precipices, mountain peaks, rivers, springs, unusual boulders, caves; in short, they could be "whatever natural object which appears notable and made different from the rest" (Polo de Ondegardo 1916–1917:189). Worshippers recognized these natural objects as *wak'as* because they appeared unusual or unique in some way (Figure 5.3). These kinds of natural objects had the capacity to evoke a sense of the uncanny, of latent, incompletely comprehended power. They were not inert objects but were, rather, deeply affect laden, possessing the capacity to inspire awe, fear, respect, and other emotions in the mind of the observer. Yet their latent potential as *wak'as* was not realized unless and until they became the objects of social recognition

5.3. The "Chingana" stone, a *wak'a* at the site of Chinchero, Cuzco region. Note the modification of the original stone with an inset stairway motif. (Photo ©Edward Ranney, from *Monuments of the Incas*, by John Hemming, Thames and Hudson, Ltd., London, 2010)

and exchange. Their oracular power was not inherent; rather, it was relational, constituted and mobilized only in the context of communication with their cult adherents. *Wak'as* only became *wak'as* when they engaged in reciprocal communication with humans. For this reason, *wak'as* could be made and unmade. The Quechua term for an unmade *wak'a* was *atisca*, or vanquished, exhausted. If a *wak'a* could not speak, as in the case of the destroyed Catequil, it was no longer a *wak'a*. Andean people made their gods, as their gods made Andean people.

So *wak'a* and human were not ontologically distinct categories. Andean *wak'as* were deeply social entities. They were linked in kinship networks just as were their human adherents. They spoke with each other and with humans. They symbolically ate and drank the food and libations offered by humans through designated intermediaries, and, in exchange, they provided their human brethren with life-giving water, fertile agricultural fields, healthy livestock, and political counsel. Attendants of *wak'as* clothed the idols that dwelled within with the costumes of their ethnic group, visually affirming the intense intimate relationship between *wak'as* and humans. In dressing the *wak'as* as they themselves dressed, ethnic groups visually expressed their sense of identity and kinship with the *wak'as* and with the sanctified forces of nature that communicated with humans through them.

In a logical extension of these relational identities between *wak'as* and humans, Salomon asserts that "*huacas* were considered by indigenous Andeans as 'persons in fact'" and possessed "vibrantly individual personalities" (Salomon 1991:18, 19). As a consequence of this indigenous merging of *wak'as* and humans into the same ontological category, Salomon remarks that "like everything else ... *huacas* are made of energized matter ... and they act within nature, not over and outside it as Western supernaturals do" (Salomon 1991:19). To understand Inca religion, we must grasp the significance of this radical conceptual difference between Andean and Western modes of thought concerning the nature of the gods and of the supernatural. When we understand *wak'as* as "persons in fact," we are no longer puzzled by the human-like agency that *wak'as* exhibit, nor by the otherwise bizarre and seemingly irrational spectacle of an Inca king waging war on a religious shrine and reducing it to ashes in a paroxysm of fury.

Wak'as, as integral parts of an ethnic group's social community, also shared in the power politics of their nation. The profound political nature of *wak'as* should not be surprising given their deeply rooted associations with an ethnic group's claims to a given territory and to the productive natural resources contained in that territory, such as its agricultural fields, its sources of irrigation water, and its population's labor. In order to advance their political claims, Inca kings avidly sought to exert control over local and regional *wak'as* throughout their domain, even, as we have seen, to the point of declaring war on existing *wak'as* and destroying some altogether. As Van de Guchte (1990:259) perceptively observes: "Dominance and the instruments of domination are crucial elements in the discourse of *huacas*. The themes which most frequently occupy center-stage in these narratives are the invention of the *huacas*, followed by the apparently equally important theme of the annihilation of *huacas*, and the conquest of and dominance over *huacas*."

Although Atawallpa's utter destruction of Catequil may be an extreme case of an emperor's will to dominance over the sacred, politics and religion were never separate realities in the Inca world. Inca statecraft demanded constant engagement with the religious beliefs and practices of the empire's subjects. We know that after conquering an ethnic group, "the Incas had the people's main idol taken away and placed in

Cuzco with the same services and cult that it used to have in its province of origin" (Cobo, cited in Gose 1996:21). Similarly, Cieza de León recounted that during the celebration of the *qhapaq ucha*[2] ritual,

[I]t was the custom of the Incas of Cuzco to have all the statues and idols in the *huacas* ... brought into that city each year. They were transported with great veneration by the priests and *camayocs*, which is the name of the guardians. When they entered the city they were received with great feasts and processions and lodged in places set aside and appointed for that purpose. And people having assembled from all parts of the city and even from most of the provinces, men and women, the reigning monarch, accompanied by all the Incas and *orejones*, courtiers and important men of the city provided great festivals and *taquis* [collective drinking bouts accompanied by song, dance and theatrical performances]. They encircled the entire square of Cuzco with a great cable of gold, and inside it they placed all the treasure and precious stones.... [A]fter that was done, they went through their annual ceremony, which was that these statues and images and priests came together and announced what was going to happen during the year, whether there would be abundance or scarcity; whether the Inca would have a long life, or might, perchance, die that year; if enemies might be expected to invade the country from some side, or if some of the pacified people would rebel. In a word they were questioned and questioned again ... and this was asked of not all the oracles together, but one by one. (Cieza de León 1976:190–191)

The idols of subject populations were, in essence, held hostage and personally called to account for their utterances. The questioning of the subject peoples' *wak'a*-idols by the Villac Umu, the Inca high priest, and by the Inca king himself became a virtual inquisition, an implicit test of the political loyalty of the subject population. Cieza de León reported that "if by the end of the year it turned out that one of these dreamers [priests of the idols who gave the oracular predictions] had by chance made a prediction that came true, the Inca joyfully ordered him to become a member of his household" (Cieza de León 1976:192). In stark contrast, we have already seen the unhappy fate of a *wak'a*-idol and its priest if the prediction turned out not to be to the king's liking.

   Why did Inca kings invest so much of their personal energy and political capital in inventing new *wak'as*, deconsecrating others, and controlling the shrines and idols of their subjects? As Rowe (1982:109) remarks, "[S]ince the Incas believed that almost everything had some supernatural power, it was natural for them to accept the deities and sacred objects of the people they conquered, insofar as the native cults did not conflict with Inca religious values." But Inca kings went much

---

[2] Literally, "royal obligation."

further than simply accepting foreign deities and oracular objects – they actively sought them out and had the conquered ethnic groups' portable idols and sacred bundles brought to Cuzco where they could be consulted through their oracle-priests. The Inca "carefully remembered every [provincial] oracle's predictions and kept an overall track record for each, constantly reevaluating its position in the imperial hierarchy of deities and its system of sacrificial rewards. These outlays in goods and services were considerable and would not have occurred if the motives behind oracular consultation were entirely cynical. In short, we must assume that the Incas and their subjects believed in oracles and gave them a certain degree of political autonomy" (Gose 1996:14).

A political realist might observe that this was simply one pragmatic tactic among others to exert power over subject populations: hold the *wak'as* of ardent believers hostage, and you control the adherents' destiny. There is a significant amount of truth to this claim. By co-opting the deities of subject provinces, by endowing them with rich offerings and publicly honoring them in the imperial capital, the Inca kings acknowledged the local deities' essential role for the ethnic groups. They thereby gained a measure of loyalty from their subject populations at the same time as they were asserting their hierarchical authority over them. But the intimate relationship between *wak'as* and Inca divine kings was more complex and more nuanced than this solely instrumental perspective would have it. Inca kings did not self-consciously manipulate religious belief as a technique of power. They were themselves enmeshed in cultural structures of religious belief and practice that were essential to the legitimacy and efficacy of kingship. That is, Inca kings did not merely use the *wak'as* as a tool of command; they believed in the *wak'as*. They did not consult the *wak'as* of subject populations solely as a kind of cynical religious theater, to gain the political favor of potentially rebellious populations. They did so in search of efficacy, believing that the *wak'a*-idol complexes of the populations they conquered might possess vital spiritual essences and special knowledge that they could acquire to enhance their own prestige, authority, and universal renown. The conquest of foreign ethnic groups, of course, entailed the eminently pragmatic appropriation of land, labor, and natural resources. But Inca kings as warrior-priests were perhaps equally motivated by their search for privileged access to the supernatural realm in which circulated the *élan vital*, the vitalizing force that animated all things – *camay*. Accumulating, concentrating, and distributing *camay* in public works, in finely crafted objects, and in the reproduction of their own noble lineage imbued Inca kings with majesty and supreme social power. As we shall see, Inca kings conceived of their empire as a hyperextended household of which they were the progenitors and, ultimately, the ancestral figures to which the population of the empire would pay homage. In this belief system, Inca kings considered themselves concentrated sources of the *camay* that brought into being and vitalized all of creation, just like Viracocha, the Lord of Creation.

Ancestor Worship

Belief in *camay*, the essential force that animated all things material, and in the concepts and practices surrounding the worship of *wak'as* were core tenets of Inca religion held by commoners and royalty alike. A third element of indigenous belief and practice played an equally significant role in Inca spirituality: the worship of ancestors. In many of the ethnic groups conquered by the Inca, as well as among the Inca themselves, the biological (or culturally defined, and even mythical) progenitor of the lineage was a principal figure of worship. Ancestors were, in fact, *wak'as extraordinaire*. In this belief system, most likely broadly shared and of great antiquity in the Andean world, ancestors were recognized as once-living members of the social community, the progenitors and principal authorities of the ethnic group's stem lineage, who upon death transitioned into a new state of being and consciousness intensely charged with spiritual power. Not surprisingly, in such a framework of belief, cremation was not a preferred method of treating the dead since the very corporality, the material matter of the once-living person, carried enduring *camay* and substantive social power and therefore the capacity to positively influence the community of the living.[3] Thus the bodies of these illustrious ancestors were frequently preserved in elaborate, richly clothed mummy bundles and installed in temples or in highly visible mortuary towers where they continued to engage with their extended families in emotional rituals of remembrance and consultation. The ancestors gave counsel and moral guidance during these séances in which they shared food, drink, religious chants, epic songs, and dance with their living descendants. The cult of the ancestors became one of the principal vehicles for expressing spirituality and for coming to grips with profound anxiety over death's approach. Although their anticipation of death surely caused existential pain to indigenous Andean

---

[3] We can now see the even deeper political significance of Atawallpa's murder of Catequil, the idol and the priest, burning them both and grinding them into dust to be cast off the mountain. Atawallpa's fury was a graphic demonstration effectively proclaiming that the once influential *wak'a* of Catequil was not merely vanquished, but was irrevocably severed from the human community, incapable of sociality and therefore no longer a social being at all.

people, ancestral cults ensured that corporeal death though an ineluctable reality was not coupled with social death. As long as they were still
remembered, feted, and incorporated as social actors in the life of their
community the Andean dead never truly died. Thomas Jefferson's aphorism that "the earth belongs to the living and not the dead" may have
rung true in the eighteenth-century society of the nascent United States,
but for the Andean people, the more accurate statement would be that
the earth belongs to the living *and* the dead, and, reciprocally, that both
the living and the dead belong to the earth.

These three mutually implicated elements of Andean spirituality –
wak'a, *camay*, and ancestor worship – received extraordinary public
salience and expression among the noble households in the imperial
capital of Cuzco. Exploring the spiritual practices of the Inca nobility
reveals much not only about the belief systems that were widely shared
in the Andean world but also about the workings of sociality and political power through religious belief and practice. Recall that by the end of
the fifteenth century the Inca elite in Cuzco were organized into twenty
distinct social groups, or *ayllus*. These *ayllus* maintained separate residential compounds constructed on a grand scale in the heart of the city.
Ten of the *ayllus* were considered royal, invested with supreme status as
direct descendants by blood of former kings – these were the *panaqas*.
Panaqa members, as consanguineal relatives of former kings, controlled
vast wealth in natural resources, goods, and labor service that had been
accumulated during the reign of the monarch who was in life the founder and, in death, the divine ancestor of the *panaqa* that bore his name.
After the death of the reigning king, his patrimonial estate passed under
the control of his principal male heirs, who became the political leaders
of the *panaqa*. *Panaqa* members were obliged to perpetuate the memory of the deceased king who had originally founded the *panaqa*. In this
sense, ancestor worship was the bedrock of indigenous Andean religion
and the focus of intensive ritual activity in the social unit of the *ayllu*.

Among the elite of Cuzco, ancestor worship took the form of an elaborate cult of the royal mummies, which both fascinated and repelled
Spanish chroniclers who vividly recorded this key element of Inca spirituality. Acosta described the exceptional care that the bodies of Inca
kings received upon death in order to preserve or even enhance the sense
that the kings remained alive and possessed of vitality, even if they had
transitioned into another ontological status:

In Cuzco, the Licentiate Polo found this Incas's house [King Pachakuti, founder
of the empire], and his servants and the priestesses who served his memory, and
he discovered the body.... The body was so well preserved, and treated with a
certain resin, that it seemed alive. The eyes were made of gold leaf so well placed

that there was no need of the natural ones; and there was a bruise on his head that he had received from a stone in a certain battle. His hair was gray and none of it was missing, as if he had died that very day, although in fact his death had occurred more than sixty or eighty years before. This body, along with those of other Incas, was sent by Polo to the city of Lima under orders from the viceroy, the Marqués de Cañete, for it was necessary to root out the idolatry in Cuzco. (Acosta 2002:364)

Acosta's comment on the need to "root out the idolatry in Cuzco" by taking custody of the royal mummies and, in effect, holding them hostage in the Spanish coastal city of Lima alludes to the profound anxiety that the Spanish legal authorities felt once they realized how critical these ancestral bodies were to the religious sentiments of the Inca people.

Pedro Pizarro, participant in and eyewitness to the Spanish conquest of the Inca, similarly noted that the Inca "had the law and custom of taking that one of their Lords who died and embalming him, wrapping him up in many fine clothes, and to these Lords they allotted all the service which they had had in life, in order that these dandles [mummies] might be served in death as well as they had been in life" (Pizarro 1921:202). Cobo provides even more telling details about the treatment of the royal mummies:

[The *panaqa* members] brought out [the royal mummies] with a large retinue for all solemn festivals. In the square they were seated in a row according to their seniority, and there the servants and guardians ate and drank.... Also placed before these bodies were large tumblers made of gold and silver like pitchers, which were called *vilques* [Figure 5.4]. Into these tumblers they put the *chicha* with which they would drink a toast to their deceased, but before drinking, they would show it to the deceased. The deceased would toast each other; the deceased would toast the living, and vice versa. The toast of the dead bodies was done in their name by the attendants. With these *vilques* full, the *chicha* was poured over a round stone idol located in the center of the square. There was a small reservoir made around the stone where the *chicha* filtered through hidden drains. (Cobo 1990:40) (Figure 5.5)

Cobo's passage provides subtle insight into the multiple material essences of *wak'as*. The mummified bodies of the dead royals were powerful *wak'as* but so too was the "circular stone set up as an idol in the middle of the plaza." This stone was nothing else than an *usnu*, an Inca term conventionally glossed as a ceremonial throne of the Inca from which the king presided at public celebrations. But the pouring of libations over the stone into "hidden channels and drains" clearly draws a direct analogy to the body of the king himself, who was obliged to drink copious amount of maize beer at these public celebrations, in sequential and seemingly never-ending rounds of reciprocal toasts with noble

5.4. *K'ero* decorated with silver studs, similar to vessels used for toasting deceased rulers and other important personages. (Image © Seattle Art Museum, #2006.123, Peru – Inca-Spanish colonial culture 1500–1600, 7 5/16″, wood and silver. Gift of anonymous donor. Photo: Paul Macapia)

compatriots and provincial elites. In other words, the *usnu* in Cuzco, as well as those installed in the principal plazas of Inca colonial towns such as Vilcashuaman and Huanuco Pampa (Figure 5.6), were essentially "body doubles" of the king, *wak'as* in their own right but always associated cognitively and in social practice with the king himself. Chapter 7 explores the concept of the *wawqi*, the kings' "object-brothers," which, like the *usnu*, served as avatars and political delegates of the king in death as in life. In essence, *usnus* were elaborate architectonic versions of the portable *wawqi*.

The seemingly lurid spectacle of the descendants of dead kings ministering to their ancestors' elaborately costumed, desiccated corpses with offerings of food, drink, and toasts in the plazas of Cuzco obscures the political and religious nuances embedded in the cult of the royal mummies. Although grounded in the virtually pan-Andean religious practice of ancestor worship, the elite cult was something more than the simple veneration of a dead lineage ancestor. In the first instance, the elaborate feasting of the dead royals was organized around, and intended as, ceremonies of agricultural fertility. "When there was need for water for the cultivated fields," Cobo made clear, "they usually brought out

5.5. Beakers of *chicha* were offered to the mummies of royalty, both kings and queens. (Adapted from Guaman Poma de Ayala 1615)

[the dead king's] body, richly dressed, with his face covered, carrying it in a procession through the fields and *punas*, and they were convinced that this was largely responsible for bringing rain" (Cobo 1979:125). Dead kings, furthermore, were frequently addressed in the protocols of *panaqa* toasts as Illapa, the weather deity who personified the atmospheric forces of wind, rain, hail, lightning, and thunder – all the meteorological phenomena responsible for the growth or destruction of agricultural crops.

The public display of the royal mummies, arranged in order of seniority, in the principal plazas of Cuzco during state occasions was also a graphic affirmation of the legitimacy of Inca dynastic rule. On these occasions, the reigning king would participate in majestic ceremonial processionals throughout Cuzco quite literally in company with the

5.6. Although *usnu* complexes were created in a variety of forms, the best-recognized version consists of a stone platform in a central plaza, as seen in this example from Caramba, Peru. (Image ©Megan Son)

complete line of his royal ancestors, who were physically represented by their richly adorned, relictual bundles. Who could contest the legitimacy of the Inca when the entire dynasty, the distilled history of their ruling mandate, was constantly visible and present to the nation? By these ritual actions, the deceased monarchs and the living emperor symbolically became one – embodiments of legitimate power, emblems of agricultural fertility and abundance, powerful icons of national identity, and concentrated essences of *camay*. The cult of the royal mummies was an intense expression of social and ritual solidarity within the Inca ruling caste, particularly among the ten *panaqas* that exploited and benefited materially from the patrimony of their kingly ancestors. Other cults and esoteric beliefs promoted this same sense of solidarity and imperial destiny among the Inca people as a whole.

The Inca Pantheon

According to the conventional imperial narratives, at some point after his victory over the Chanka in the mid-fifteenth century, the great Inca king Pachakuti reformed and systematized the state cults, just as he reorganized social structures, implemented a new legal and moral code, redistributed land and natural resources to his family and close political allies, and rebuilt the city of Cuzco to befit its supreme status as the capital of the largest native empire of the Western Hemisphere. King Pachakuti's reorganization of religious life and practices recognized a formal pantheon of state deities arranged, as were all things social in the Inca world, in a hierarchy of prestige. These deities, however, shared an essential underlying identity as manifold aspects of nature. Viracocha, the creator deity, was the most abstract of the Inca deities, held responsible for the initial act of cosmogenesis: the creation of the sun, the moon, the stars, people, the earth – in effect, the creation of all of human space and time (Figure 5.7). One of the creator deity's revelatory titles was Ilya-Tiqsi Viracocha Pacha-yachachic, or "Ancient Foundation, Lord, Maker of the World" (Rowe 1946:293; cited also in D'Altroy 2002:145). Most imperial subjects did not actively worship Viracocha, unlike other nature deities. Furthermore, the cult of Viracocha did not enjoy the wealth of royal endowments bestowed upon other nature deities such as Inti, the solar deity, and Illapa, the Lord of Thunder, Lightning, Hail and Rain. The Lord of Creation appears almost as an abstract foundational proposition in comparison with the more tangible deities of nature that received daily acts of reverence and sacrifice. At a moment of political crisis during his epochal wars against the Chanka ethnic groups, Pachakuti claimed to have a trance-induced vision of Viracocha who gave him political counsel, assuring him of his eventual victory and charging him with the obligation to bring order and civilization to the Andean world (Betanzos 1996:29; Sarmiento 1999:90). Betanzos relates that upon winning the Chanka wars, King Pachakuti began rebuilding Cuzco and reorganizing the moral codes and religious practices of the Inca. One of his first acts was to construct the lavish Qorikancha, or Golden Compound, the single most important religious structure in Cuzco. Betanzos (1996:45–46) explains that Pachakuti dedicated the new temple to Viracocha, the figure he saw in his trance-dream. The king subsequently reflected on his encounter with this deity: "[H]e took into account that the one he had seen there [in his trance], whom he called Viracocha, he saw with great brightness.... As he was planning on building this house [Qorikancha], he judged by the brightness of the one he saw that it must have been the Sun, and on coming near the first word he spoke, 'Child, fear not'; thus, his people called him 'child of the Sun.'" In this account, Pachakuti calls the bright vision he saw in his trance Viracocha and addresses this deity as the Lord of Creation: "'Lord God who created me and gave me the form of a man'" (Betanzos 1996:29). Yet, upon the dedication of Qorikancha, the principal deity of this most prestigious temple was referred to not as Viracocha, but as Inti, the god of the sun. So, despite the evident importance to Pachakuti

5.7. The two-story temple at Raqchi, built of stone and adobe, was dedicated to the deity Viracocha. (Image ©Ricardo Espinosa)

of his vision of the Lord of Creation, our sources remain ambiguous about the actual hierarchical position of Viracocha in the presumed pantheon of Inca deities. At times, the figure of Viracocha seems to merge seamlessly into that of Inti, as if the two were one and the same or, more likely, were distinct avatars of the same underlying cosmological principles of procreation focused on the energy and life force that emanated from the sun.[4]

Whatever the relationship between Viracocha and Inti, the solar deity became the focus of the most ubiquitous state cult in the empire. Inca kings asserted that Inti was the immediate ancestor and the spiritual paterfamilias of the royal dynasty (Rowe 1946, 1982). By identifying themselves as descendants of Inti, Inca kings symbolically appropriated the brilliant, life-giving essence of the resplendent sun. As a result of this intimate association with royalty, the solar cult received enormous endowments of temples, lands, goods, and labor service. Cult temples were staffed by large numbers of *aqllakuna* and priests serving at the pleasure of and patronized by Inca nobility. Upon the completion of the Qorikancha, King Pachakuti endowed the temple with priestly attendants, five hundred *aqllakuna,* and two hundred young married men who served as *yanakuna* to farm land specifically set aside for the

[4] See Demarest (1981) for an elaboration of this theme and the overlapping qualities of the various Inca deities, particularly Viracocha, Inti, and Illapa.

support of the cult (Betanzos 1996:45–46). Pachakuti commissioned two idols for the dedication of the temple: one a natural, sugarloaf-shaped stone covered with a strip of gold intended for public reverence by commoners and nonroyal elite in the main plaza of Cuzco; and the other a golden idol in human form depicting the young, rising sun referred to as Punchao, reserved for private worship by the royal household and highest-ranking nobility (Figure 5.8). Punchao was dressed in "a tunic of very finely woven gold and wool in a variety of styles" and installed with great reverence in an inner sanctum of Qorikancha on a "seat made of wood and well covered with iridescent feathers of various colors" (Betanzos 1996:47). This idol was reputed to contain in its hollow stomach a paste made of gold dust and the ashes of the ritually cremated hearts of former Inca kings. Punchao became a powerful political emblem of the royal dynasty and by extension of the Inca nation itself.[5] Betanzos reported the magnificent ceremonies celebrated during the installation of the twin idols upon completion of the Qorikancha:

> The day the idol was placed in the temple of the Sun, the stone was placed in the middle of the square. Ten days after the idol was put on the seat which you have heard about, Inca Yupanque [King Pachakuti] ordered a small litter made and covered with a certain gold cloth. With it ready, he ordered the most important lords, who were his three friends and the caretaker of the Sun, to take the litter, and Inca Yupanque himself went in where the idol was and put it on the litter. Then, saying that the Sun blessed the city and all of its residents, he ordered it to be carried all around the city. The lords who were carrying the litter said that it was the Sun who blessed his town and his children. Therefore when some *orejón* noble from Cuzco left town, no matter how poor he might be, the people in the provinces worshipped him as the child of the Sun wherever he went…. And they gave him food and full service with the solemnity they used in offering a sacrifice to their idols. (Betanzos 1996:48)

Although the idol of Punchao, symbolic of the dynastic authority of the royal house, was mobile, its twin, the sugarloaf stone installed in Cuzco's principal plaza, was rooted in place. According to Betanzos, the Inca built a font around the statue and buried around the sugarloaf *wak'a* a series of golden statuettes: "[T]hey made as many small squadrons as lineages of the city of Cuzco. Each statuette represented the most important lord of each of those lineages. After these squadrons were set up and put in order, all were buried under the earth by the wall

---

[5] Given Punchao's role as a commanding symbol and source of Inca dynastic authority, it is not surprising that during their conquest of the Inca the Spanish went to enormous lengths to track this idol down and destroy it, something they were able to do in the wild, trackless lands of Vilcabamba only some four decades after the conquest began.

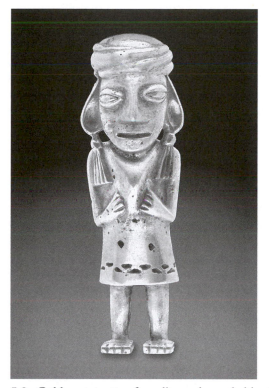

5.8. Golden statuette of an elite male, probably similar to the image of Punchao kept at Qorikancha. (Image ©The Field Museum of Natural History, #A114463_02d)

of the font. In the middle of the font they put the stone that represented the sun. Putting these statues around the font that way was an offering which they made to the Sun of the generation of people of Cuzco and the lineages from the time Manqo Qhapaq had founded it up to the lineages of that time" (Betanzos 1996:48–49). The mimetic statuettes of the *ayllu* and *panaqa* leaders buried at the base of the sugarloaf-shaped, gold-banded *wak'a* in Cuzco's main plaza speaks volumes about the Inca elite's internal hierarchy, sense of solidarity, and claims to divine authority. Their gold doubles buried in the heart of the empire's spiritual center opened up continual lines of communication with the forces of nature that animated all material reality.

These passages reveal many subtle details about Inca spirituality, particularly among nobles and in the royal household. Inca state religion was elitist and hierarchical: the public, commoners and the lesser elite, worshipped some idols; nobles of the highest rank worshipped others, reserving a special mystique and exclusive spiritual knowledge and practices for themselves. Inca elite considered themselves to be chosen people, destined to bring order, morality, and good governance to their subjects. This sense of spiritual exclusivity justified and consolidated their authority to rule since only the highest-born Inca nobles had immediate access, through their chosen king, to the cosmological powers of the sun and to the other deities of nature. All the Inca shared in the belief that *wak'as*, idols, and oracles brought them into communication with these divine forces. After the construction of Qorikancha, Inca kings commissioned temples of the cult throughout the highland and coastal regions of their empire and assiduously propagated the myths, narratives, beliefs, and sacrificial practices that identified the royal household with the life-giving properties of the sun. The network of solar temples constituted, in effect, a politically and culturally influential religious foundation. Collective and widespread worship of Inti served as one of the principal religious practices that unified the subjects of the empire culturally while simultaneously reminding them of their subordinate position to the Inca elite.

The third major deity in the Inca pantheon was Inti-Illapa, the emblematic force of nature manifested in powerful meteorological phenomena: thunder, lightning, wind, sweeping rain, hail, and snow. All of these elemental forces had a direct impact on the lives of Inca subjects as they pursued their daily acts of farming, herding, and fishing. Not surprisingly, sacrifices and prayers addressed to this weather deity, who could be either beneficent or malevolent depending upon circumstance, were widely distributed throughout the empire. In fact, Inti-Illapa was a deity based on more ancient, pan-Andean ritual practices associated with the propitiation of the natural forces that create the changeable and often highly unpredictable weather patterns that Andean farmers, herders, and fishermen had to confront each day. The composite name alone associates the weather deity with the solar deity Inti, but this solar element is likely a later, elite Inca–inspired accretion. As an astute move of political propaganda, as well as most likely a sincere belief, Inca nobility attached the name of their patron deity, Inti, to that of the more broadly distributed and deeply rooted cult of Illapa, the god of weather.

This deity cuts a complex figure in the historical record, appearing in the Andean *altiplano* as Thunupa, the Aymara deity of thunder, lightning, rain, hail, and other celestial phenomena (Rowe 1946:295). As we have seen, the Lake Titicaca region around the ancient archaeological site of Tiwanaku (ca. 400–1150) was one of the principal venues for Inca myths of the cosmogony of the ancient Andean world. The

so-called Gateway God of Tiwanaku (see Figure 2.7) represents an
ancestral image of Thunupa, the Aymara nature deity closely associated with both agricultural production and human social reproduction.
The image of the Gateway God, reflecting an early representation of
Thunupa, combines attributes of the Inca deity Viracocha with those of
Illapa (Demarest 1981:49; La Barre 1948). In the image, the god wears
a resplendent headdress with solar rays associated with feline heads,
raindrops fall from his eyes, and he holds two scepters furnished with
avian (condor, eagle, or hawk) heads. One of the scepters appears in
the form of a double-headed serpent; the heads of this scepter, held
in the deity's left hand, are represented as eagles or hawks. This scepter may reference shafts of lightning (Demarest 1981:81). The scepter
in the Gateway God's right hand has been convincingly interpreted as
a spear-thrower. Bernabé Cobo described Illapa as a celestial storm
god carrying a spear-thrower with which he hurled thunderbolts to
the earth (Rowe 1946:295). Arrayed around the central figure of the
Gateway God are secondary figures that face the principal image of the
deity. These figures have been interpreted as "attendants" of the creator deity (Demarest 1981:78), but more likely they represent the ethnic groups created by the deity as his kindred. This, of course, evokes
the myth that the Inca narrated regarding Viracocha's creation of the
earth, the elements, the celestial realm, and humankind. The entire
iconographic ensemble evokes the Gateway God's powers of creation
and destruction.

Inca elite consistently referenced Lake Titicaca in their dynastic lore
and established on the Islands of the Sun and Moon major temple complexes that became focuses of religious pilgrimage (Figure 5.9). These
Inca temples built upon and embellished sacred places that had been
present at least as early as the mid-sixth century during the apogee of
the Tiwanaku state (Bauer and Stanish 2001; Seddon 1998). In addition to constructing these island temple complexes and endowing them
with precious goods and servants, the Inca reshaped the agricultural
landscape of the adjacent mainland peninsula of Copacabana in Bolivia
and Peru into massive, stepped terraces in order to provide the crops
necessary to support these temples and the religious pilgrims who visited them at times of major festivals. The intense association of Lake
Titicaca with extensive religious pilgrimage implies that the powerful
Aymara-speaking kingdoms that developed in the region after the dissolution of the Tiwanaku state around 1150 AD maintained substantial
cultural and religious influences over their Inca conquerors. We can infer
with reasonable confidence that the Inca weather deity Inti-Illapa was
conceived directly from a more ancient *altiplano* model with origins in

5.9. The religious precinct of Pilko Kaina was one of several complexes
that the Inca built on the Island of the Sun in Lake Titicaca, Bolivia.
(Image courtesy of A. Guengerich)

the culture of Tiwanaku (or perhaps even earlier) and continuing in the
later Aymara kingdoms, such as the Colla, Lupaqa, and Pacajes, arrayed
around Lake Titicaca. The Inca, like other indigenous Andean peoples
before them, readily adopted the deities and shrines of other ethnic
groups, creating a complex, pluralistic, but always hierarchical religious
world.

These three major deities of the Inca – Viracocha, Inti, and Illapa –
represented different but substantially overlapping aspects of the same
phenomena: the celestial forces of nature (the sun, rain, winds, hail, and
snow) and the powers of social reproduction (the *camay* of the ancestor)
that the Inca believed controlled their fate as a people fundamentally
dependent on tilling the soil. The Inca people worshipped other nature
deities with similar existential powers. If the troika of deities, Viracocha,
Inti, and Illapa, were represented as males, there were equivalent female
deities that played complementary roles in the worship and propitiation
of the forces of nature. The principal female deities were Mama Quilla,
the Goddess of the Moon; Mama Cocha, the Goddess of Lakes and
the Ocean; and Pachamama, the Goddess of the Earth. These goddesses
were worshipped by all, but they were served by separate religious orders
of priestesses. Whereas male priests and religious practitioners may have
focused their practices of sacrifice and worship on the male deities, the
priestesses focused their attentions on these female deities, forming a

5.10. Gold statuettes of elite males and females reflect the centrality of gender complementary to Inca thought and religion, in which
humans and deities of both genders played important roles. (Image
©Dumbarton Oaks, Pre-Columbian Collection, Washington DC)

separate but complementary socioreligious structure (Silverblatt 1978,
1987) (Figure 5.10). This system of organized worship is entirely distinct from that of the traditions of the Judeo-Christian-Islamic worlds,
in which men constitute the principal religious practitioners as rabbis,
priests, and imams conducting worship on behalf of all, men and women
alike.

In the Andean religious tradition, men and women played complementary roles in worship, focusing on those deities and elemental
forces of nature with which they had particular symbolic associations.
Males were associated symbolically with the celestial realm, particularly with the genesic properties of solar heat and rain, as well as with
the more violent forces of thunderstorms, lightning, wind, and hail.
Females retained symbolic affinities with the fertile, chthonic forces

of nature – with the earth itself, with caves, and with groundwater, springs, lakes, oceans, and vegetation that issued from the earth (Silverblatt 1978:46). Sexual intercourse between men and women and the creation of human progeny was analogized to the life-giving rains fertilizing the rich but dormant soils of the earth to produce abundant agricultural crops. That is, males and females possessed complementary powers of fertility, but this capacity, latent in each gender, became actualized only when males and females were brought together. This gender-inflected symbolism also served as a master metaphor for structuring social relations and made clear to everyone that social reproduction was possible only when the complementary male and female members of the kin group actively united in biological, social, and ritual acts. From this perspective, males and females were essentially mirror images of each other, dependent on one another as husbands and wives and as brothers and sisters but also reliant on maintaining solidarity with their same-sex relatives. The Inca kinship system of bilateral descent and parallel transmission of inheritance recognized the importance of the intricate web of social relations that stemmed from this comprehensive form of gender parallelism.

In this belief system, priests and religious practitioners were both male and female, although, of course, still arrayed in a prestige hierarchy in which the male solar-creator deity was the highest ranking. Like those of their male counterparts, the principal shrines and temples of Mama Quilla, Mama Cocha, and Pachamama received rich endowments of dedicated agricultural lands, pastures, precious goods, and labor service. The moon goddess, Mama Quilla, was believed to play a significant role in the Inca ritual calendar, as well as in the timing of agricultural production. Phases of the moon were carefully tracked to regulate the Inca ceremonial cycle in which many important ritual events were scheduled according to the lunar calendar (Cobo 1990:29–30, cited in D'Altroy 2002:148). Close astronomical observation of lunar phases, as well as observation of other celestial phenomena, particularly the star group known as the Pleiades, was also used to predict the most propitious time for the planting and harvesting of crops, as well as to manage the seasonal rounds of camelid herds to and from the pastures distributed across the empire's multiple elevations and ecological zones (Orlove 1977). Similarly, sacrifices to Mama Cocha focused on the productivity of agricultural crops irrigated from lakes and groundwater, and on the health and welfare of the camelid herds that depended on cochas, high-altitude lakes, groundwater seeps, and artificial reservoirs for their drinking water. Finally, the deity known as Pachamama was a female counterpart to the male creator deity Viracocha in the sense that

Pachamama represented the female principle of creation. A personification of the latent powers of the earth, Pachamama received virtually daily worship from the farmers who depended on the agricultural crops produced in and on her. In Inca cosmogonic narratives, it was from the very stuff of the earth, from the rock, clay, and soil of Pachamama herself, that humans were created and ethnic groups emerged. That Pachamama remains an important figure of worship among indigenous people in the rural reaches of the Andes today attests to the tenacity of this animistic belief in the elemental forces of nature critical to people's daily lives and livelihoods.

All of these deities were emblematic of natural forces that enveloped, interacted with, and tangibly affected the life course of Inca subjects. Most religious worship at the folk level occurred in the households and open-air *wak'as* of the ethnic *ayllus*. Sacrifices of food, drink, llama fat, guinea pigs, textiles, seashells, and other commodities with deep symbolic and social value constituted the material elements of worship. These material sacrifices, which were burned, buried, or otherwise consumed at the shrines, were coupled with prayers, most often for life-giving rain during the growing season and for the health, well-being, and security of the *ayllu*. At critical moments in the seasonal agricultural cycle, community members converged on the shrines to direct their petitions for well-being and to engage in dialogue with the divine through their intermediaries: the shamans, priests, priestesses, and political leaders of the community. Communication with the divine occurred frequently in the social context of a feast in which the participating members shared food and drink, and, not trivially, moments of intimacy and social solidarity. Songs, dance, and theatrical narratives that recounted the history of the *ayllu* and its ancestral founders accompanied the important, periodic festivals of planting and harvesting. At these festivals the historical memory and commemoration of the ancestors merged with concerns of the here and now: like the *wak'as* themselves, the ancestors were appealed to and engaged to ensure rainfall and a productive harvest, and therefore the prosperity and continuity of the lineage itself. So, for the bulk of the population subject to the Inca, daily life was a repeated round of work and worship, and the two merged seamlessly in belief and practice. The ordinary, daily acts of making a living – planting, irrigating, weeding, harvesting, managing the herds, fishing, cutting wood, drawing water – unfolded in a seemingly eternal, seasonal cycle. The animate *wak'as* and lineage ancestors that spoke to the community through their mediums were critical social actors in ensuring the continuity of this cycle by virtue of their capacity to communicate directly with the elemental forces of nature that held the fate of the community in the balance. Worship at the corporate shrines of the community underlay and substantively constituted a sense of social solidarity and an ethic of mutual aid that permitted the Andean people to survive in an often harsh and intractable environment.

State Ceremonies and the *Zeq'e* System of Cuzco

If folk religion in the Inca realm revolved around community worship at local shrines and communication with the elemental forces of nature, so, too, did the elaborate cults of the state promoted by the royal dynasty. Folk and elite religious beliefs and practices did not vary greatly in kind, but they did differ markedly in organization, formality, and scale. Moreover, as might be anticipated, the state cults, unlike folk religious practices, were intensely associated with the politics of the royal dynasty and were intended to reflect, represent, and ensure the dynasty's social dominance in the hierarchy of power that was the Inca Empire.

As they did for many of the organizational forms that structured the empire, Inca historical narratives attributed the formalization of shrines, sacrificial practices, ritual calendars, and religious ceremonies to King Pachakuti, the architect of Inca expansionary politics in the mid-1400s. According to these narratives, Pachakuti's epochal victory over the rival Chanka polity generated enormous wealth and consolidated his political power. Victory in war permitted him to concentrate on reorganizing the physical, sociological, economic, and religious infrastructure of Cuzco to befit its new status as the imperial capital. Under his urban renewal project, Pachakuti redistributed water sources and arable land in and around Cuzco, dispossessing some subjects and rewarding his political allies and other lineages with which he maintained close bonds of kinship and affiliation. His vision for the capital entailed an audacious, labor-intensive canalization of the Tullumayo and Saphy Rivers, construction of aqueducts and covered surface channels to provide fresh water to city dwellings, creation of a subterranean sewage system, and development of an urban core of plazas, roads, palaces, temples, fountains, and terraces. The physical result of Pachakuti's urban renewal scheme for Cuzco was an elegant ensemble of residences, expansive public spaces, and richly endowed temples built of the finest ashlar masonry.

The splendor of this new Cuzco, though subsequently elaborated by later kings of the Inca dynasty, filters through the first impressions of the city recorded by the Spanish conquistador Pedro Sancho de la Hoz, who witnessed life in the native capital before its utter destruction in 1535: "The city of Cuzco is the principal one of all those where the lords of this land have their residence; it is so large and so beautiful that it would be worthy of admiration even in Spain," he wrote. "It is full of the palaces of the lords, because no poor people live there.... The streets are laid out at right angles; they are very straight, and are paved, and down the middle runs a gutter for water lined with stone.... There are many houses upon the slope and others below on the plain.... And in the valley, which is surrounded by hills, there are more than five thousand houses.... [T]he others are storehouses" (Sancho de la Hoz 1917:153, 158).

Sancho de la Hoz's fascinating remark that no poor folk lived in Cuzco reflects the intensely hierarchical nature of Inca social reality and the manner in which this hierarchy became physically inscribed on the landscape. If the central core of the city was the residence of nobility, the concentric outer rings were inhabited by a socially heterogeneous population that included provincial elite, Incas by privilege, *yanakuna*, *mitmaqkuna* resettled from other parts of the empire, and local commoners.

During Pachakuti's long reign, Cuzco became the unchallenged seat of the Inca ruling class, the pivotal locus of both the royal court and of the holiest shrines of the imperial religion. All Inca subjects viewed Cuzco as a virtually mythical city, redolent with the symbolism of royal power and the divine aura of the sacred. The imperial capital became an icon of Inca rule as well as a cosmogram, a mimetic representation of the world, reflecting in the spatial arrangement of its public architecture the structure of the natural and social orders. The city was the origin point for the royal roads extending into and symbolically partitioning the four quarters of the realm; it was self-consciously conceived as the *axis mundi*, the city at the center of the world that bound together the complementary universes of the sacred and the secular. Cuzco, as the political, economic, religious, and symbolic center of the Inca world, was, above all else, a monumental representation of power. Here the Inca elite intentionally designed and audaciously displayed their own conception of themselves as Lords of the Andean world. They invested Cuzco with the powerful resonances of constructed public images: the image of the secular power of the empire, suffused with the vast, differentiated wealth of its many subject nations; the image of the sacred power of the Inca ruling classes, who appropriated for themselves the essential role of ritually mediating between society and the forces of nature; and the image of dynastic power, the city as seat of a long lineage of divine emperors, both living and dead, engaged in the exercise of legitimate authority. Cuzco was, in short, an image of concentrated imperial power, a representation of an ideal social order, and the ultimate Inca *wak'a*, the nexus and arbiter of wealth, power, prestige, social identity, cult, and command.

Given the centrality of religious practices to Inca identity and social power, it is not surprising that Pachakuti's first act in raising

5.11. Interior of the Qorikancha. Note the fine masonry and the wall niches for placement of important objects. (Image courtesy of L. Guengerich)

this new Cuzco was his design and construction of the Qorikancha (Figures 5.11 and 5.12). As we have seen, the Qorikancha housed many of the principal icons of the imperial pantheon, most importantly that of Punchao, the young avatar of the solar deity, Inti. More importantly, it was from the Qorikancha that the Inca conceived a comprehensive sacred landscape of Cuzco, and, by extension, of the Inca Empire itself, ordered in a complex and hierarchical logic of religious shrines arrayed along lines of sight. This sacred landscape was central to the Inca people's notion of their own identity as an ethnic group, and to their belief in their right to rule other nations. Bernabé Cobo's description of a complex system of shrines provides us with an entrée into this critical dimension of Inca politico-religious belief: "From the *Qorikancha*, as from the center, there went out certain lines which the Indians call *ceques*," he wrote. "They formed four parts corresponding to the four royal roads that went out from Cuzco. On each one of those *ceques* were arranged in order the *guacas* which there were in Cuzco and its district, like stations of holy places, the veneration of which was common to all. Each *ceque* was the responsibility of the *parcialidades*

5.12. Interior of the Qorikancha. (Image courtesy of L. Guengerich)

[the Spanish name for groups of people who formed related parts of a larger ethnic whole] and families of the city of Cuzco, from within which came the attendants and servants who cared for the *guacas* of their *ceque* and saw to offering the established sacrifices at the proper times" (Cobo 1990:51).

This remarkable conceptual organization of Cuzco and its near environs incorporated a total of forty-one directional sight lines, or *zeq'es*, radiating out from the origin point at Qorikancha, along which the Inca recognized more than four hundred individual *wak'as* imbued with the capacity to communicate with the supernatural (Figure 5.13). As Rowe explains:

In the account of the shrines of Cuzco summarized by Cobo, the shrines or *guacas* ... are grouped by location in four divisions, each division relating to one of the main Inca roads leading out of Cuzco, respectively the Road of Chinchaysuyu, the Road of Antisuyu, the Road of Collasuyu, and the Road of Cuntisuyu. Within each of the four divisions, the shrines or *guacas* are assigned to *ceques* or lines which ... radiate from Coricancha, the Temple of the Sun. Ceque (Inca *zeq'e*) simply means a line of any kind. There are nine *ceques* in each of the first three divisions, and these *ceques* are enumerated in sequences of three by the special classifying and ranking words Cayao, Payan, Collana. (Rowe 1979:3)

In this hierarchical system, *collana, payan,* and *cayao* describe a descending order of social rank from highest to lowest that the Inca applied

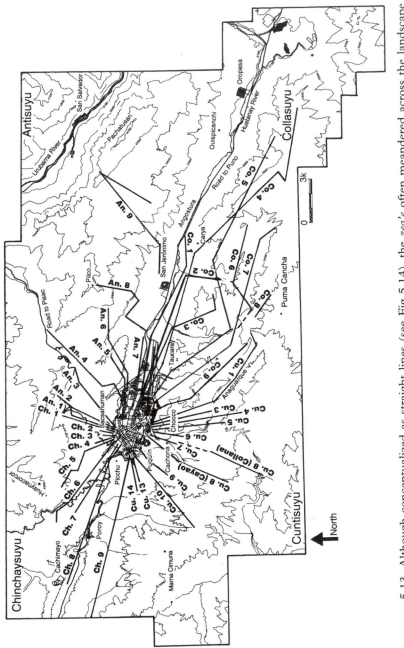

5.13. Although conceptualized as straight lines (see Fig 5.14), the *zeq'e* often meandered across the landscape in zigzag pathways to accommodate the mountainous terrain around Cuzco. (Image ©University of Texas, Bauer 1998)

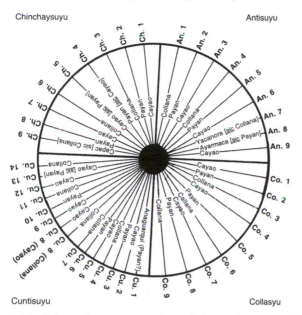

5.14. Schematic representation of the *zeq'e* system. The lines within each of the four *suyus* are ranked according to the system of *collana*, *payan*, and *cayao*. (Image ©University of Texas, Bauer 1998)

to multiple dimensions of life, including the Inca kinship system, the political relationships among the elite and subject populations, and the organization of religious shrines (Figure 5.14). Cobo observed that different sets of related *ayllus*, or larger social groups (*parcialidades*), were charged with the responsibility of maintaining the *wak'as* along the *zeq'e* line designated to that group. Responsibility for the *zeq'e* line included the obligation of offering periodic, ritually prescribed sacrifices at these sacred shrines.

The *zeq'e* system of Cuzco carried multiple layers of significance that bound together Inca concepts of topographic and symbolic space, time, cosmology, dynastic history, and social organization. As a result, this complex system of lines and shrines was mutable, dynamically accounting for changing historical circumstances, yet, at the same time, inherently stable, establishing permanent points of communication with the deities who personified the capricious forces of nature. From time to time, new *wak'as* were commissioned by Inca nobility and incorporated into the overarching system. Frequently, these newly designated *wak'as* were shrines intended to commemorate significant events in the lives and political careers of the royal dynasts, both men and women. So, one significant function of the *zeq'e* system was to serve as a vast, landscape-scale memorial to the lives of the emperors and their consorts. Another meaning embedded in the *zeq'e* system was reflected in its role as the physical expression of the Incas' sidereal-lunar agricultural calendar. Throughout the agricultural cycle of the seasons, members of at least one Inca *ayllu* or *panaqa* resident in Cuzco were engaged in performing rituals, sacrifices, and offerings to the *wak'as* along a designated *zeq'e* line designed to ensure rains, abundant harvests, and the fertility of camelid herds. These fertility ceremonies, organized according to the principles of the *zeq'e* lines, were trenchant reminders to the noble classes of Cuzco that their success as a people destined to rule other nations hinged on group solidarity and on their ability to sustain a concordance between the social and natural orders. This meaning of the *zeq'e* system was stable: a designated number of *wak'as* served as permanent physical markers for days in the sidereal-lunar agricultural calendar. Many of these *wak'as* either were particularly beautiful and highly productive terraced agricultural fields or were sources of abundant irrigation water – fountains, springs, marshes, and groundwater seeps. Others were gnomons used for observations of the sun and important star clusters such as the Pleiades. According to Betanzos, the emperor Pachakuti systematized the Incas' agricultural calendar, gave names to each of the months in the seasonal cycle, established religious rituals appropriate to the agricultural activities of each month, and finally, "so that, as time passed, they would not lose count of these months and the times of sowing and celebrating the fiestas ... he had made those *pacha unan chic*, which means 'clocks.'" Betanzos's "clocks" refer to stone pillars set along the hills above Cuzco that were used as solar observatories to mark the passage of the sun across the horizon. Specifically, according to Betanzos, Pachakuti carefully observed the positions of the sun and the moon throughout the year, calculating that each month contained 30 days and each solar year included 360 days. Subsequently, Pachakuti placed "four clocks where the sun comes up and four others where it goes down that mark the courses and movements made by the sun during the year," so that "by this means, the common people kept track of time" and therefore knew "when to sow or to harvest" (Betanzos 1996:68). By Betanzos's account, Pachakuti became not only the Incas' greatest political, religious, and social reformer but also the empire's most sagacious astronomer. These gnomons placed atop Cuzco's hills as arms of a landscape-scale sundial were incorporated into the *zeq'e* network of agricultural and commemorative shrines arrayed along sight lines. In this respect, the *zeq'e* system of religious shrines served as a technology of production, permitting the Inca to forecast critical moments in the agricultural cycle, especially the times for planting and harvesting, upon which they depended for their wealth and well-being (Zuidema 1990).

Inca kings, their queens, and the most highly ranked aristocracy of the realm publicly participated in agricultural rituals conducted at the agricultural shrines of the *zeq'e* system. These rituals, like the *zeq'e* system of shrines, also constituted a technology of production by concentrating labor during the time of festivals to perform communal acts of plowing, planting, and harvesting that provided the economic underpinnings of this agrarian empire. The first tilling of the soil – the preparation of fields and sowing of seeds in August and September – and the harvest at the end of the agricultural season in April and May were two of the most important of these royal rituals. Cobo related that these two critical ritual events, one initiating the agricultural cycle and the other marking its closure, occurred on a particularly valued *chacara* (agricultural field) called Sausero that constituted a major shrine of the *zeq'e* system: "The third [*wak'a* on a particular *zeq'e* line] was named Sausero. It is a *chacara* of the descendants of Paullu Inca to which, at sowing time, the king himself went and plowed a little. What was harvested from it was for sacrifices of the Sun. The day when the Inca went to do this was a solemn festival of all the lords of Cuzco. They made great sacrifices to this flat place, especially of silver, gold, and children" (Cobo 1990:71). Sacrifice of the most precious substances in the realm, most especially children, publicly affirmed the solemnity and magnitude of this ritual, as did the fact that the king himself, in the company of his queen, put his hand to the *chaki-taqlla*, or foot plow, to symbolically initiate the breaking open of the earth for the planting of maize, or corn, the most valued prestige crop of the Inca (Murra 1960). The act of farming was worthy of royal labor, even if the king and queen only worked the fields in a highly symbolic gesture of solidarity with their kin and subjects. Cobo adds subtle details concerning the ritual practices that accompanied this corn-planting ceremony on Sausero, relating that the Inca sacrificed many "sheep" (llama) and "*cuis*" (guinea pigs) during this ceremony that focused specifically on propitiation of the elemental forces of nature linked to agricultural success:

These sheep were from the livestock of the Sun, and with this sacrifice the *chacara* called Sausero was sown. This job of seeding was done with great solemnity because this *chacara* belonged to the Sun. What was harvested from it was for the ordinary sacrifices made in addition to the ones described above. All during the time that the seeding was done, in the middle of the field there was a white sheep with its ears of gold, and with this sheep there were numerous Indians and *mamaconas* of the Sun pouring out much *chicha* in the name of this sheep. Since they were finishing the sowing, a thousand *cuis* [guinea pigs] were brought by shares from all the provinces.... This sacrifice was made to the Frost, the Wind, and the Sun, and to all things that seemed to them capable of making their sown fields grow or capable of harming them. (Cobo 1990:144)

These passages succinctly convey critical elements of Inca religiosity among nobles and commoners alike: communal labor; sacrifice of precious goods; invocations to the capricious, personified forces of nature; and celebratory shared meals among kin.

The king and his court also participated in the complementary harvest ritual in April and May at Sausero and at other agricultural terraces commissioned by royalty, such as Colcampata on the hillslopes under the fortified temple of Saqsawaman. As in the case of the first plowing in the month of August, the harvest of these special terraces, emblematic of agricultural productivity and success, entailed elaborate rituals in which the royal household and the expanding Inca aristocracy played highly visible, interactive dramaturgical roles. According to Cobo, the harvest ritual began with young nobles who had recently been initiated into the ranks of elite warriors. The young males, elaborately dressed in newly bestowed ceremonial tunics, harvested the corn while they sang *haylli*, a warrior's song of triumph that analogized the acts of farming to warfare (Figure 5.15). The Spanish chronicler Garcilaso de la Vega, himself partially of Inca blood, provided penetrating insight into the indigenous meaning of the *haylli* in the context of the plowing and harvest ceremonies on the royal agricultural terraces of Cuzco designated as shrines in the *zeq'e* system:

> This terrace was tilled and cared for by those of the royal blood, and none but Incas and Palla [women of royal blood] could work in it. The work was done amidst the greatest celebrations, especially at ploughing time, when the Incas came dressed in all their insignia and finery. The songs they recited in praise of the Sun and their kings were all based on the meaning of the word *hailli*, which means triumph over the soil, which they ploughed and disemboweled so that it should give fruit. The songs included elegant phrases by noble lovers and brave soldiers on the subject of their triumph over the earth they were ploughing. The refrain of each verse was the word *"hailli,"* repeated as often as was necessary to mark the beats of a certain rhythm, corresponding to the movements made by the Indians in raising their implements and dropping them, the more easily to break the soil. (Garcilaso de la Vega [1543], cited in Bauer 1996:328)

The Inca, like most indigenous people of the Andes, integrated songs and chants into their work parties, converting the drudgery of hard labor into joyous, communal acts of religious worship, competition, and, not infrequently, bawdy sexual innuendo played out across the fields of the lords. In the moment of ritually breaking open the earth to sow the seed that would sustain them, the Inca viewed this quotidian act of farming as a sexual penetration of Pachamama achieved by virtue of the most vigorous, *camay*-infused members of Inca society – the Inca king, the highest-ranked male aristocracy, and the ranks of virile warriors dedicated to the service of the king.

5.15. During planting and harvest ceremonies, young royalty sang and chanted the genre of song known as *haylli*, which metaphorically compared warfare to the process of cultivating the land. (Adapted from Guaman Poma de Ayala 1615)

The Spanish cleric Bartolomé de Segovia witnessed the last great corn harvest ceremony celebrated by the Inca aristocracy in April of 1535, three years after the Spanish invasion of the empire. Segovia's rare and revealing account conveys the extraordinary pageantry and ritual theater that accompanied this royal harvest ritual. Despite the trauma of the ongoing conquest of their realm, and the assassination of the competing, half-sibling kings, Atawallpa and Waskhar, the Inca still managed to stage a majestic ritual in which some six hundred nobles participated. The surviving aristocracy was arrayed on the field of Sausero in two moiety lines of three hundred each, in the company of Manco Inca, newly crowned as the ersatz emperor by the Spanish invaders, and of the principal idols and ancestral effigies of the state cults. According to Segovia's account, "[T]hey brought out all of the effigies from Cuzco's temples onto a plain at the edge of Cuzco, toward the area where the Sun dawned. The effigies with the greatest prestige were placed beneath rich, finely-worked feather canopies, which had an elegant appearance.... The space [between the canopies] formed an avenue over thirty paces wide, and all the lords and other principal figures of Cuzco stood in it" (Segovia [1553], cited in D'Altroy 2002:154). Segovia related that Manco Inca, the assembled lords of the realm, and presumably the living mediums of the cult idols and ancestral effigies began to chant *sotto voce* at dawn as the sun broke the eastern horizon above the Cuzco basin. Throughout the morning hours, the celebrants sang in increasingly louder intonations until the sun reached its zenith around noon – its point of most intense solar heat. Subsequently, they began gradually to diminish the volume of their chants in mimetic imitation of the sun's waning power as it descended toward the western horizon, ceasing their song suddenly as the last solar rays dissipated at nightfall. The harvest festival continued in the same fashion for some eight consecutive days, during which enormous quantities of food, alcohol, coca leaves, and animals were consumed in sacrifices and communal meals.

Two other religious-political festivals, Qhapaq Raymi and Inti Raymi, were also symbolically associated with Inca concepts of fluctuating solar intensity. These two festivals were respectively celebrated at the times of the December and June solstices, when the sun's apparent directional path across the sky ceases and then reverses direction (Bauer and Dearborn 1995). The celestial path of the sun tracked the waxing and waning of the agricultural cycle. The December solstice occurred at the moment when the crops planted at the beginning of the rainy season in September were maturing in the fields, vitalized by the sun at its nearest and most powerfully radiant position in the sky. Qhapaq Raymi was an intensely political festival for the Inca aristocracy that symbolically analogized the emergent vigor of the maturing crops, particularly maize, with the ceremonial ear piercing of young male nobles who, at that moment, became full-fledged warriors, or, as the Spanish chroniclers referred to them, "knights" of the realm. The rituals that accompanied Qhapaq Raymi were numerous, extending over many days and designed exclusively for the young Inca nobles and their families (Figure 5.16). Female members of the young nobles' families wove special tunics, cloaks, headbands, and slings (a critical weapon of war) and brewed enormous quantities of alcohol in the form of *chicha*, or maize beer, for the celebrants. The young nobles themselves were expected to

5.16. Drumming and processions by men and women were an important part of Qhapaq Raymi and other royal festivals. (Adapted from Guaman Poma de Ayala 1615)

fast, eating only raw maize, and to abstain from sexual intercourse from the time the tunics were being woven until the day the youths received the ear piercing that symbolized their incorporation into the ranks of adult warriors. During this fast, they were required to journey alone to the sacred mountain of Huanacauri, the highest-ranking *wak'a* in the *zeq'e* system of Cuzco after the temple of Qorikancha. This aspect of the young noble's rite of passage to adulthood resembles the inner-directed vision quest of North American natives, which also occurred at a critical time of reflection and transition to adulthood and warrior status. Each young noble was required to sacrifice copious quantities of llama, maize, and coca leaf to the sun, petitioning for prosperity, and to take a private oath "to revere the Sun, farm his lands, and be obedient to the Inca, always tell him the truth, be a loyal vassal … loyal to the city of Cuzco, and whenever the Inca or the city of Cuzco goes to war, he will offer himself with his weapons in that war … and he will die in defense of the city and the Inca" (Betanzos 1996:62). After these private actions and reflections, the youth eventually rejoined the group of young aspirants to compete in a wild, high-speed footrace from Huanacauri in order to earn personal merit and familial honor. Upon returning to Cuzco, the young nobles had new red tunics bestowed upon them by their relatives, and each was forced to "hold out his arms, and his relatives, who were waiting there with him like godfathers … beat him on the arms with slings so that he will remember … the oath he took there" (Betanzos 1996:62–63). All celebrants then joined in a month-long festival of drinking, eating, dance, song, and spectacular theatrical performances by noble warriors dressed in red tunics with "lions' skins on their backs, the heads of the lions over their own heads and the faces of the lions in front of their faces"; these martial costumes of "lions' heads" (i.e., pumas or mountain lions and tropical forest–dwelling jaguars) had gold ear ornaments equivalent to those of the human warriors (Betanzos 1996:63).

Only Incas of the blood participated in Qhapaq Raymi. No foreign-born or provincial nobles could aspire to become knights of the realm. The latter served as allied warriors in the field. They could obtain gifts of property, labor service, and precious goods for conspicuous success in battle on behalf of the Inca, but they could never become part of the true-blooded aristocracy of the empire. Qhapaq Raymi was an intensely class-based religious festival focused on publicly recognizing the social identity of Cuzco's nobility. Cristóbal de Molina provides a richly detailed description of twenty-three intense days of ritual activities, fasts, sacrifices, and feasting, culminating on the twenty-third day when the young nobles received their ear piercing and on the subsequent final day when "they carried the statue of the Sun called *Huayna punchao*, to the houses of the Sun called *Puquinque*, which are on a high hill, a little more than three arquebus shots from Cuzco. Here they sacrificed to the Creator, the Sun, the Thunder, and the Moon, for all nations, that they might prosper and multiply" (Molina 1873:47). After the festival of Qhapaq Raymi, the newly knighted nobles, or, as the Spanish called them, *orejones* ("big ears"), were viewed as mature adults who had achieved a position in Cuzco's social hierarchy in which they were now expected to contribute to the social reproduction of their lineage and the empire itself. As adults, they were now progenitors, providers, and warriors, required to produce and support a noble house, as well as to participate in the wars of conquest waged by their royal patron.

Inti Raymi occurred at the other end of the solar spectrum from that of Qhapaq Raymi. It was celebrated during the June solstice, as the sun reached its northernmost, weakest position in the sky and when Cuzco's agricultural fields were cold, barren, and dormant. Inti Raymi was conceptually linked to the maize-planting festival in August and September. During Inti Raymi, the young warriors who had received their golden ear spools in December, at the beginning of the Inca solar year, cooperated in the task of breaking the barren earth to prepare the ground for planting later in August and September. Inti Raymi was also celebrated as a solar festival, but as one accompanied by a measure of social and psychological anxiety that the sun's rays had reached their nadir of intensity. At the same time, all understood that, barring some catastrophe, the sun's radiance would increase in strength until the December solstice when the people of Cuzco would again celebrate Qhapaq Raymi and the rite of passage of the young nobility.

Apart from the four solar-based religious festivals that celebrated the planting, harvest, and solstice events, each of which was associated symbolically with the life cycle of males connected to the royal household, a fifth major sequence of ritual activities, the Citua festival, took place in Cuzco during the onset of the rainy season, an anxiety-filled period that was essential to agricultural livelihood. The festival was held during the month referred to as Qoya Raymi, the Queen's Festival. The Citua rituals were associated particularly with royal females, lunar phases, rainfall, rivers, and flowing irrigation waters. They formed a symbolic counterpart to the solar, male-focused rituals of the state religion, underscoring the importance of gender complementarity in Inca religious thought.

The Citua water festival was framed around elaborate rites of purification and expiation of misdeeds to eliminate potential harms that might impede the rains so critical for the empire's agrarian economy. In the Inca world, chronic drought was the most devastating natural catastrophe, one that could readily undermine the political stability of the empire. Inca emperors understood this risk, and so the Citua festival was of supreme importance to the success of their political careers. Molina's fascinating, highly detailed description of the Citua festival reveals many of the religious, economic, and political preoccupations of the Inca royal household and their imperial subjects:

The month of August was called *Coya-raymi*; and in it they celebrated the *Situa*.[6] In order to perform the ceremonies of this festival, they brought the figures of their *huacas* from all parts of the land, from Quito to Chile, and placed them in

---

[6] Other chroniclers write that the Citua festival was celebrated in mid-September to early October, coincident with the first rains in Cuzco; this seems to be the most logical conclusion given that Molina concurs that the festival began with the onset of rains.

the houses they had in Cuzco....The reason for celebrating the feast called *Situa,* in this month, was because the rains commenced, and with the first rains there was generally much sickness. They besought the Creator that, during the year, he would be pleased to shield them from sickness, as well in Cuzco, as throughout the territory conquered by the Yncas. On the day of the conjunction of the moon, at noon the Ynca, with all the chiefs of his council, and the other principal lords who were in Cuzco, went to the Ccuricancha [Qorikancha] which is the house and temple of the Sun, where they agreed together on the way in which the festival should be celebrated; for in one year they added, and in another they reduced the number of ceremonies, according to circumstances. All things having been arranged, the High Priest addressed the assembly, and said that the ceremonies of the *Situa* should be performed, that the Creator might drive all the diseases and evils from the land. A great number of armed men, accoutred for war, with their lances, then came to the square in front of the temple. The figures called *Chuquilla* [Illapa, the Thunder God] and *Uiracocha* [Viracocha, the Creator God] were brought to the temple of the Sun from their own special temples.... The priests of these *huacas* joined the assembly, and, with the concurrence of all present, the priest of the Sun proclaimed the feast. First, all strangers, all whose ears were broken, and all deformed persons were sent out of the city, it being said that they should take no part in the ceremony, because they were in that state as punishment for some fault. Unfortunate people ought not to be present, it was believed, because their ill-luck might drive away some piece of good fortune. They also drove out the dogs, that they might not howl. Then the people, who were armed as if for war, went to the square crying out: "O sicknesses, disasters, misfortunes, and dangers, go forth from the land." In the middle of the square, where stood the urn of gold which was like a fountain, that was used at the sacrifice of *chicha,* four hundred men of war assembled. One hundred faced towards Colla-suyu, which is the direction of the Sun-rising. One hundred faced to the westward, which is the direction of Chincha-suyu. Another hundred looked towards Anti-suyu, which is the north, and the last hundred turned towards the south. They had with them all the arms that are used in their wars. As soon as those who came from the temple of the Sun arrived in the square, they cried out and said: "Go forth all evils." Then all the four parties went forth to their appointed places. Those for Colla-suyu set out with great speed, and ran to Augostura de Acoya-puncu, which is two short leagues from Cuzco, crying out as they ran, "Go forth all evils." The people of Huvin-Cuzco [Hurin Cuzco, the lower moiety of the city] carried these cries, and there they delivered them over to the *mitimaes* of Huayparya, who in their turn passed them to the *mitimaes* of Antahuaylla, and thus they were passed to the *mitimaes* of Huaray-pacha, who continued them as far as the river at Quiquisana, where they bathed themselves and their arms. (Molina 1873:20–22)

Molina subsequently names the other Inca *ayllus* and *panaqas* responsible for bearing misfortune and maladies out of Cuzco along the principal roads of the three other quarters of the realm: Chinchaysuyu,

Antisuyu, and Cuntisuyu. Once beyond the immediate confines of the royal capital, each *ayllu* and *panaqa* passed on responsibility for the purification ritual to a chain of non-Inca *mitmaqkuna* of lower social status. The last and most distant participants in the chain finally washed away the burden of accumulated sickness and ill luck in the powerful currents of distant rivers.

During subsequent days of the festival, other purification rituals were performed in private houses and public spaces. Cuzco's residents smeared a porridge of coarsely ground maize called *sancu* on their bodies to extract perceived toxins and then bathed in rivers to purge themselves of the maladies drawn into the *sancu*. They also applied this extractive porridge to the lintels of their house, to the coffers in which they kept their food and clothes, and to the preserved bodies of their dead relatives, so that, as Molina recounts, "they also might enjoy the benefits of the feast." In this quintessentially Andean animist perspective, ordinary objects such as houses and furniture, as well as the apparently inert mummified corpses of the dead, participated in the social life of the community and therefore could harbor sickness and ill fortune. So these entities, too, needed to undergo a process of ritual shriving. The gods and dead royals also participated in this festival:

In the night, the statues of the Sun, of the Creator, and of the Thunder, were brought out, and the priests of each of these statues warmed it with the before mentioned *sancu*. In the morning they brought the best food they could prepare to present at the temples of the Creator, of the Sun, and of the Thunder; which the priests of those *wak'as* received and consumed. They also brought out the bodies of the dead Lords and Ladies which were embalmed, each one being brought out by the person of the same lineage who had charge of it. During the night these bodies were washed in the baths which belonged to them when they were alive. They were then brought back to their houses, and warmed with the same coarse pudding called *sancu;* and the food they had been most fond of when they were alive was placed before them, and afterwards the persons who were in charge of the bodies consumed the food. (Molina 1873:24–25)

Citua was a purification festival, but it was also a celebration of the abundance that would come to the Inca if they performed all of the prescribed religious protocols with perfect fidelity. During the days of Citua, the Inca emperor hosted an enormous public feast in the principal plazas of Cuzco that literally overwhelmed the senses of participants by the sovereign's conspicuous generosity. According to Molina,

All the people of Cuzco came out, according to their tribes and lineages, as richly dressed as their means would allow; and, having made reverences to the Creator, the Sun, and the lord Ynca, they sat down on their benches, each man according to the rank he held, the Hanan-Cuzcos being on one side, and the Hurin-Cuzcos on the other. They passed the day in eating and drinking, and enjoying themselves and they performed the *taqui* called *alancitua saqui,* in red shirts down to their feet, and garlands called *pilco-casa* on their heads; accompanied with large or small tubes of canes, which made a kind of music called *tica-tica.* They gave thanks to the Creator for having spared them to see that day, and prayed that they might pass another year without sickness; and they did the same to the Sun and to the Thunder. (Molina 1873:26)

The gods, dead royals, living Inca aristocracy, and king and queen at the pinnacle of the social hierarchy celebrated the feast in a spectacle of shared emotions meant to reaffirm and consolidate the bonds of social solidarity on which the political power of the emperor and nobles depended. The Inca drew on the state granaries and herds from all of the four quarters of the realm to provide an overwhelming abundance of food and drink for the feast. Molina remarked that:

The number of animals was so great, according to those who made this declaration, that they amounted to more than one hundred thousand, and it was necessary that all should be without spot or blemish, and with fleeces that had never been shorn.... When they had distributed the flocks, the sheep were killed in great numbers, to be eaten on that day. Then a vast quantity of *chicha* was brought into the square, from the storehouses where it was kept. It was made of boiled white maize, in the valley of Cuzco. The flocks that were used at this festival were the property of the Creator, the Sun, and the Thunder, from their estates set apart in all the provinces of Peru. Having finished eating with much rejoicing, they performed their *taquis,* and drank in the same order as on the day before. This continued for four days.... On a subsequent day, people of all the nations, that had been subdued by the Yncas, came with their *huacas* and in the richest costumes, peculiar to their respective countries, that they could procure. The priests, who had charge of the *huacas,* carried them on litters. When they entered the square, coming from the direction of the four *suyus* already mentioned, they made reverences to the Creator, the Sun, and the Thunder, and to the Huanacauri, a *huaca* of the Yncas, and then they did the same to the Ynca, who was in the square on that occasion. Having made these obeisances, they proceeded to the places, assigned to them, and, in order to make more room, the families of Hanan-Cuzco and Hurin-Cuzco formed themselves into one, and thus left more space in the square.... Each nation passed the rest of the day in performing the *taqui* and in singing and dancing, according to the custom of their respective countries before they were subdued by the Yncas. On this day all the deformed persons, who had previously been expelled from Cuzco, were allowed to join the feast.... Then those who had to return to their homes, sought permission from the Creator, the Sun, the Thunder, and the Ynca, which was granted, and they left at Cuzco the *huacas* they had brought there in that year. They returned to their homes with the *huacas* they had brought for the festival of the previous year, and, as a recompense for their trouble in having come from such great distances, their chiefs were given gold and silver and clothes and servants, and permission to travel in litters. Their *huacas* were also granted estates and attendants to wait on them, and so they returned to their homes. (Molina 1873:27, 32–33, 34)

Molina's detailed description of the Citua festival lays bare much of the inner structure of the religious thought, social hierarchy, and principles of governance in the Inca Empire. Inca religious and political concepts and practices entailed a systematic, recursive, and dialectical process of differentiation and integration. The Citua festival perfectly exemplified that process. The royal household and aristocracy of Cuzco celebrated the first stages of the festival by expelling all foreigners, deformed people, and even unclean animals from their capital. In a powerful, symbolic demonstration effect of cultural superiority, the purification rituals of Citua began with the expulsion of foreigners in order to cleanse the royal capital of the "ethnic impurities" vested in their bodies. Simply phrased, the first differentiation was "us versus them," put into stern effect by restrictive protocols of ritual-religious participation. Only full-blooded ethnic Incas were permitted to begin the feasts and rituals of purification. This took the form of all the lineages of Inca Cuzco assembling in the principal plaza of the royal capital. But, as Molina noted, this assembly itself was internally differentiated "according to their tribes and lineages" with "each man [read here "family"] according to the rank he held, the Hanan-Cuzcos being on one side, and the Hurin-Cuzcos on the other" (Molina 1873:26). So even the "pure" Inca ethnic group was finely differentiated into separately recognized moieties (Hanan Cuzco vs. Hurin Cuzco), constituent lineages, and social ranks. Subsequently, the four hundred elaborately costumed Inca warriors, one hundred from each designated quarter of the realm (the result of the further bifurcation of the Hanan and Hurin moieties into the four quarters of Chichaysuyu, Collasuyu, Antisuyu, and Cuntisuyu), raced out from the center of Cuzco bearing their symbolic burdens of maladies and misfortunes. Once well beyond the confines of Cuzco's self-consciously sacred center, they passed their burdens along to imperial subjects of progressively lower social rank, the various *mitmaq* groups resident in the peripheries surrounding the capital. Thus in this process of differentiation, the Citua ritual encodes a second, spatial distinction between center (the sacred ethnic, residential, and religious focus of Inca life) and periphery (the wilder, less cultured, less civilized hinterlands in which the subjects of inferior status worked and lived).

Once these prescribed rituals of purification were completed, the Inca lineages in Cuzco commenced celebrating the *takis*. Again, these initial stages of the feast were restricted to the ranked lineages of the

Inca, in communion with their gods, ethnic *wak'as*, and royal ancestors. The Citua festival began as an exclusively Inca religious event that
symbolically and materially confirmed the Incas' unique ethnic identity
and sense of belonging to a special and, from their perspective, a superior, social collectivity. This intimate sense of Inca ethnic identity, of kin
relatedness, and of solidarity was publicly reaffirmed and emotionally
intensified in the collective song, dance, and drinking spectacles of the
takis. During these *takis* "all the principal Indians, very richly dressed,"
danced in the principal plaza of Cuzco with the reigning monarch; as
they danced, they all held a "woolen chain of many colors, garnished
with gold plates and two red fringes at the end" (Sarmiento 1999:101,
102). The "chain" described by Sarmiento, and which he claims attained
an extraordinary length of 150 fathoms (ca. 270 meters), was an elaborate, thickly braided wool cable entwined with multicolored fabric and
extruded gold thread. Incas of the blood held the cable as they danced
together in the most exclusive and most sacred precincts of their capital.
This cable possessed multiple symbolic meanings, not only as a reference to the *amaru*, the celestial, double-headed serpent associated with
rain and flowing water, but also as a symbolic umbilical cord that linked
people together as consanguines, a set of self-identified blood relatives.
Only Incas of the blood could handle and interact with this braided
cable, which was maintained in a special structure called Muru-urco.

To this point, apart from the passing on of the symbolic burden of illness and misfortune to non-Inca *mitmaqkuna* of lower social rank on the
peripheries of Cuzco's sacred urban landscape, the Citua rituals were
an intensely Inca affair. But on the final day of the festival, the Inca king
invited the previously excluded foreigners, as well as the deformed and
other "defective" humans, to reenter Cuzco in order to participate in the
culminating feast and reciprocal drinking bouts. This was the moment
of symbolic reintegration of rulers and subjects. Foreign subjects were
now given a seat at the table, but only after having first been dramatically excluded from the festivities to illustrate in no uncertain terms
the hierarchical superiority of the Inca ruling classes. The foreign lords
and their entourages literally waited in the wings, on the periphery of
Inca-centric religious stagecraft, for this moment of return. Upon entering Cuzco, the foreign lords brought their ethnic *wak'as* with them so
that they, too, had a place in the hierarchy of the state cults, even if this
place was subordinate to that of the principal deities and *wak'as* of the
Inca. The foreigners came into the presence of the assembled Inca people with songs of praise for the Inca *wak'as* and king as a sign of respect
and an explicit recognition of their own subordination. They took their
assigned positions in the main plaza next to the Inca lineages of Hanan

and Hurin Cuzco, which, at that moment, "formed themselves into one, and thus left more space in the square." Molina's observation that the Inca lineages formed one group in order to make room for the foreigners misses the deeper significance of this dramatic moment of reintegration of alien subjects into the body politic. This was not a simple matter of logistics to accommodate a swelling crowd in the public square. This act was, more importantly, a vital political statement in which the previously differentiated and profoundly competitive Inca lineages affiliated with the moieties of Hanan and Hurin Cuzco were themselves reintegrated so that they became, at that moment, a single, recognized social body displaying solidarity in counterpoise to their foreign subjects. So the politically charged, culminating moment of Citua entailed a double dialectical reintegration from states of "us versus them" to one of "us *and* them." The previously differentiated Hanan and Hurin moieties of Cuzco became as one, as did the Inca masters and their provincial subjects, in a shared religious and political feast. Yet, implicitly recognized by all, underneath the shared solidarity of the feast the fault lines of sociopolitical differentiation remained (*hanan* vs. *hurin*, masters vs. subjects), even if sublimated in the moment.

After having been forcibly expelled from Cuzco at the opening of the Citua rituals, on the last day of the festival the participating foreign lords and their *wak'as* received the solace of subordination: value-laden gifts of textiles, gold, silver, servants, private estates, and the right to be borne in litters in recognition of their Inca-derived status. In turn, by recognizing and capitulating to the authority of the Inca king, lordly vassals from the provinces gained resources useful in conducting their own local politics.

Religion and Politics

In the imperial cults of the Inca, politics and religion clearly interpenetrated to the point at which they became virtually indistinguishable. State rituals were political, and politics was ritualized. As in the case of the Citua rituals, most acts of worship, and of sacrifice, began in Cuzco under the patronage of the king, and then emanated out from this source of divine authority to circulate along *zeq'e* lines to participants of subject ethnic groups of lesser social status at increasing remove from the capital. Perhaps most emblematic of this radial "moving wave" model of religious worship was the empire-wide performance of the *qhapaq ucha* ritual. Unlike the solar and water rituals associated with cyclical agricultural production, the largest *qhapaq ucha* sacrifices were not performed on a fixed schedule. Rather, *qhapaq ucha* was primarily a situational ritual, one that was instituted at critical, yet unpredictable, moments, such as at the investiture or death of a king, or during the occurrence of biological and natural calamities such as epidemics, earthquakes, chronic droughts, and killing frosts. *Qhapaq uchas* required human sacrifice, but even more profoundly, the sacrifice of the most beautiful, unblemished, and perfectly formed children. Although performed in different situations and at distinct scales, the most solemn *qhapaq ucha* sacrifices involved participants from each of the four quarters of the realm. Molina, again, provides a detailed recounting of an Inca ritual, revealing the *qhapaq ucha*'s essential political nature and its merging of worship, politics, and the sustenance of the empire:

The provinces of Colla-suyu, Chincha-suyu, Anti-suyu, and Cunti-suyu brought to this city, from each lineage or tribe, one or two male and female children aged about ten years. They also brought cloth and flocks, gold and silver. Then the Ynca seated himself in the Huacay-pata, or great square of Cuzco. The children and the other sacrifices walked round the statues of the Creator, the Sun, the Thunder, and the Moon, which were placed in the square, taking two turns. The Ynca then called to the Priests of the provinces, and commanded them to divide the sacrifices into four parts, in token of the four provinces, Colla-suyu, Chincha-suyu, Anti-suyu, and Cunti-suyu, which are the four divisions into which the land is divided. He told them, "Take, each one of you, his part of these offerings and sacrifices, and offer them to your principal *huacas.*" So the children were strangled and buried with the silver figures of sheep, and the gold and silver figures of men and sheep, and they burnt the cloth, with some bags of coca. The people of Cuzco carried these sacrifices as far as Sacalpiña, about a league from Cuzco, where they were received by the Indians of Anta, and in this way they were passed on until they were delivered at the places where they were to be offered up. In the same way, they were passed on to the other provinces. The Lord Ynca offered these sacrifices when he began to reign, that the *huacas* might give him health, and preserve his dominions in peace. No *huaca* or place of worship, how small soever, was left out in the distribution of the sacrifices....
At each place was offered up the portion that was assigned for it at Cuzco; for in Cuzco there was the *Quipucamayu*, or accountant, who took an account of each portion of the sacrifice, and of the province to which each was to be sent.... The order of marching with the sacrifices was that all the people who went with the *Ccapac-cocha* took ways apart from each other. They did not follow the royal road, but traversed the ravines and hills in a straight line, until each reached the places where the sacrifices were to be made. They ran, and as they went they raised cries and shouts which were commenced by an Indian who was deputed to perform this duty. Having given the word, all the others continued the same cries. The cries were to beseech the Creator that the Ynca might ever be victorious and be granted health and peace. They carried on their shoulders the sacrifices and the lumps of gold and silver, and the other things destined to be offered up. The children that could walk went on foot, and others were carried in their

mothers' arms. When they reached their destinations, the *Huacacamayoc,* who had charge of the *huacas,* received those that were intended for their *huacas* and sacrificed them, bringing the gold and silver and other things; and the children, having first been strangled, were burnt in sacrifice, with the sheep, lambs, and cloth. It is worthy of remark that children were not sacrificed at all the *huacas,* but only at the chief *huaca* of each lineage or province. In this way they travelled over all the dominions of the Ynca, with these sacrifices, until each one reached the extreme point of the empire, in the direction in which he travelled.... They held this sacrifice ... in such veneration that, when those who were making journeys over uninhabited tracts with the sacrifices met other travellers, they did not raise their eyes to look at them, and the travellers prostrated themselves on the ground until the sacrifice-bearers had passed. (Molina 1873:54–55, 57–59)

Some of the young children sacrificed during *qhapaq uchas* were interred as male and female pairs in remote burial shrines on the crests of snowcapped mountain peaks, particularly in the southernmost provinces of the empire. Archaeological evidence of these *qhapaq ucha* sacrifices comes from southern Peru, Chile, and Argentina, where astonishingly well-preserved remains of the young victims have been recovered, some at altitudes above six thousand meters, along with offerings of gold and silver statuettes of llama and alpaca and finely woven textiles (Bray et al. 1995; Reinhard, 1992, 1993, 1996, 1998; Reinhard and Ceruti 2000; Schobinger 1995, 2001; Wilson et al. 2007) (Figure 5.17). The male-female pairing of these sacrifices, together with the miniature silver and gold votive offerings of ordinary household implements and ceramic tableware deposited with the bodies, suggests to some scholars that these children were ritually married in Cuzco before beginning the preordained pilgrimage to their place of sacrifice. The paired male–female sacrifices may have been intended to symbolically represent an archetypal conjugal couple, the fundamental unit of social reproduction that was the source of labor, and therefore of wealth, for the empire (McEwan and Van de Guchte 1992). The remote *qhapaq ucha* shrines appear to mark highly visible political boundaries between imperial provinces, or the territorial boundaries between subject ethnic groups. To reach these points of demarcation, the sacrificial entourage had to cross the territories of distinct ethnic groups, each of which provided high-ranking officials as escorts to the limits of its territorial domain, whereupon representatives of the adjoining province would assume this responsibility (MacCormack 1991:152–154, 2000). As in the Citua ritual, this radial, centripetal process of religious practice distributed the responsibility and benefits of participation across subject populations, socially incorporating them into the Inca's political project of building an empire based simultaneously on differentiation and integration

5.17. The mummy of a young boy who had been sacrificed in a *qhapaq ucha* ritual; it was recovered from the mountain of El Plomo in Chile. (Image © Loren McIntyre)

of diverse ethnic groups. The various *qhapaq uchas* themselves became *wak'as*, spiritual custodians and guardians of the ethnic provinces, whose worship was shared by master and subject alike (Hernández Príncipe 1923; Zuidema 1977/1978:141).

As Molina astutely noted, *qhapaq uchas*, the most sacred of all Inca sacrifices, were not distributed to all *wak'as* or ethnic provinces, but rather were distributed in a pattern of calibrated reciprocity with the principal *wak'as* of a province, particularly those that provided correct (i.e., desired) prophesies for the king (MacCormack 1991). This is why the imperial *khipu kamayuqkuna*, who recorded everything from agricultural production, to population, to tribute levels, to oracles, was such an important functionary in the ceremonies surrounding celebration of the *qhapaq ucha*. Social reciprocity demands close accounting to ensure that the participants believe the exchanges have a certain measure of equivalence. In theory (if not in practice), obsessive accounting of services rendered to and benefits received from the divine seems alien to Western notions of authentic religious expression. But this was simply an inherent, structural given in the indigenous Andean context in which reciprocity between humans, nature, and the ancestors formed the core of religious belief and sociality. Inca kings and commoners argued with, upbraided, and even punished their *wak'as* when the expected exchange of services never materialized. The careful calibration of religious cost-benefit ratios was a consummately Andean approach to the divine. This kind of seemingly cold-blooded, rational calculation even extended to local *kurakas* of ethnic groups aspiring to enhance their economic and political positions in the state hierarchy, who willingly gave their children as *qhapaq uchas* to the king (McEwan and Van de Guchte 1992; Zuidema 1982b). In these regal-religious transactions, the fathers received enhanced prestige and tangible resources as rewards from the king for their sacrifice; the children who were sacrificed received the profound ontological honor of transitioning from a living human being to a *wak'a* that became the focus of community worship. If our sources are to be believed, the children who were selected or offered by their parents to become a *qhapaq ucha* sacrifice did not attempt to avoid their fate but actively embraced the opportunity to become, in effect, a local deity, remembered and worshipped by their living compatriots (Zuidema 1982b). From this perspective, these children were not victims – they were gods. Yet who can imagine parents willing to sacrifice their children for some presumed worldly gain? This transaction does not seem so emotionally incomprehensible when we fully grasp the indigenous Andean concept that death does not mean irrevocable loss of personal identity or of participation in the social life of the community. The *qhapaq ucha* metamorphosed into a *wak'a* that then communicated constantly with kin and kith and became an even more vital participant in community affairs. What did the Inca king receive in this transaction? By offering the *qhapaq ucha* throughout the empire, the king received spiritual assurance of his personal health and of his ultimate success in the conduct of state affairs. He also was perceived by his subjects to be acting on behalf of their security and economic well-being. Perhaps most importantly, these imperial-scale rituals became effective instruments for cultural integration, a powerful technique of statecraft and nation building that brought diverse ethnic groups into an imagined moral community of faith and practice. Shared religious belief and practices such as the Citua and *qhapaq ucha* rituals became among the most subtle and pervasive means that Inca kings employed to achieve integration of their subjects and, in so doing, to deepen Inca cultural hegemony.

The Inca political project, one that was only partially successful, was to intensify these moments of participatory integration, to recognize but sublimate difference, to create, in effect, a multicultural, one-world *ayllu*. The Inca apparently understood that they existed in "greater historical fields of cultural others" and that the success of their empire required a means of recognizing, accounting for, and integrating alterity into their realm (Sahlins 2010). They realized that their own identity, their status as a unique and superior social body within their expansive empire, necessarily involved them in interdependent relations with cultural others as a precondition for their internal political coherence. Shared religious sentiment and practice was one instrument for achieving integration of cultural others. At the same time, Inca kings used other persuasive tactics to advance their imperial project, including royal patronage, conspicuous generosity, economic development, and redistribution of wealth, but also the converse – strategic violence, ethnic cleansing, battlefield atrocities, and naked coercion. That is, with various degrees of nuance, Inca kings deployed a profoundly Machiavellian combination of persuasion and force. I explore the instruments and meaning of political power in the Inca state in the following chapter.

6   The Political Order: Kingship, Statecraft, and Administration in the Realm of the Four Quarters

> The Inca emperors were absolute rulers with power checked only by the influence of ancient custom and the fear of revolt. They not only ruled by divine right, but claimed lineal descent from the Sun and were worshipped as divine during their lifetimes. While the Emperor and his government were merciless toward their enemies and demanded an obedience which amounted to virtual slavery from their subjects, they were in theory obliged to care for their people in every sort of need and keep them comfortable and happy.... The unquestionable success of the system is due chiefly to a sincere effort by the Imperial Government to live up to its theoretical obligation.
>
> John H. Rowe, "Inca Culture at the Time of the Spanish Conquest"

The vision of the Inca as a totalitarian but enlightened monarchy still finds considerable resonance in historical accounts of the empire. Although recent scholarship has begun to question and modify this interpretation of the Inca political order, the exceptional rapidity and thoroughness with which the Inca kings subjugated and incorporated the better part of the Andean world into their empire implies the application of overwhelming force and, at the same time, the effective deployment of social and economic incentives that induced newly subject populations to acquiesce in their own subjugation. This chapter explores the specific political instruments, social institutions, and forms of power that brought structure to the Inca Empire, and how these structures of power changed over time and space.

Politics organizes, embeds, and justifies power relations in society. Society, even in the most egalitarian social arrangement imaginable, cannot exist without the systematic exertion of political power. Social reproduction depends on political decisions made on a daily basis in households and communities. Empires attempt to intervene with varying degrees of success in the social reproduction of their subjects at the base level of households and communities by exerting overwhelming political and cultural force. Such political power is exerted through imposed structures of governance, through systems of tribute and taxation, and through social and religious institutions and practices that induce the acquiescence, obedience, or collusion of imperial subjects. Whether the obedience demanded or attained by the Inca was ever tantamount to "virtual slavery" as John Rowe (1946:257) suggested may be questioned, but we can certainly assert that the Inca kings did manage to put into place, in a remarkably short time, instruments of political power that permitted them to create and, for a time, effectively govern the largest and most geographically, ethnically, and linguistically diverse empire in the Western Hemisphere prior to the Spanish conquest.

As the empire exerted and consolidated its hold over its subjects, patterns of personal and institutionalized power in the Inca realm changed over time and space. Some subjects of the empire were more thoroughly incorporated than others into the social and political world of the Inca. Large swaths of the Andean *altiplano*, ancestral homeland of Aymara-speaking ethnic groups, remained resolutely resistant to Inca expansion. Spanish chroniclers vividly describe cycles of warfare, resistance, rebellion, and subsequent reprisals in the Aymara kingdoms around Lake Titicaca (Figures 6.1 and 6.2). The later Inca emperors such as Thupa Inka Yupanki and Wayna Qhapaq were compelled to repeatedly reconquer their kingly rivals in the *altiplano* (Sarmiento 1999:121–125). Similarly, some ethnic groups in the Pacific coastal valleys and the northern highlands and eastern slopes of the Andes in modern-day Peru and Ecuador vigorously contested the loss of their political sovereignty. At times, native resistance inflicted nearly catastrophic losses on Inca military forces (Sarmiento 1999:161–163) and, as in the case of the Araucanian ethnic groups in the south of Chile, fended off Inca attempts at conquest altogether. In most instances, however, local resistance was met with ferocious Inca reprisals that at times rose to the level of genocide in which entire ethnic groups were exterminated, as happened in the coastal valley of Cañete where the Lunahuaná and Mara people were systematically slaughtered by the forces of Thupa Inka Yupanki after a four-year-long campaign of resistance (Cabello Balboa 1951:339; Cieza de León 1976:344). The bones of vanquished warriors remained strewn about the battlefields well into the Spanish colonial era. Local women and children, if not executed, were taken into servitude, transformed into the social category of *piña*, or captives of war, and absorbed into their conquerors' households. Similar episodes of extreme violence directed at stubbornly resistant ethnic groups virtually depopulated stretches of the Ecuadorian highlands.

These instances of determined resistance to Inca dominion indicate that the form and effectiveness of Inca imperial power varied over time and space. In some regions, such as the Chincha polity, the Inca

6.1. The star-shaped *porra* (mace head) was one weapon available to the Inca with which to subdue groups that resisted incorporation into the empire. (Image courtesy of A. Guengerich)

6.2. Woven slings were another important weapon in the Inca military arsenal. (Image ©Loren McIntyre)

achieved a true viral hegemony in which conquerors and the conquered came to share a hierarchical ideology of social relations and governance that bound rulers and subjects in enduring structures of mutual recognition and dependence. In these cases, subjects became collaborators and, in some sense, true "citizens" of the empire, even if they remained in a perpetually unequal status in socially subordinate positions. In other areas of protracted resistance, such as among the autochthonous Aymara kingdoms, the Inca were able to establish only a form of laminar hegemony that depended principally on sustained coercive and disciplinary subjugation. Here the Inca did not manage to produce citizens of the realm but rather only subjugated, compliant populations, resistant to ideological conversion to the belief propagated by the Inca that they were the sole natural lords of the Andean world. Aymara historical consciousness of political autonomy and their capacity for self-determination were never entirely lost nor transformed beyond recognition. As a result, these native kingdoms were prone, whenever possible, to acts of subversion, resistance, and outright rebellion.

Empires inevitably create enemies and collaborators, both within and between subject polities. As a result, the hegemonic power of the state assumes different forms and intensities depending on local historical contingencies and power imbalances. In their ambition to rule the Andean world, Inca kings deployed different political strategies and instruments of social power, shrewdly tailoring their application to local conditions and political possibilities. Our task here is to examine the specific forms and workings of personal and institutionalized power that made this unprecedented political achievement possible.

How did the Inca kings exert social power? How did forms of social power in the empire change over time and space? What political innovations in statecraft permitted Inca kings to assemble an empire on a geopolitical scale never imagined (or at least never achieved) by their predecessors in the Andean world? The answers to these questions, not surprisingly, implicate the dynamic interplay of social, economic, and religious institutions, beliefs, and practices, as well as the powerful but evanescent force of individual ambition. The Inca kings built on preexisting, deep-seated, socially embedded forms of power, but they created new instruments to exercise that power as well. The Inca political order was conservative and innovative at the same time – it built on traditional Andean social institutions and simultaneously transformed them by inserting them into new structures of governance. To analyze the political order of the Inca Empire requires us first to understand the nature of Inca power in its most general form, and then to explore the specific beliefs, social institutions, and instruments of statecraft that the Inca deployed to conquer and govern their world.

The Inca Empire was a political structure ruled by individuals who claimed to possess a divine mandate. But the empire was not the product of individuals alone. Indigenous Andean states, including that of the Inca, were essentially patrimonial in character: power was vested in and flowed through oligarchic or princely households (Kolata 1990, 1996).

These households constituted themselves as related or allied lineages of nobles with rights and obligations framed in terms of customary law and habitual social practice. Noble lineages were organized in hierarchical arrangements, culminating often in some institutional form of kingship. That is, the most concentrated form of social power in the native Andean world was kingly authority. To understand the political order that the Inca imposed in their realm, we must first explore the social ontology of kingship and how the practices of royal authority influenced structures of governance and their social and political relationships with subject populations.

In the pre-European world of the Inca, the social interactions and interdependencies established and played out within the court among the aristocratic lineages shaped the form and content of royal authority. How can we understand the nature of Inca kingship, its ontology, social context, and meaning? First, Inca kingship, and political power more generally, was not constituted in terms of abstract rules that demarcated arenas of social action. There is little evidence of a formal legal framework that constructed Inca conceptions of social order. Power was not defined by a set of transcendental, universal principles against which all social and moral action was tested. That is, Inca kingship was not conceived of and legitimated in terms of legal texts, as was the case in Europe by the time of the late medieval period (Kantorowicz 1981:93–94). This relatively late Western European legal framework substantially shapes our own cultural understandings of what kingship means and how it operates. But the legitimacy of Inca kingship was constituted exclusively in the pragmatic arena of social action: through daily acts of rule, marriage alliances, hospitality, gift giving, conquest, and religious ceremony. The king's power and legitimacy were not tested against or confirmed by formal legal frameworks, but instead by the mobilization of personal networks and social consensus that was continuously redefined.

In this regard, Inca kingship may be considered an instance of charismatic rule, a metastable form of leadership that required of the king exquisite sensitivity and constant personal attention to his leading subjects' attitudes and behaviors. Inca kings had to constantly prove themselves by displaying their superiority as warriors on the battlefield and as politicians in the imperial court by effectively deploying the supremely valued power of discourse, the capacity to convince others of their unique capacities for governance. Success as an Inca king demanded all those personal qualities described so perceptively by Max Weber (1978) in his analysis of charismatic power: the special "gifts of mind and body" that demonstrated the king's physical, social, and moral superiority. To survive in the intensely competitive social arena of Cuzco's noble lineages and *panaqas*, Inca kings needed to demonstrate preeminence as warriors, at times by visibly placing themselves at risk on the front lines in their wars of conquest. At the same time, the kings' exceptional prowess as warriors was seen as proof that they were imbued with divine authority, with a supernatural ability to prophesy, to work miracles, to perform almost incomprehensibly heroic deeds. The legendary biography of the Inca king Pachakuti perfectly reflects the centrality of charismatic power in the concepts and practices of Inca royal authority. As several Spanish chronicles related, at the defining moment of Inca history, when the Chanka ethnic group threatened the very existence of the people of Cuzco and their nascent empire, Pachakuti went into seclusion to pray to the creator god, Viracocha Pacha-yachachic. While in a trance, Pachakuti received a personal revelation from the deity, who told him: "My son, do not be distressed. The day that you go into battle with your enemies, I will send soldiers to you with whom you will defeat your enemies, and you will enjoy victory" (Betanzos 1996:29). The miraculous intervention of Viracocha's promised warriors, who in some accounts were said to spring to life from the very stones of the battlefield, turned the military tide in favor of the embattled Pachakuti and his devoted coterie of kinsmen and followers. The forces of Cuzco defeated Usovilca, the rival Chanka king, and subsequently absorbed the prosperous and once powerful Chanka ethnic group into the emergent Inca Empire. Pachakuti's personal political power intensified dramatically after these events, which were perceived and later commemorated as proof of the king's privileged, mystical access to divine providence; the stones of the battlefield, called *pururaucas*, were subsequently enshrined and venerated as *wak'as*.

Apart from the perception that Inca kings possessed almost uncanny access to supernatural forces, Inca kingship as a form of charismatic power also depended on a deeply ingrained cultural pattern of sociability. The mode of consciousness of this kind of power is subject oriented, in contrast to the legally enmeshed frameworks of absolutist rule. Subject-oriented rule demanded constant engagement, or at least the perception of engagement, with subjugated populations at all levels of the social hierarchy by the king himself, by his delegated representatives, or by his supernatural avatars (Figure 6.3). Not surprisingly in this charisma-based political system, Inca kings were peripatetic. They were often absent from the capital in Cuzco for many years at a time, constantly on the move as they engaged in military campaigns, suppression of rebellions or often simply on extended inspection tours in the provinces. Following his enthronement, Wayna Qhapaq, the last independent Inca emperor, rarely spent more than a few months at a time in Cuzco. As Betanzos relates, "[T]he Lords of Cuzco knew that he was given to making inspections throughout the kingdom and to waging war" (Betanzos

6.3. As a charismatic ruler, the Inca king sustained legitimacy through his continued, personal participation in military conquest. Here, King Wayna Qhapaq enters battle carried on a litter by his attendants. (Adapted from Guaman Poma de Ayala 1615)

1996:177). Wayna Qhapaq, like his predecessors, spent most of his reign on the road "visiting and inspecting the provinces, towns and lands that each province contained. He marked the boundaries of all of them and gave order, reason, and good government to all" (Betanzos 1996:175). Inca kings moved throughout the realm in itinerant circuits that brought them into continual personal contact with their subjects, especially with the provincial elites upon whom local governance depended.

Yet, despite their arduous efforts as warriors and on the road, Inca emperors could not be everywhere at once, distributing and displaying their awesome, divinely bestowed power. In a literal sense, the Inca political system hinged upon a dense network of delegated authority, a proliferation of people and sacred objects that functioned as administrative proxies for the king himself. Close kinsmen of the Inca served as governors of provinces and heads of politically critical institutions such as the military and the priesthood. As one scholar perceptively describes this pervasive pattern of delegated authority, the Inca surrogate

> periodically delegated his military duties to various "generals," his religious duties to the high priest of the Sun, and his administrative duties to a figure called the *Inkap rantin*, or "Inka's substitute." Descriptions of an Inka's exploits frequently included everything done by these delegates in the Inka's name. Thus the Inka became something of an umbrella figure or corporate persona who hierarchically subsumed under his identity an entire supporting cast of lesser individuals. (Gose 1996:17)

Although a designated *Inkap rantin* who served as the king's official representative and public intermediary evidently existed within the Inca governance structure, the "Inca's substitute" was, in reality, not simply a single person or office but, more importantly, an operational principle of multiple surrogates who operated in virtually all domains of social, political, religious, and cultural life. The most powerful surrogate administrators of the empire, the *tokrikoq*, or provincial governors, and the *willaq umu*, the holder of the most exalted religious office in the empire, were close blood relatives of the reigning emperor, full or half-siblings who survived the periodic struggles for succession and retained the emperor's personal confidence. These highly placed political surrogates of the emperor enjoyed all the prerogatives of royalty: they traveled in richly adorned litters protected by a cordon of heavily armed warriors and accompanied by a retinue of wives, concubines, and personal servants who attended to their daily needs (Poma de Ayala 2002:349). Tellingly, in a society in which clothing reflected personal identity, status, and power, the provincial governors were permitted to dress like the emperor himself with only subtle differences, such as wearing the *mascaypacha,* the exquisite woven fringe emblematic of the emperor's political authority, askew rather than over the forehead as only the emperor himself could do (Ramos Gavilán [1621], as cited in Gose 1996:18). Like the Inca emperor, these noble avatars circulated constantly and visibly through the province in their charge, appointing local *kurakas* to imperial offices, administering justice, officiating at religious festivals, recording tributary obligations with the aid of their *khipu kamayuqkuna* (Figure 6.4), and distributing imperial boons – in other words, performing all of the functions of leadership in the name of their emperor. From the perspective of provincial subjects, these political surrogates did not simply speak on

6.4. *Khipu kamayuq* officials used *khipus* to closely monitor the contents of *qollqas*, as seen here, and also kept records for many other aspects of Inca administration. (Adapted from Guaman Poma de Ayala 1615)

behalf of the Inca emperor; they were, in effect, a bodily extension of the emperor and of his supernatural power. By virtue of their appointment as the king's delegates, they were imbued with some of his concentrated charismatic power, even if only temporarily, while executing their office on behalf of the king.

But this infusion of charisma carried considerable political risk for the Inca king, since many of these highly placed proxies for the Inca emperor were nobles possessed of exalted bloodlines, and therefore were potential claimants to the throne. Virtually every royal succession among the Inca became embroiled in intense political infighting that often entailed violent military confrontations among noble factions, enforced exile of unsuccessful claimants to the throne, strategic assassinations, and even wholesale slaughter of competing rivals and their families (Rostworowski 1960; Sarmiento 1999:155). Part of the reason for this structural instability in succession derived from the logic of charismatic rather than rules-based kingship. That is, any claimant to the throne who proved himself most able as a warrior and a politician could seize the crown. There was no single rule based on genealogical principles of inheritance, such as primogeniture, as was common among the noble houses of Europe. If the eldest son of a deceased Inca monarch was less capable than a younger brother or a rival from among the ranks of another noble lineage related to the king, he would be passed over, or even assassinated. At times the entire families of failed aspirants to the throne were brutally murdered to prevent protracted blood feuds and the emergence of effective oppositional parties.

The principle of charismatic rule, with its inherent capabilities' test for would-be kings, ensured that vigorous, politically shrewd and socially adept leaders ascended to the throne. But the cost of charisma as a principle of succession was a permanent state of factionalism among competing noble houses that undermined solidarity and a shared sense of purpose among the ruling classes. This deeply rooted, violence-inflected factionalism became a major contributing factor to the destruction of the Inca Empire at the hands of the invading Spanish, who, upon their arrival in 1532, astutely grasped and took full tactical advantage of the internecine blood feud that was raging between the forces of Atawallpa and Waskhar. Constant intrigue in the palaces of the king, the *panaqas,* and the noble families became the normal way of conducting politics. Then, too, these crises of royal succession repeatedly precipitated rebellions in the provinces among conquered ethnic groups aspiring to regain lost sovereignty and throw off tribute obligations to the lords of Cuzco. For this reason, competing noble factions often kept the death of a reigning monarch as a closely guarded state secret until a new emperor could be proclaimed and publicly accede to the throne. The first act of a newly installed Inca king was often to repacify these rebellious groups, thereby demonstrating his own charismatic gifts of mind and body and, in doing so, consolidating his personal power.

Charismatic authority, then, based as it was on highly personalized qualities of power, brought to the Inca Empire both significant benefits and a significant measure of structural instability. Charisma is, by definition, a concentrated rather than a distributed form of social power. Yet effective governance of a rapidly expanding empire demanded that the Inca kings delegate power (and thereby impart charisma) to others,

despite the potential risk of diluting, or even dissolving, their own charismatic authority. In the absence of a universally accepted legal framework for legitimating political power, Inca kings were forced to take this
risk at the cost of constant surveillance of the *tokrikoq* and other highly
placed and well-connected rivals, including the monarch's many noble
uncles, siblings, half-siblings, and cousins holding significant administrative positions in the empire.

In a quintessentially Andean perspective that made no unequivocal
ontological distinction between animate and inanimate entities, Inca
kings also commissioned other kinds of "Inca's substitutes" to serve as
their delegates and to extend their corporeal and political reach into the
provinces. Unlike the human delegates of the Inca such as the *tokrikoq*,
these proxies did not represent the same kind of political and existential threat to the emperor. Yet they held the same political and religious
capacity to act on behalf of the king, in his name and as his religiously
sanctioned avatar. Betanzos provides a detailed description of these nonhuman proxies in reference to the reign of Atawallpa:

> [F]inding himself lord, he ordered that a statue be prepared of his own nail
> clippings and hair, which was a representation of his person. He ordered that
> this statue be called Incap Guauquin, [*wawqi*] which means brother of the Inca.
> Once this statue was completed, he had it placed on a litter and charged one of
> his servants named Chima with guarding and watching over it. Giving this statue
> many other young men as servants, he ordered that it be taken and carried on
> its litter by the messengers to where his captains Chalcochima and Quizquiz
> were so that the peoples of the subjugated provinces could render obedience to
> that statue in place of his person. Thus this statue was carried and given to the
> captains, who received it and were very pleased with it. They performed many
> and great sacrifices and served and respected this statue as if the very person of
> Atahualpa were there. One should understand that the constitution of this statue
> in this way was ordained by the Inca Yupanque [Pachakuti]. When he sent some
> captains or his sons on a conquest, they carried one of these statues through the
> towns and provinces as if it were the Inca in person. (Betanzos 1996:205)

Betanzos's description of these *wawkis* or "object-brothers" of the
Inca emperor makes clear that the creation of multiple substitutes for
the king extended well back into Inca history, putatively to the time of
the great ideological and political reorganizations initiated by Pachakuti
(reigned ca. 1438–1471). Sarmiento claimed an even deeper antiquity for the *wawki* phenomenon, stating that the first king claimed by
the Inca, Manqo Qhapaq, was responsible for initiating this cult of
the object-brother: "From this Manco Ccapac were originated the ten
[royal] *ayllus* mentioned above. From his time began the idols *huauquis*,
which was an idol or demon chosen by each Inca for his companion

and oracle which gave him answers" (Sarmiento 1999:61). These sculptured images of the king were made of gold, silver, and wood and had parts of the king's own body (hair, nail clippings) infused in them. The *wawkis* incorporated bodily elements of the reigning monarch so that, in a real sense, rather than just *represent* the king, as in Betanzos's interpretation ("as if it were the Inca in person"), they *were* the king. In other words, the Inca did not treat the *wawkis* as merely a static icon of royalty but as an animated object-body infused with both the corporeal and the soul-like qualities of the king himself. *Wawkis* communicated in oracular form, giving counsel to the living king on affairs of state and in times of personal crisis. In the politico-religious worldview of their subjects, Inca kings possessed multiple bodies, and the *wawkis* were the most intimate exemplars of the king's presence and authority outside of his living, mortal body. Inca ministers and subjects prayed, sacrificed, and socially related to the *wawkis,* but, again, they did not regard the *wawkis* as passive, iconic representations of royalty meant to evoke religious sentiments or as vehicles for supernatural intercession. Rather, the *wawkis* literally spoke to the king's subjects through trusted human intermediaries, akin to spirit mediums. These intermediaries presumably had intimate knowledge of the living monarch's intentions, which they conveyed to his subjects in the physical presence of the statue. These spirit mediums spoke on behalf of the king, who had imbued the *wawkis* they served with his social power and corporeal essence.

These "object-brothers" of the king shared in the charismatic power of the monarchy and thereby fully participated in the governance of the realm. The *wawkis* went into battle in the company of the Inca kings and became rallying points for the Inca military forces, much like the religious statuary, icons, and emblems of Catholic saints that accompanied the armies of medieval city-states in Italy and Spain. Inca kings feted, socialized, and consulted with the *wawkis* through their human mediums, who gave the desired oracular pronouncements. Moreover, the importance of these "object-brothers" continued after the death of the Inca king. Additional *wawkis* were fabricated in gold to commemorate the king's death and to ensure, along with the king's mummified remains, that the dead sovereign had a tangible and eternal social presence in the empire (Betanzos 1996:138). As José de Acosta recounts, "[The Incas] were not content with this idolatrous worship of dead bodies but also made statues of them; and each king during his lifetime had a stone idol or statue of himself made, which was called *guaoiqui* [*wawki*], meaning 'brother,' for both in life and death the same veneration had to be paid to that statue as to the Inca himself. These statues were taken to war and carried in procession to pray for rain and good growing seasons, and different feasts and sacrifices were made to them" (Acosta 2002:265–266). Bernabé Cobo observed further that the kings "gave their *guauques* a house and servants. They also assigned some farmland to support those who were in charge of each statue. From the day that they made their *guauques* their brothers, the Inca kings would order the people, especially those of their lineage and family unit, to treat the *guauques* with the same reverence as the king himself" (Cobo 1990:37). The *wawkis* or "object-brothers" of the Inca kings, in sum, had a soul (*camaquen*); a body; a unique name; communicative capacity; kinship relationships; ongoing political and religious responsibilities; a house, tangible property, and servants bestowed by the king and his family; and, upon a king's death, an honored place of interment beside the mortal body of their human brother. The *wawkis* were, in indigenous Andean terms, living brother-companions of the king, possessed of a unique personhood bestowed on them by the king himself; they were not simply static images of the king's authority.

The mystical power of the king to infuse his animating force (his *camay*) into multiple human and object proxies, to make them literal extensions of his own body permeated with divine authority, underscored his uniqueness among men and his status as the charismatic Sapa Inca, the Unique Lord. Gose (1996:21) succinctly captures this dimension of Inca delegated authority: "By working through the multiple embodiments of 'substitutes,' statues, and mediums, a ruler extended his influence in space and time and delegated enough power to govern effectively. At the same time, he demonstrated his divinity by 'animating' these far-flung subdivisions of himself, thereby making an ideological virtue out of administrative necessity. This style of delegation reinforced the personal, patrimonial emphasis of Andean divine kingship, which discouraged strong governing institutions."

Given its origins in charismatic authority, the legitimacy of Inca kings required a peculiarly intense and continuous form of social interaction between the king and his subjects. Relations between them were not framed solely in terms of the circulation of labor services and commodities in tribute or gift form, but consisted of a constantly shifting and strategically deployed manipulation of social solidarity, religious sentiment, political power, and instrumental resources. The principal forms of this social interaction included reciprocal feasting and drinking bouts linked to a ceremonial calendar, periodic hosting of foreign gods and dignitaries in religious festivals, gift giving, marriage alliances, and everyday acts of court ritual and etiquette. The substantive contents of this social exchange included the circulation of status-indexed marriage partners to and from the king and his court, grants of rights to labor, the distribution of proprietary rights to land and water, and the reciprocal exchange of meaningful, value-laden gifts such as food, livestock, textiles, jewels, and other luxury commodities. How did this comprehensive system of social exchange between the king and his subjects actually work?

In a nonmonetary, nonmarket economy such as that of the Inca, two resources apart from labor were especially critical for the production and reproduction of social power: land, along with the right to irrigate the land, and marriage partners. The different social characters of these two instrumental resources set up a potential tension. The Inca appropriated and alienated land from subjugated communities, frequently deploying these lands in sustaining social exchange and sociability between the king and the provincial nobility (Rostworowski 1999). Gifts of land, or perhaps more accurately, gifts of the right to irrigate and cultivate land, extended a potentially autonomous power base to the elite recipients that could constitute a political threat to the Inca king. In theory, through this instrumental resource, local elites could maintain a power base independent of the king and could attract followers, just as did the Inca kings, by virtue of conspicuous acts of generosity. At the same time, however, these gifts of land and irrigation rights were often tied to long-term, reciprocal relationships in the form of a hierarchical circulation of marriage partners to and from the king. In this system of social exchange, one kind of gift (land, labor, and irrigation rights) potentially afforded provincial elites a means to distance themselves politically and economically from the king, to weaken bonds of dependency; yet, at the same time, the other instrumental resource, marriage partners, drew the elites back into a network of mutual dependencies, mutual surveillance, and increased interdependency.

The circulation of status-indexed marriage partners was critical to the construction and legitimacy of royal authority and to the pragmatics of governance among the Inca (Zuidema 1964, 1989a) (Figure 6.5). In some sense, royal authority itself, and all of the adhering practical entailments of authority, such as the right to receive labor and the right to irrigate parcels of land, circulated with these marriage partners and through the offspring that resulted from these unions. The essence of the indigenous logic underlying this social exchange can be glossed by two terms: "asymmetry" and "hierarchy." From the perspective of the Inca, the king formed two kinds of marriage bonds: one endogamous (and, in the extreme case of endogamy, incestuous) and the other exogamous. The offspring born of these unions were hierarchically ranked according to their origin: the children of endogamous, primary spouses were considered legitimate heirs of the Inca king and elder siblings, whereas the children of exogamous unions were classified as secondary children

Chympo Coya

6.5. Royal and elite women played an important role in Inca politics as status-indexed marriage partners, but also made political decisions in their own right. Here, a seventeenth-century image of the queen Chimpo Qoya by Martín de Murúa. (© The J. Paul Getty Museum, Los Angeles, Ms. Ludwig XIII 16, fol.25v. Martín de Murúa, Chimpo, 1616) and younger siblings. Children of these distinct marriage partners were distinguished socially among the Inca through an indigenous, triadic classification into status groups called *collana, payan,* and *cayao* (the same categorical designations operating in the *zeq'e* system of Cuzco, as described in Chapter 5). In this system of asymmetrical and hierarchically ranked kinship relations, "*collana* referred to the legitimate descendants of the Inca's union with the *coya* [i.e., with his queen, the primary, legitimate wife who was actually, or culturally, defined as his sister]; *payan* alluded to secondary children, or those born of the Inca's union with foreign women; and *cayao* referred to the non-Inca population from whom the Inca acquired his secondary wives in a system of reciprocal exchanges in which he would exchange his own female kin with these non-Inca groups" (Ossio 1996:231–232). These distinct kinds of marriage exchanges established well-defined social and political classes that provided the underlying rationale and the pragmatic armature for governance in the empire.

Royal incest in which the newly crowned king publicly married his own sister at the time of his investiture was simultaneously a religious and a political act. Only the newly enthroned king could wed his full-blooded sister, breaking a virtually universal social taboo, and with her produce "doubly royal" heirs to the throne. The practice of royal incest reinforced the charismatic power of the king: he alone, by virtue of his divine status and his mystical "powers of body and mind," could commit incest and thereby engender progeny possessed of this ultimate royal status. One cannot gainsay the importance of the underlying religious rationale for royal incest. Yet the Spanish chronicler Cieza de León astutely observed another dimension of this marriage practice, revealing the pragmatic political logic of royal incest that, by traditional historical accounts, was formally instituted during the reign of Thupa Inka Yupanki (ca. 1471–1492):

It was ordered by them that he who was to be the Lord-Inca should take his sister, the legitimate daughter of his father and mother, to wife, so that the succession to the kingdom should be confined to the royal line, for it seemed to them that in this way, even if the woman in question, the sister of the Lord-Inca, were unchaste and, knowing another man, should become with child by him, the child who was born would be descended from her and not from an alien woman....

And if it so happened that he who was to become Lord-Inca had no sister, he was permitted to marry the woman of highest rank there was, that she might be considered the principal among all his wives, for there was no one of these lords who did not have more than seven hundred women for the service of his house and with whom to take his pleasure. Thus all of them had many children by these women who were their wives or concubines, and they were well treated by him and held in high regard by the natives.... When the sons of these Lord-Incas had by these women were grown, they bestowed upon them lands and estates which they call *chacaras*, and from the storehouses they were provided with clothing and other things for their needs. They did not, however, give them authority, for in the event of any disturbance in the kingdom, they did not want them to seize power on the grounds that they were sons of the Lord-Inca. Thus none of them was put in command of a province, although when they went out on wars of conquest, many of them were captains and favored above the rest of troops. (Cieza de León 1976:40–41)

Royal incest was the most exclusive and religiously charged form of marriage exchange among the Inca. But, as Cieza's passage reveals, Inca kings did not limit their political marriages to their own sisters. In addition to the *qoya*, their principal sister-wife, the later Inca kings took hundreds of additional wives and concubines in an extreme practice of polygamy common to rulers in premodern empires throughout the world. Depending on their social status, these wives and concubines produced large numbers of progeny who served as war leaders or held low-level administrative posts. Only the sons and daughters of the highest-born female consorts of the king, however, could aspire to positions of significant authority, and in the case of the provincial governors, access to power was strictly limited to the king's closest blood relatives.

From the perspective of the Inca king, these multiple marriage exchanges permitted him to simultaneously preserve the identity, legitimacy, and status of his unique, endogamous power base and still project his personal, kin-based authority through exogamy into the broader, foreign world of non-Inca peoples. This system effectively made affines of potential political rivals and gave the children of these unions an elevated, though still subordinate, status in the emerging cosmopolitan world that the Inca Empire created in the course of its conquests. So the circulation of marriage partners both reaffirmed the boundaries of the social order and conferred new kin-based status, rights, and obligations on foreigners incorporated into the system.

The extension of kinship bonds to provincial elites was a strategic and, evidently, extremely effective political instrument of the Inca kings. In the absence of text-based, contractual relations between the Inca and provincial elites, these wife and consort relations constituted what I have called "kintracts." To prevent or weaken the emergence of independent power bases, the Inca developed formal, reciprocal social bonds framed in the idiom of kinship. These kintracts enlarged the boundaries of the social order beyond the immediate, consanguineal bonds of the royal family to an expansive understanding of kinship in which, in effect, "all the world's" a potential affine. Relations between the king and provincial nobles and subjects were perceived and acted on not as arms-length contractual arrangements between unrelated individuals but as intimate social exchanges between kin, whether defined biologically or socially. The Inca, in fact, provide a fascinating counterexample to Sir Henry Maine's dictum that the state as a form of political organization required a transition from status to contract. In theory, and certainly often in practice, the Inca king considered all of his willing subjects to be his kin, and he behaved toward them as though they were. From his standpoint, this audacious concept of universal kinship converted the empire into a vast, one-world *ayllu* in which every subject was considered to be related to every other one as biological or culturally conceived (fictive) kin.

Of course, in the intensely hierarchical social world of the Inca, not all subjects as kin were equal or possessed equivalent rights and responsibilities. The highly elaborated class system, as well as considerable ethnic differentiation, crosscut the sociological concept of the empire as a single *ayllu*. All subjects were fitted into the empire's social structure along a complex gradation of status from "poor relatives" to Incas by privilege to nobles of pure blood to the king himself, who served as the supreme leader of this imperial-scale *ayllu* in life and as its divine ancestor in death. A comprehensive interpretation of Inca society requires recognition that economy, ideology, politics, social organization, and religious belief were mutually constitutive. These specifically Inca institutions and cultural forms were most certainly not articulated in a formal bureaucracy that bore any significant resemblance to modern state bureaucracies. As a result, the nature of social power in the Inca state cannot be captured by an analysis of political economy alone or of processes associated with capitalist economies, such as the accumulation of wealth through market exchange. Instead, in the noncapitalist world of the Inca, sources of state power were prefigured in the relations of domination and subordination worked out in the kinship structures of Andean societies. In this respect, state power in the Inca world flowed naturally from a shared sense of meaning that linked the natural, social, and spiritual worlds and from social experience grounded in and shaped by fundamental networks of kinship.

Specific political practices engaged in by the Inca king emphasize the critical importance of this kin-based theory of governance and its underlying principles of reciprocal obligations and sociality. The Inca king and his counselors paid close attention to the marriage status of their subjects, and they intervened directly by making and ratifying arranged marriages in the context of religious festivals, particularly in the provinces surrounding Cuzco. Betanzos related that the Inca king Pachakuti initiated a systematic program of strategic arranged marriages intended to consolidate his own authority:

In this fiesta both the lords and the rest of their subjects took part. This fiesta lasted thirty days, after which the Inca ordered a certain number of lord *orejones* to leave the city. They were to go through the lands of those lords who were there to find out about and bring him the number of unmarried young men and girls there were. He sent word to the caciques and important men to inform their foremen, *llacta camayos*, as they call them, of what the Inca wanted.... Once the Inca understood the number of young unmarried men and women in these towns and provinces, he ordered his three friends the lords [his principal political allies and counselors] to leave right away for those towns and provinces and to take with them all those cacique lords who at present were there with him. In their presence in each town and province where they went they should marry the young men of a province to the young unmarried women of another province.... They should continue doing this throughout the lands and dominion of those lord caciques ... so that their numbers would grow and multiply and they would share perpetual friendship, family ties and brotherhood. With this arranged, the Inca did great favors for those lord caciques, giving them many gifts.... Inca Yupanque [Pachakuti] stayed in Cuzco with the people of the city itself and some lords of those living within about one league, a half league or less of the city. He ordered them and those of the city to each bring before him the unmarried men and women that they had in their towns. When they were brought before him, the Inca himself performed the marriage of all those young men and women. (Betanzos 1996:57–58)

Betanzos went on to note that the Inca personally gave these newly wedded couples from the circum-Cuzco region gifts of blankets; garments, including two sets of clothing to both men and women; rations of maize, dried meat, and fish; and llamas and earthenware for their daily use – all the essential domestic goods for them to begin their productive adult lives as a conjugal couple. According to Betanzos (1996:58), Pachakuti ordered that these couples receive provisions drawn from the imperial storehouses every four months. In other words, the couples were to be the beneficiaries of royal patronage, the recipients of a permanent public dole that was intended to ensure their loyalty and bind them firmly to the personal authority of the king.

Revealingly, these arranged marriages of near-Cuzco and provincial subjects were explicitly exogamous in nature. They were intended to join together people from geographically and ethnically distinct communities through marriage ties and to encourage the procreation of new subjects who possessed mixed, cross-provincial identities. In a real sense, this program of arranged marriages was an audacious attempt at social and genealogical engineering on an imperial scale, designed to create, in Betanzos's words, "perpetual friendship, family ties and brotherhood" that would dissolve, or at least diminish, the political salience of pre-existing ethnosocial boundaries. The underlying political rationale from the perspective of the Inca king was to produce loyal, compliant subjects who shared the characteristic of being dependent upon the Inca for their social and biological identity. In analytical terms, this comprehensive imperial-scale program of arranged marriages was an effective biological and social instrument for creating a state of viral hegemony based on the acquiescence, collaboration, and consent of subjects rather than on tactical violence and sustained repression.

The Incas' political involvement in assigning marital partners to their subjects entailed other instruments of social control. As we have seen, the special status group of the *aqllakuna*, or chosen women, concentrated large numbers of young females in the principal towns and temple precincts of the empire. The *aqllakuna* lived communally in dedicated residential compounds referred to as *aqllawasis* (houses of the chosen women). The chosen women performed a variety of state services, including producing high-quality textiles and clothing and brewing maize beer for public ceremonies. But just as important as their labor output was, the *aqllakuna* were critical vehicles for extending Inca power by virtue of their status as women of prestige, chosen and sanctified by the Inca king. All *aqllakuna*, who were young women in their prime child-bearing years, could become highly coveted marriage partners distributed by the Inca king or by his noble delegates to subjects as rewards for loyal and distinguished service to the crown. Much like the progeny of the interprovincial marriages engineered by the Inca, the descendants of *aqllakuna* given in marriage as diplomatic gifts owed their existence and social status to the king.

In this comprehensive system of arranged marriages, the king was perceived to be the originator and the royal patron of kintracts that extended social relations and kin networks across perceived ethnic and territorial boundaries. These cross-provincial marriage ties under royal patronage began to subtly reshape the geopolitical landscape for Inca subjects. Cross-provincial marriages served to complicate, if not eradicate, deep-seated parochial attachment to well-defined territories and local shrines and deities. For better or for worse, the Inca subjects' social world expanded dramatically upon their incorporation into the empire.

Of course, the extent to which this self-conscious attempt by the Inca kings to produce a unified nation based on notions of universal kinship actually succeeded on an empire-wide scale can be questioned. As we have seen, the historical record makes clear that many of the subjects of the Inca, such as those living in the Aymara kingdoms of the Andean *altiplano*, resisted incorporation into the empire, and most likely rejected any notion that they were anything less than autonomous peoples with a unique social identity, one for which they were prepared to fight implacably. The idea of creating close ties of kinship with their Inca overlords that would be framed in terms of a permanently inferior social status as *huaccha concha*, or poor relatives, would have been anathema to the proud and powerful Aymara-speaking peoples. Their willingness to risk annihilation by the Inca armies during repeated rebellions underscores their determined resistance to the Inca-inspired concept of a one-world *ayllu*. Similar rejection of Inca attempts to propagate a viral form of hegemony occurred all along the Inca Empire's northern, southern, and deeply forested eastern frontiers among ethnic groups such as the Kañari, Kayambe, and Caranqui, as well as among Guaraní- and Araucanian-speaking groups (Figure 6.6). In these regions and among the most resistant ethnic groups, rather than implementing the "soft power" of extending kin and fictive kin status to newly incorporated populations, the Inca kings of the late empire often resorted to brute force and tactics of sustained military occupation to subdue local populations and to enforce their political will. In these regions of obdurate resistance, Inca emperors could only achieve a costly and evanescent form of laminar hegemony that repressed local populations but never truly incorporated them into the Inca king's imagined one-world *ayllu*. Although a concept of universal kinship in which the Inca and their king occupied the hierarchical apex of a one-world *ayllu* may not have been effectively implemented throughout the entire empire, the principle of kintract was nevertheless a powerful strategy of statecraft and administration, particularly in the Inca heartland around Cuzco and among Quechua-speaking groups of the central Andean sierra.

Thus, kintract, *not* contract, was the operative political principle of the Inca state. Political office in the empire depended on one's kin ties to important Inca nobles and, for the most highly placed subjects, to the king himself. Diplomatic relations between the king and local rulers in subject provinces were framed and conducted through the idiom of kinship. Betanzos provided a revealing account of another political practice, from the reign of Wayna Qhapaq, that publicly displayed and reaffirmed the intensity of the king's personal, kin-based bonds with his subjects. Wayna Qhapaq

decided that it would be well to take some things with him to give as gifts to the caciques [*kurakas*] of the towns and provinces he visited.... With this done, he left the city, ordering those lords whom he was taking with him always to be sure to make his arrival known before he reached a certain town or province so that the people could come out to meet him on the road and to get him a garment like the ones used in that town.... Since sometimes they would go to a town where they wore long hair [the Inca customarily wore their hair cut short], the Inca ordered that, along with the garment, a hairpiece should be brought for

6.6. Many groups along the frontiers of Tawantinsuyu, such as the Kayambe, Kañari, and Chachapoya in modern Ecuador and northern Peru, offered strong resistance to Inca incursion. (Adapted from Guaman Poma de Ayala 1615)

him to wear.... When the Inca arrived, they offered him that garment. The Inca put it on and also put on the hairpiece. He looked like a native of that province. Thus he entered the most important town [of the province] where they had in the plaza a certain seat which resembled a high platform and in the middle of the platform, a basin full of stones. On reaching the town, the Inca climbed up on the platform and sat there on his chair. From there he could see everyone in the plaza, and they could all see him. They brought out before him many lambs [llamas] whose throats they slit in his presence, and they offered them to him. Then they poured out much *chicha* into that basin which was there for sacrifices. The Inca drank with them, and they with him. Then he came down from there, danced and sang with them, clasping hands, joining to make a circle, and he ate with them.... After this, he gave them what he brought and did them favors.... After doing this, he left that province, and in the next one they found out that the Inca was traveling. When he reached the border he found that they had the accustomed garment ready there. The Inca took off the garment of the town he had just left and put on the other one. Thus he entered every province in the local attire, and the Inca celebrated with them as if they were his equals. To some he gave women, to others livestock, to others tumblers of gold and silver, and to others valuable garments like the ones he wore. (Betanzos 1996:168–169)

Although this passage refers specifically to the reign of Wayna Qhapaq, the regal protocol of the king's adopting local hairstyles and dress, as well as distributing precious gifts, including women, while touring the provinces was standard in Inca statecraft (Cieza de León 1976:74). This strategy of identity politics also was a powerful motivating force when the Inca kings needed to mobilize ethnic groups to take part in military campaigns. Cieza de León states that "his informants" recounted that when the "Lord-Inca Yupanqui" decided to wage war on the Wanka peoples of the central Andean highlands near Xauxa, he issued a call to arms to different allied ethnic groups. When these groups had assembled, "he ordered banquets and feasts given for them, and to delight them, he appeared every day in different garb or attire, that of the nation he wished to honor that day, and the next he put on another, such as those invited to the banquet or drinking feast wore. With all this their hearts were merry beyond power to describe" (Cieza de León 1976:117). During these military campaigns and in their extended serial encounters while touring the provinces, Inca kings not only made painstaking efforts to appear in public looking like the locals in each province but also used these appearances to interact with their subjects as paragons of proper kin behavior. On these occasions, the Inca kings distributed culturally valued gifts, sponsored royal banquets, and personally performed in local festivals. The king made a dramatic point by first appearing to the public from the exalted heights of his throne in the middle of a town plaza, thereby visually asserting his authority and superior status, and then descending to circulate freely among his subjects, eating, drinking, clasping hands, dancing, singing, and celebrating with them "as if they were equals." This latter gesture, the charismatic, affect-laden moment of face-to-face participation with subjects, together with the exchange of highly valued gifts, reaffirmed the psychological and political status of the Inca king as the most senior and exalted kinsman of the province and, by extension, of the whole empire.

In analyzing its significance, we should not make the mistake of assuming that this practice was merely a crowd-pleasing gesture of political theater without deeper social meaning, the equivalent of a U.S.

president's wearing tribal dress in Africa or Asia while on a state visit, or donning the baseball hat of a local sports team when presiding over a political rally. Clothing and hairstyles among the indigenous peoples of the Andes carried profound, even foundational, significance as vehicles of social identity. By wearing the clothes of provincial ethnic groups and appearing adorned in local hairstyles, the king proclaimed literal, not merely symbolic, kinship with his subjects. Although always maintaining a clear hierarchical distinction between himself and his subjects through complex sumptuary laws, courtly etiquette, and rigorously implemented codes of behavior, Inca kings strove mightily to portray themselves as the benevolent patriarchs of an enormous, patrimonial household (the one-world *ayllu*) that constituted their empire. This royal claim of real kinship with all of his subjects was not inconsistent with Inca sumptuary laws that required ethnic groups to maintain their own styles of headdress and clothing as markers of their unique identity. In creating imperial subjects and subjectivity, the Inca did not try to eradicate all cultural difference in the interest of creating a monolithic, normative citizen. Rather, the Inca concept of empire imagined it as a hyperextended patrimonial household that was pluriethnic, multilingual, and culturally diverse, but still bound together by the commonality of kinship.[1] This was not a chauvinistic, parochial, or exclusionary notion of kinship. Difference was recognized, embraced, and articulated at the imperial scale by its insertion in a comprehensive, hierarchical social order with the king at its apex.

The Inca system of social exchange between lords and subjects that I have characterized as a "kintract" obviated the need for legal contracts or an impersonal, text-based system that detailed mutual rights and obligations. Such rights and obligations were understood and acted on in the personalized idiom of kinship. That is, the relations between a lord and his subjects at all levels of the political hierarchy were embedded in a thoroughgoing, subjective framework of social exchange. The subject-oriented system of the Inca was substantially different from that of feudal society in Europe in which the essential relationship between lord and vassal was mediated by legal principles presumed to have an objective, universal validity independent of any particular social context. The crux of the vassal-lord relationship in medieval Europe turned on the possession of land and the products taken from the land (Bloch

---

[1] Even today Andean *ayllus* may consist of members with different native tongues, such as Quechua and Aymara, possessing distinct occupational specializations, modes of dress, and other cultural traits emphasizing the sociological flexibility of this mode of social organization (Bastien 1978).

1965). The feudal lord granted vassals the right to a parcel of land in return for a designated portion of the products of the land. These mutual rights were recognized in courts of law; in the event of nonperformance, vassals could appeal for redress to higher legal authorities outside of their specific social context, such as parliament or the assembly of the estates. This is not to say that the European feudal relationship was devoid of personal social content, affect, or sentiment. Lords and vassals sustained other forms of social rights and obligations, such as the right of vassals to security on the land and to political protection, or the obligation of the vassals to contribute military service to the lord. One can readily imagine that bonds of mutual sentiment between lord and vassal did on occasion result in social relations that resembled the direct, personal, or familial relationships characteristic of the Andean system. But the fundamental formal character of the European vassal-lord relationship was framed in material, objective, and contractual terms: in this system, social exchange was more narrowly construed in mutual economic relations and was mediated by the possession of land.

The subject-oriented system of authority that structured social relations in the Inca Empire finds counterparts in other premodern states. Similar indigenous conceptions of royal authority characterized many pre-Columbian Mesoamerican societies, such as the Maya. Further afield, the nature of authority in premodern Japan bears great similarity to the Andean system. As Eisenstadt notes: "In Japan relations between vassal and lord were generally couched, not in contractual terms based on fully formalized mutual legal rights and obligations, but in terms of familial or filial obligations.... Indeed, Japanese feudalism is characterized by the extension of strong familial obligation to frameworks broader than the nuclear family ... and by the vesting in the lord of control over such frameworks and the use of and access to their resources" (Eisenstadt 1996:165–166). In its general contours, Eisenstadt's analysis of traditional Japanese conceptions of social power fits comfortably within the Inca experience of kingly authority.

For such a concept of royal authority to be effective, there must be a strong emphasis on social inclusiveness and on the mutual loyalty of subjects and lords. In this regard, subjects generally act with the understanding that they are in league with, rather than in conflict with, their lords. Under such a system of authority, subjects and lords consider themselves, self-consciously, a social collectivity. Even if lords and subjects were believed to have distinct social ontologies and, accordingly, markedly different statuses, rights, and privileges, their subjective natures were nevertheless bound by shared cultural understandings and social practices. Furthermore, political authority in the Inca Empire was not experienced or legitimized through objective, externally validated rules, but rather by interpersonal relationships grounded in a shared understanding of the "naturalness" of Inca royal power.

What specifically were these cultural understandings and social practices that rendered Inca royal power not only acceptable but, in fact, a "natural" element of the social and moral order? In native Inca concepts of kingship, religious thought, experience, and practice determined, or at least profoundly influenced, concepts of proper governance. Just as kingship depended on sociability and on the creation of consensus, the structure and perceived legitimacy of the social order was directly embedded in and interpenetrated by religious conceptions of the natural world. Unlike European societies after the late Middle Ages, ancient Andeans did not consider the relationship between the mundane and the transcendental worlds an analytical problem for rational contemplation. Nor, indeed, were these worlds even conceived as separate realities, one the realm of the sensual and experiential, and the other of belief. Rather, there was an indigenous assumption of immanence, habitual communication, and continuity between the quotidian and spiritual worlds. As we have seen, this continuity was materially manifest in everyday life in essential aspects of Inca religiosity, such as sacrificial practices, ancestor cults, and hierarchical networks of *wak'as* and temples. Again, Eisenstadt's analysis of the premodern Japanese state presents a strikingly similar perspective on native conceptions of the relationship between nature and society: "The Japanese emphasis on the mutual embeddedness of nature and culture does not entail the perception of reality as homogenous. On the contrary, it entails a perception of reality as structured in multiple, continually shifting contexts, between which it flows.... This basic attitude to the world entailed a certain sanctification of the phenomenal world, of nature, the possibility of the sanctification of almost any object" (Eisenstadt 1996:321). This portrayal of underlying native attitudes toward nature and culture applies equally well to the Inca. But, as we have seen, among the Inca the sanctified objects of everyday life, animate or inanimate, were also organized in a hierarchical, kin-based system of social relations in a manner directly homologous with society itself. Agricultural shrines, temples, and pilgrimage sites were considered related to one another explicitly in the social idiom of a kinship network (mother to daughter, elder brother to younger brother, and so forth). In short, in this system of cognition, familiar to all scholars of indigenous American societies, nature was cultural, and culture natural, and every entity was considered to share a relationship of kinship to all others (Descola 1994, 1996).

The role of the king in this ideological system was unique, underpinning his power in both sacred and secular actions. The social collectivity of lords and subjects acted as a sacral community of which the king was the principal representative. In life, as sometimes in death, the king, as the highest-ranking member of this community, mediated between the phenomenological and the spiritual worlds on behalf of this social collectivity. The power of the king to mediate between heaven and earth was grounded in his unique twin nature: he was simultaneously embedded in and an essential part of the social collectivity but, by virtue of his unique, hierarchical position at the pinnacle of that society, he was also capable of communicating beyond the boundaries of the social world directly with the spiritual forces that structured the cosmos. In this respect, royal interlocution was a liturgical act. To grasp the political character of Inca kinship, we must understand and appreciate the power of religious belief and practices to shape structures of governance.

Inca kingship was conceived as a form of natural theology, and the practice of royal power was construed simultaneously as a social and as a liturgical act. But this kind of liturgical kingship is not purely theological, constructed by faith and collective belief alone. Rather, this kingship is fundamentally concerned with exercising power – material and economic power to be sure, but most especially social power in which the king defines the terms of value in the system of social exchange. Inca conceptions of kingship and the liturgical and social acts of royal mediation constitute more than a coda of religious beliefs. They represent a fully articulated political theology in which cult and command, the spiritual and the material, interpenetrated to an extraordinary degree. Among the Inca, the liturgical aspects of kingship were ubiquitous and publicly expressed in various kinds of social interactions between ruler and ruled. The calendar of politico-religious observances followed by the king and the royal family was full and demanding, from the first plowing ceremony to the investiture of young nobility. The burdens of empire building intensified the need for the king and his representatives to engage in highly social public acts, such as hosting feasts or distributing marriage partners, that were framed as shared religious beliefs.

The essence of this Inca political theology was distilled materially and conceptually in the sacred geography of shrines, ritual pathways, and sacrificial practices referred to as the *zeq'e* system (Zuidema 1964, 1990). As we have seen, the *zeq'e* system, a complex collection of shrines arrayed along lines of sight, was a symbolic and social landscape of the capital city of Cuzco and, by extension, of the Inca Empire. Different sets of related lineages (*ayllus*) were charged with the responsibility of maintaining the shrines along the *zeq'e* line assigned to that group. Responsibility for the *zeq'e* line included the obligation to offer periodic, prescribed sacrifices at these shrines (Zuidema 1990). To grasp the significance of the *zeq'e* system for understanding Inca concepts of kingship, we can discriminate two salient classes of symbolic associations of the constructed shrines and landscape *wak'as* arrayed along the *zeq'e* paths of Cuzco and its near environs: water and irrigation associations on the one hand, and dynastic lore and "history" on the other (Sherbondy 1982, 1986, 1992). These two dominant symbolic classes relate to distinct principles of legitimate authority (Kolata 1996). The first of these associations relates symbolically to the autochthonous people of Cuzco – the original inhabitants of the valley who lived and cultivated lands in the region before their domination by the Inca elite. Recall that these non-Inca peoples would be classified in the Inca system of asymmetrical and hierarchically ranked kinship relations as *cayao*. Fully one hundred and nine, or nearly one-third, of the *zeq'e* shrines relate directly to springs, streams, rivers, and pools that are actually or symbolically sources of flowing water for irrigating adjoining lands. These water-related *zeq'e* shrines can be interpreted in one sense as boundary markers, delimiting and sectioning arable land among various social groups (Sherbondy 1982, 1992; Zuidema 1986). The sacrifices made at these water shrines, such as offerings of the highly coveted *mullu*, the marine *Spondylus* shell associated in the Andes with royalty, emphasize associations with telluric phenomena and with the fertile and generative properties of land fed by flowing water. The principle of legitimate authority expressed by these associations emerges from the rights of the autochthonous populations as the original holders of usufruct title to the land.

The second dominant set of symbolic associations in *zeq'e* shrines concerns the myth-history of the Inca kings and queens and the class of royalty as a whole. This "history" includes those mythical events relating to the origins of the Inca as a distinct ethnic group and as a royal dynasty that derived its authority from outside of the Cuzco environs. But it also includes events that commemorate significant actions and achievements in the lives of historical Inca kings, such as episodes of the conquest and incorporation of foreign peoples. The lineages specifically indexed in these shrines would be classified as *collana* and *payan* in the Inca kinship system. By imposing the conceptual framework of the *zeq'e* system over both urban and imperial space, and incorporating Inca, Inca by privilege, and non-Inca lineages into the system, the Inca achieved a tacit integration of ideology and politico-religious practice that ideally came to be experienced by Inca and non-Inca alike as "natural."

Although here we may perceive a dialectic between opposing principles of authority, this is not a case of equivalency of power in counterpoise. One side of this dialectic is clearly dominant and the other subordinate. The special sociological characteristic of the first Incas is that they are outsiders. The source of their authority stems from their very foreignness and their aggressiveness. According to the dynastic origin myths of the Inca, they did not originally possess legitimate authority to rule the autochthonous inhabitants of Cuzco; rather, they had to appropriate that authority by force. Further, the Inca kings needed to continually assert and reaffirm their authority by continuing peregrinations through their conquered territory.[2] By definition, the power and de facto legitimacy of the successful usurper is superior to the authority derived from original possession, given that autochthonous groups are dislodged from the source of their authority – the exclusive and exclusionary right to irrigate and cultivate their land.

In some sense, the *zeq'e* system was the Inca solution to integrating these opposing principles of authority into a social and symbolic whole. By encapsulating foreign, non-Inca groups in the *zeq'e* system, the Inca, via collaborative, habitual social and spatial practice, effectively dampened the social contradictions and tensions that arose from their usurpation of authority. That is, the conquered and the conquerors shared an ideology and practice of worship focused on the *zeq'e* shrines of Cuzco and its environs. Encoded in this symbolic landscape of shrines were metaphorical and material referents to both the autochthonous inhabitants of the land who possessed legitimate authority and the foreign kings who, by force of arms, usurped and appropriated legitimate authority. The relationship between and among these groups was a form of hierarchical solidarity mediated by the king in a double sense: instrumentally, through individual acts of social exchange in which marriage partners and rights to land, labor, and water were distributed between the conquerors and their subjects; and spiritually, on behalf of the social totality through royal intercession with the forces of nature.

Thus, Inca royal power in the Andes was constructed through habitual acts of social exchange and through acts of rule that were naturalized in terms of shared politico-religious beliefs. By the late Middle Ages in Europe the concept and legitimacy of royal authority was transferred from liturgical to law-based kingship (Kantorowicz 1981). Among the Inca, such a transition never occurred. Social power was constituted transactionally through intersubjective relations rather than as rules of privilege and behavior codified in legal texts. Inca kingship remained subject oriented and embedded thoroughly in local social contexts and in notions of a shared sacral-liturgical community. Here the principle of royal immortality necessary for a concept of social continuity was not

---

[2] This, of course, is nothing other than the Inca version of Sahlins's (1985) "stranger king."

vested in an abstract legal construct of a king's twin natures, one mortal and the other eternal, as Kantorowicz brilliantly shows for medieval Europe (Cieza de León 1976:57). Instead, kingly immortality among the Inca was literal, a tangible social construct expressed in the king's postmortem inclusion in the social life of the community, in the physical presence of the dead king's mummified body, and in the continuing exertion of political force by these deceased kings through their successor corporate bodies of kindred known in the Inca context as *panaqas*. Recall that the *panaqas* held land in common, perpetuated the memory of their royal founders, and continued to fulfill the acts of social exchange required of their deceased ancestors.

This is not to say that some notion of the twin nature of kingship similar to the formal legal principles that emerged in medieval Europe was necessarily absent in the Andes. Kings do physically die, and heirs take their place, so some kind of distinction between kingly successors and their individual actions must have been made. But the Inca solution to this paradox of the mortality of individual kings counterpoised against the political imperative for the immortality of kingship was to affirm the social participation of kings in the life of the community even after they died. In the social experience of the Inca, neither the king nor kingship ever truly died. The earthly mortality of Inca kings was not experienced as a removal from the social community; nor was the entombment of the king's body and the apotheosis of his memory experienced as an alienation from the community or, for that matter, from the levers of political power. Upon the Inca king's death, his mortal body was multiplied in the corporate body of the *panaqa*.

An expansive concept of kinship on an imperial scale, focusing on and emanating from the king, shaped the political order of the Inca Empire. The deeply embedded cultural principle of sociability expressed and mobilized through an idiom of kinship gave specific form to imperial politics. This kin idiom of sociability revolved around mutual recognition of relatedness (whether biologically or socially constructed), commensalism, gift giving, reciprocal labor services, and marriage exchanges between the king and his subjects. Moreover, the cultural sense of immanence between the quotidian and spiritual worlds inherent in the Inca political theology of kingship, and the religious aspects of royal legitimacy in which subjects shared in an empire-wide community of worship with the king and noble lineages, profoundly shaped the Inca Empire's structures of governance.

As we have seen, the king's delegation of political authority and decision making to human and nonhuman surrogates (the *wawkis*) became a key operative principle of the Inca system of governance. The highest imperial offices, those that required unquestioned loyalty and trust, devolved upon the king's closest blood relatives. Even these close relatives of the king were subject to surveillance to ensure their compliance with the king's wishes and to prevent the emergence of oppositional factions that could threaten the crown. But as the realm expanded rapidly through aggressive military campaigns and strategic alliances, the logistics of empire demanded both expansion and innovation in the administrative infrastructure. The physical capital of empire – roads, bridges, agricultural estates, irrigation works, centralized warehouses, and specialty-built installations such as colonial new towns and military garrisons – depended upon the human and social capital that conceived, organized, executed, and maintained this material infrastructure. Although numerous, the king's blood relatives could not possibly fill all positions of authority, particularly during the late empire as the geopolitical boundaries of the realm expanded across nearly four thousand kilometers of western South America to incorporate some of the most rugged, ecologically complex, and ethnically diverse landscapes in the Western Hemisphere. Not surprisingly, then, a fundamental principle of Inca statecraft in the imperial provinces, reflecting the political pragmatism of the ruling elite, was to confirm the traditional authority of the local political leaders, or *kurakas*, in dealing with their own communities. Cieza de León, among other Spanish commentators intrigued by Inca principles of command, described this phenomenon in his chronicle of Peru: "And they had another device to keep the natives from hating them, and this was that they never divested the natural chieftains of their power. If it so happened that one of them … in some way deserved to be stripped of his power, it was vested in his sons or brothers, and all were ordered to obey them" (Cieza de León 1976:57).

This system of preserving the local mandate of the native elite has been aptly termed indirect rule, though perhaps a more precise term would be delegated rule by local proxy. For an empire that was frenetically expanding and only in the nascent stages of generating formal principles of colonial governance, this system of rule by proxy was simple to implement, relatively efficient, and the least intrusive in altering the daily rhythms and decision-making autonomy of potentially hostile local communities.

The key to the success of delegated rule was the ability to secure the cooperation and at least the overt political loyalty of the local *kurakas*. As we have seen, one strategy for co-opting these local lords was worked out through marriage alliances with the Inca elite that established irrevocable bonds of kinship. The ritualized exchange of daughters as marriage partners between the Inca and the local elite created powerful incentives for the provincial political leaders to "buy into" the Inca system. The highest-ranking ethnic rulers in the provinces also had an obligation to maintain a residence and retainers in Cuzco so that they could attend court functions and account to the Inca king for their stewardship of the villages and towns subject to their authority. This residence requirement, which may have obligated them to live in Cuzco for as much as four months per year, would have had the effect of binding these local ethnic leaders even closer to the cultural influence and political fate of the Inca royal dynasty. Moreover, Inca kings required the eldest sons and potential heirs of provincial elites to reside in Cuzco for a number of years to receive education in the language, history, religious thought, and customs of the Inca. This period of formal cultural and political indoctrination intensified the process of converting local elites with exclusively parochial loyalties into cosmopolitan agents of empire.

The network of real and fictive kinship ties engendered by these alliances provided rich opportunities to local lords for the strategic manipulation of the resulting patron–client relationship. Of course, this strategy of enticing the local *kurakas* into the patronage system by extending the promise of wealth and enhanced social prestige was effective only as long as the *kurakas* were able to deliver the labor and productive capacity of their people. The Inca kings realized this critical linkage and helped the local *kurakas* resolve potential conflict by massive displays of state generosity, "making the people joyful and giving them solemn banquets and drinking feasts, great *taquis*, and other celebrations that they use, completely different from ours, in which the Incas show their splendor, and all the feasting is at their expense" (Cieza de León 1976:191). Like the Romans' policy of bread and circuses, intended to defuse the potentially explosive problem of a malcontent underclass by occasional distribution of free staples and the staging of massive public entertainments, the Inca kings' practice of periodically redistributing warehoused food, drink, and clothing to commoners during state-sponsored festivals served to dissipate social tensions and to incorporate commoners into the new economic and social order of the Inca world. Repeated displays of conspicuous generosity intensified the sense of awe and obligation that subjects felt in the presence of the king or his noble delegates.

At the same time that the Inca governed newly absorbed provinces through practices of indirect rule and delegated authority at multiple hierarchical levels from provincial governors to local headmen, their statesmen began to interject more formal, centralized channels of labor recruitment, resource extraction, and tax assessments based on a decimal system of administration (Julien 1982, 1988). In this system, labor obligations were assessed on an ascending numerical series of tributary households that began with a minimal unit of 10 households (termed *chunka*) and terminated with the maximal unit of 10,000 households (*hunu*). Between these limits, there were decimal groupings for 50 (*pichkachunka*), 100 (*pachaka*), 500 (*pichkapachaka*), 1,000 (*waranqa*), and 5,000 (*pichkawaranqa*) tributary households. An official who, at least at the lower levels of the household groupings, was drawn from the local community headed each decimal unit. Officers of the various decimal units were ranked in a pyramid-like hierarchy. Higher-ranking decimal administrators appointed some officials to their offices, whereas others appear to have inherited their positions. The chain of command and reporting responsibility began with the basal *chunka* leader and proceeded progressively upward to the *hunu* officials. Above the rank of the *hunu* heads of 10,000 households, administrative responsibility was vested in individuals with direct consanguineal or political ties to the royal households of Cuzco. These were the emperor's surrogates, and they served as provincial governors or as members of the imperial council, which included extremely high-ranking representatives from each of the four quarters of the realm.

The Inca periodically took a census to account for fluctuations in the size, residential patterns, and resources of the empire's population. Based on these census figures, they adjusted membership in the decimal groupings of tributary households to reflect changing demographic realities. Service in the military causing extended absences and high mortality rates among adult males, along with the state-directed *mitmaq* forced relocation and colonization scheme, meant that the population dynamics of the empire were extremely fluid. In the late empire, in particular, great numbers of able-bodied men and their families, uprooted from their natal communities, were on the move, so that tracking and managing their movements became a critical technical challenge for state administrators. The decimal system was a logical tool for managing these population flows. Implementation of the decimal organization required development of a comprehensive, standardized, and relatively accurate accounting system. To politically reorganize several million subjects into new, numerically based demographic units, to allocate tribute obligations, and to track the resulting flows of labor and goods demanded a powerful accounting system that could be implemented throughout the empire. The Inca's technical solution to this formidable administrative problem was the accounting device of the *khipu*, the multicolored knotted cords that encoded both binary-based arithmetical data (numbers of human tributaries, quantities of goods) and mnemonic prompts to oral histories, narratives, chants, and songs that included, most notably, panegyrics and eulogies recording the great events in the lives of the Inca kings (Urton 2003). As we have seen, *khipus* were complex, sophisticated devices that required a professional class of accountants (the *khipu kamayuqkuna*), specially trained technicians who could produce, manipulate, read, and interpret the *khipu*. Betanzos provided an extended account of the use of *khipus*, putatively from the reign of Pachakuti, the emperor to whom he attributed the implementation of this accounting system:

> The Inca ordered them [local *kurakas*] to tell him what they had in their lands and what each one could produce. And they were to tell him the truth, for the Inca had given orders to place in each province ... an *orejón* lord born of the people of Cuzco. Each one of them was to respect this lord in their land as if he were the Inca. This lord would know what each one possessed, and if the Inca found out that someone lied to him ... they should understand that the culprit would die. Then the caciques sent for the *quipos*, records that they keep, and also for paintings of what they had and of the type of land and province of each one of them.... Having seen this, the Inca called the important lords of the city whom he had designated to keep track of what these lords and caciques brought in as tribute. And being there he ordered many woolen cords in a variety of colors. Bringing each cacique before him in the presence of those lords of Cuzco and making knots in those cords, he made a record for each one of them of what he was to bring in tribute to the Inca and to the city of Cuzco. He ordered some of them to bring in tribute in maize, others sheep, others garments, others gold and so forth.... The Inca ordered two of each one of these *quipos* and records to be made, one for the cacique to take and another to remain in the possession of the lords. (Betanzos 1996:90–91)

This extraordinary passage indicates that the Inca invented a kind of double-entry bookkeeping technique in which debits (outputs of tribute) on one *khipu* were matched against credits (inputs of tribute to the Inca king's patrimonial household and other state institutions) on another. This double-entry bookkeeping system reduced the chance for fraudulent manipulation by the local lords of tribute obligations. Moreover, Betanzos alluded to a parallel accounting system in the form of paintings that provided an independent, graphical record of provincial resources. Draconian legal practices imposed by the Inca offered a final device for ensuring accuracy in the tribute records: embezzlement, fraud, and deceptive practices by local administrators were punished by death.

As the Inca consolidated their authority in a conquered province, they attempted to gradually streamline the complicated political mosaic of the local lords' claims to power and traditional prerogatives by imposing the decimal system of administration. Tellingly, this system as a technique for imposing and tracking tribute obligations appears to have been implemented in the fifteenth century during the reigns of the last few emperors. Furthermore, decimal organization did not extend throughout the empire. The best evidence we have for its implementation derives from demographically dense, core areas of the empire, such as among the Aymara-speaking populations of the *altiplano*, and in the central Andean highlands (Julien 1982). We have little evidence for the system in the far northern or southern provinces except among *mitmaq* colonists forcibly resettled among local populations (D'Altroy 2002; Salomon 1986). These temporal and spatial patterns strongly imply that the reorganization of the empire's population according to new principles of decimal administration was a strategic innovation in governance implemented by the late Inca kings to deepen their personal control over provincial populations by circumventing traditional political organization and demographic bases of power.

The regrouping of provincial populations in a decimal system of accounting necessarily reconfigured both preexisting ethnic territorial boundaries and the scope of local political authority. Provinces and ethnic groups with more than 10,000 households were subdivided in order to maintain the maximal *hunu* accounting unit. Similarly, provinces and ethnic groups with fewer than 10,000 households were aggregated to form the ideal *hunu* unit. This process of population subdivision and aggregation transformed not simply the local accounting of tribute obligations but also the entire spectrum of local political, social, and territorial concepts and practices. People who previously maintained social and economic relations with a restricted, familiar group of compatriots suddenly found themselves in a transformed social world in which they shared tributary and other social obligations with strangers. Under such transformative circumstances, these new social arrangements would, over a generation or two, have led to different political affiliations, patterns of power, and cultural dispositions.

Similarly, aspirants to political office under the new decimal system of administration no longer gained their positions from traditional sources of authority. Julien (1988:272) observes, for example, that in the northeastern province of Chachapoyas no paramount lord existed prior to Inca rule, but that "during the relatively brief period of Inca rule, five different men were given the highest position in the decimal hierarchy," and "of the five men who were elevated to local prominence by the Inca dynasty, only two had validated claims to local prominence at the time they took office.... [T]hose remaining had ascended to prominence through service to the Inca state." In other words, the system of indirect rule through existing local *kurakas* widely implemented in the earliest phases of empire was gradually being transformed into a system of delegated authority directly bestowed by the Inca kings. Loss of political autonomy most likely proceeded gradually, with each new imposition and innovation in governance resulting in a further erosion of local decision-making authority. Just as importantly, traditional patterns of status, power relations, and social interactions between local populations and their "natural lords" changed, as *kurakas* increasingly came to owe their positions as leaders directly to the authority invested in them by the Inca state and not by their own constituency. The simultaneous indoctrination of the provincial *kurakas'* sons and heirs in Inca language, thought, and cultural practices accelerated this process of transformation by producing a new generation of leaders who owed their authority directly to the Inca king and who came to share the value system of the lords of Cuzco.

As Julien (1988:260) notes regarding the political impact of decimal administration, "[W]hat is really at issue is not just the particular form taken by Inca administration, but whether the Inca imposed a bureaucratic order of their own design, thus reshaping the political organization of the Andes, or simply reoriented existing political organization to meet their own demands." The answer to this question seems to be that the Inca deployed *both* techniques of rule, depending on the spatial (demographically or strategically important regions vs. peripheral or frontier regions) and temporal (early empire vs. late empire) context. One trend, however, seems clear: upon accession to the throne, each new Inca king attempted to consolidate and extend his personal power over subject populations by imposing new techniques of governance that circumvented and subjugated local authorities to the will of the king. New emperors liberally combined force (military repression, political murders, forced migration, and even genocide) and persuasion (the seductive inducements of appointed office, luxury gifts, and the exchange of high-status marriage partners) to achieve their political objectives. The Inca kings' tactics replicate with uncanny precision the recommendations for gaining and holding power expounded in Niccolò Machiavelli's *The Prince*, the cold-blooded "how-to manual" for the would-be rulers of Europe. Inca kings seemed to have had a kind of "military dream of society" that imagined their subjects as "meticulously subordinated cogs of a machine" subject "not to the general will but to automatic docility," even if they never managed to realize that dream before their own subjugation to the forces of Spain (Foucault 1977:169).

Decimal administration had clear benefits for the Inca central government, permitting the state to operate with a relatively homogeneous form of political organization and labor recruitment in a pluralistic social landscape characterized by extreme ethnic, linguistic, and cultural diversity. The advantage to local *kurakas* was not as readily apparent.

With the emergence of what was essentially an imperial class system of favored officials, those *kurakas* who were not designated as decimal officers saw many of their social prerogatives and their traditional access to local labor pools begin to dissolve. The resulting tensions generated by the imposition of the decimal system were substantial, and there are numerous accounts in the chronicles of resentful "natural lords" of the provinces promulgating rebellions against Inca rule at every opportunity. The various coercive techniques applied by the Inca state to repress these rebellions – calculated military violence, garrisoning of provinces, uprooting and resettling populations in alien social settings, replacement of native with central authority – were effective but energetically costly and short-term solutions to the problem of political integration. Coercive mechanisms such as these, when applied indiscriminately, inevitably generate disgust and hostility in volatile subject populations. In effect, these hard-edged instruments of laminar hegemony succeeded in imposing an immediate kind of law and order, but over the long run they generated resentful, seditious subjects who searched for both symbolic and tangible means to subvert Inca rule.

The relationships between the Inca and local populations were complex, fraught with insecurity for both state and local political authorities, and subject to rapid change. In terms of the extraction of surplus labor, the Inca attempted to juggle the "soft" strategy of delegated rule by proxy with more intrusive tactics such as the imposition of the decimal system to reorganize local populations, forced relocation of populations as *mitmaq* colonists, and conversion of politically autonomous populations into the status of *yanakuna*, or permanent retainers of the king and the noble households. The strategic decision or capacity to employ one or the other of these forms of labor extraction depended on the individual political context. If there was a general preference for managing tributary relationships by means of indirect rule, this was a reflection of the difficulty of maintaining strong Inca military presence throughout the widely dispersed provinces of the empire. When the Inca did employ more forceful techniques of command and involve themselves directly in developing massive agricultural reclamation projects that reshaped the physical and social environment of selected regions, this tended to occur in particularly strategic areas, such as in the immediate hinterland of Cuzco or in the fertile, subtropical Cochabamba Valley in Bolivia (Wachtel 1982). Like most premodern states without well-articulated bureaucracies or permanent standing armies, the Inca sought or, perhaps more accurately, were strategically compelled to strike a balance between force and persuasion, violence and consent in the process of constructing their empire.

These reflections on the nature of power, strategies of governance, and administrative techniques raise some final questions. Did the Inca ever seek or achieve true political and cultural integration in their empire? Did they even have the intent of producing a unified Inca nation? John Rowe and María Rostworowski de Diez Canseco, preeminent scholars of the Inca, answer this question in the negative, although in part for different reasons. Rowe claims that the brevity of Inca rule, limited to only three full generations of kings or a maximum of sixty to seventy years, meant "there had not been enough time for much cultural unification to take place, or for a sense of common identity to develop among the peoples subject to the Inca" (Rowe 1982:94). Although Rowe remarks that the dissemination of the Quechua language, along with several Inca institutions such as the *mitmaq, aqlla, kamayuq,* and *yana* labor statuses that made large numbers of subjects directly dependent upon the Inca for their well-being, should have promoted a degree of social identity with the Inca, he nevertheless concludes that "cultural unification was probably not a primary goal of the Inca government." Rowe decides that he is "inclined to agree with Bernabé Cobo, who said of the Inca in 1653, 'The whole foundation of their policy of government rested on means designed to keep their people subject and deprive them of the zeal to revolt against them'" (Rowe 1982:94). Ultimately, Rowe suggests that rather than ideological persuasion or the development of social institutions designed to promote identification with the Inca, tactics of force dominated Cuzco's imperial policies.

Rostworowski extends this line of reasoning even further, going so far as to reject using the word "empire" for the Inca altogether. She prefers to refer to the Inca polity simply by the Quechua term *Tawantinsuyu,* "the four quarters joined" (Rostworowski 1999). Rostworowski believes that Western concepts of empire simply do not accurately characterize the Inca political order. She asserts that enduring parochial affinities to land, local natural resources, shrines, and deities defined the everyday social life of individuals and ethnic groups conquered by the Inca. In her view, subjugated populations never participated in a broader social world created by the dissemination of widely distributed cultural values and practices. Rather, Rostworowski believes that the Inca state established primarily economic and tributary relations with their subjects, neither intending to promote among them nor achieving a sense of shared identity and belonging to an emergent Inca nation. Subject populations never succumbed to the ideological persuasions of Inca culture; they remained firmly embedded in the bedrock of their highly local cultural and religious beliefs and practices. Rostworowski even argues that the Inca state's policy of requiring subject populations to adopt the "common language" of Quechua was motivated by nothing more than a pragmatic desire to facilitate economic transactions. She characterizes Inca-directed dissemination of Quechua as a matter of linguistic convenience in order to propagate a trade tongue designed to smooth economic relations with diverse populations speaking many mutually unintelligible languages. In this view, adoption of the Quechua language by subject populations had no substantive effect on their modes of perception, their social status, or their local value systems. Inca ways of knowing and behaving in the world never penetrated deeply into local beliefs and practices.

In other words, neither Rowe nor Rostworowski believe that the Inca created what I have called a viral hegemony, a political and social order with the power to change their subjects' historical consciousness and sense of subjectivity. For Rowe, the Inca simply had insufficient time to produce political and cultural unification among the diverse ethnic groups that they had placed under their dominion before their own violent conquest by the Spanish. In his interpretation, they were an incompletely consolidated empire. But for Rostworowski, the Inca never created an empire at all. They confined themselves to managing the extraction of economic surplus by means of military force and the strategic extension of relations of economic reciprocity with local chieftains. For Rostworowski, the Inca state was fundamentally organized as a political instrument of economic extraction, a kind of plunder state designed to enrich the Inca elite at the expense of subject populations. Under such conditions, local ethnic lords were subordinated to the yoke of the Inca kings and increasingly impoverished relative to their former status as autonomous rulers. She maintains, therefore, that the local lords would have had little incentive to promote identification with the Inca state (Rostworowski 1999:226). As she states explicitly: "[T]he Inca state did not create feelings of solidarity among the macroethnic groups, nor did it integrate the populations of the Inca realm, owing to the persistence of local and regionalist loyalties," and "the inhabitants of the Inca state were not shaped into a single national identity. Rather, the Inca limited themselves to the recognition and exploitation of the human and territorial resources under the control of the ethnic lords" (Rostworowski 1999:181, 225).

I believe that this interpretation of the Inca political achievement is, at best, only partially accurate. Although, as Rowe aptly observed, the Inca Empire had insufficient time to create a fully realized "national identity," Inca kings clearly did deploy strategic political, administrative, and cultural instruments designed to transform their subjects' historical consciousness, to convince them by ideological persuasion and, if necessary, violent political tactics that they were subjects of an overarching social world dominated by the Inca. The Inca created several new categories of subjects, the *aqllakuna, mitmaqkuna, yanakuna,* and *kamayuqkuna,* who were directly dependent for their social identity, political status, and economic well-being on the Inca elite, and not on their affiliation with a particular ethnic group. The numbers of people in these specialized labor and identity categories grew dramatically over time and space as the empire expanded. Inca kings assiduously promoted marriage alliances, at both elite and subelite levels, intended to develop new social ties across ethnic, linguistic, and provincial boundaries. In a real sense, children from these arranged marriages owed their biological and social existence to the Inca, constituting a kind of natural constituency of the empire. The Inca trained the sons and daughters of subject ethnic lords in the customs, beliefs, practices, and language of the court in Cuzco. They sponsored religious festivals and sacrifices, such as the Citua, the planting and harvest ceremonies, and the *qhapaq ucha,* that were celebrated simultaneously throughout the empire, and they promoted state cults associated with Inca deities that subordinated, although they did not entirely replace, local expressions of religious sentiment. The Inca state took censuses, reorganized populations into distinct new communities of taxation, redistributed nonlocal resources, built regional infrastructure to stimulate agricultural production and facilitate trade, mediated political disputes, and punished reprobates. Hundreds of thousands of families, constituting upwards of 30 percent of the empire's entire population, were uprooted from their natal communities and resettled in distant lands among other ethnic groups (D'Altroy 2002). Under Inca rule, many indigenous populations left their homelands by force or persuasion for new economic opportunities that, in the end, served the state's interests. All of these policies clearly represented vigorous attempts at nation building designed to diminish the intensity of local and regional affiliations and enhance loyalties to the state. That is, the Inca implemented central governmental policies and practices intended to produce both subjects and citizens.

Yet the extent to which this audacious attempt at nation building was successful can be questioned. We know that the cultural unification of the empire at the time of the Inca encounter with the forces of Spain in the mid-sixteenth century was incomplete. The devastating, internecine warfare between Atawallpa and Waskhar, the royal half-siblings who violently competed for the throne left vacated by the untimely death of King Wayna Qhapaq, depopulated large swaths of territory and left entire provinces ungovernable over the years just prior to the Incas' fateful encounter with the Spanish invaders. This bitter personal rivalry and a deep anxiety regarding whom to back in the kingly competition left the Inca nobility deeply divided. Elite *panaqas* jockeyed for power, for influence, and for their lives as the rivalry of the half-brothers over the throne reached unprecedented levels of violence, including the eradication of entire noble families. These enormously unsettled conditions of military competition, fratricide, and the ruthless liquidation of royal lineages placed the nation-building process in abeyance. The political question of the moment was not how to consolidate the nation, but who would succeed to the throne and under what conditions. All else remained uncertain and in flux until the succession was completed. But, precisely at this moment of violent internecine competition and imperial instability, the forces of Spain erupted on the scene and changed the political equation forever.

7   The Destruction of the Inca

In the year 1524, Wayna Qhapaq reigned as the unquestioned, if not unchallenged, emperor of the largest political entity ever created by native Americans. His empire extended over an enormous, ecologically varied landscape of desert coasts, mountain valleys, high plains, and tropical jungles. The population subject to his rule was no less vast or diverse: in that year, his empire incorporated at least eighty distinct provinces populated by no fewer than six million subjects speaking more than two hundred languages and distinct dialects (Figure 7.1). Wayna Qhapaq was the heir of two aggressive warlords, Pachakuti and Thupa Inka Yupanki, who, by force of arms and unparalleled diplomatic skill, had forged an indigenous empire unlike any other in the Western Hemisphere. Their unremitting success in war and diplomacy made them seem invulnerable, transforming them into charismatic divine kings – direct descendants of gods, feared, loved, worshipped, and obeyed by their subjects. During their reigns, unimaginable wealth generated by plunder, tribute, and taxation flowed back in a continual stream to Cuzco, converting the political and religious capital of the empire into a glittering urban theater for the performance of royal power. With the mandate of heaven and literally untold wealth at their command, who could contest the authority of these kings?

Yet, by 1524, the Inca Empire had reached such an unprecedented continental scale that the logistics of rule became increasingly untenable. Despite sophisticated administrative instruments such as decimal organization, extensive road networks, rapid communication systems, accurate accounting systems, and strategic storage facilities, the Inca Empire was seriously overextended, having been created in only three generations and expanded rapidly over 4,000 kilometers from Colombia to Chile.[1] Through personal ambition for power, wealth, and renown,

---

[1] Several chroniclers claim that in response to the political difficulties of implementing rule over such a great expanse, Wayna Qhapaq decided to split the empire into two parts, north and south, with the former centered in Quito and the latter at the traditional

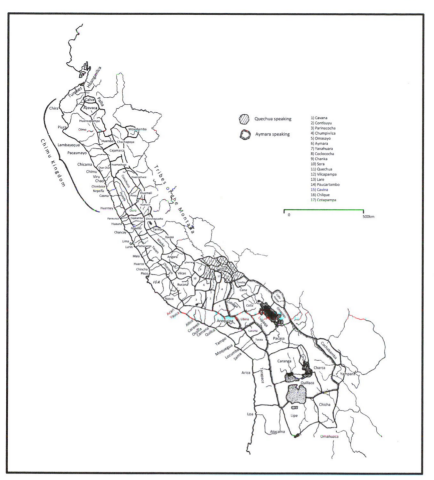

7.1. Tawantinsuyu was a highly diverse empire that incorporated more than eighty distinct ethnic groups. (Image from Rowe 1946)

and an intense desire for immortality in the memory of their kin and compatriots, Pachakuti, Thupa Yupanki, and Wayna Qhapaq drove relentlessly to expand the Realm of the Four Quarters. Their success is a testament to their ruthlessness and to the extraordinary efficacy of their charismatic leadership. But charisma demands constant renewal through the presence of the ruler among the ruled. The Inca system of

capital of Cuzco. He may have also been influenced by his personal preference for residing in the northern, Ecuadorian provinces of his birth.

delegated authority deployed through multiple "bodies double" of the king, both close kin and *wawki* avatars, could only serve as a partial, temporary substitute for the presence of the king himself. Not surprisingly, then, Wayna Qhapaq spent much of his long reign on the road,[2] accompanied by his royal entourage of warriors, women, and *yanakuna*. He became the archetype of an itinerant king, on a never-ending circuit of conducting royal visits to his far-flung provinces, sponsoring public festivals, distributing gifts and endowments, appointing and disciplining local *kurakas*, consolidating the administration of the realm, quelling ever more frequent rebellions by restive subjects seeking to recapture lost autonomy, and extending the territory of the empire in a series of protracted, though not entirely successful, military campaigns. Upon consolidating his political position in Cuzco after a contentious struggle for succession, Wayna Qhapaq was rarely resident in the capital, spending years at a time in distant provinces attempting to impose his will. But his extended absences from Cuzco posed considerable political risk. The *panaqas*, the royal *ayllus* of Wayna Qhapaq's illustrious dead ancestors who commanded their own estates and independent sources of wealth, constituted alternative and potentially deeply threatening bases of power. To retain his authority, the king was forced to pay close attention to the aspirations, internecine disputes, and machinations of these leading subjects of the realm. Ferocious competition for personal power and deepening factionalism among the ever-expanding nobility strained the fabric of ethnic solidarity upon which the Inca depended for their preeminent political strength. At the same time, on repeated occasions, Wayna Qhapaq was forced to fight costly rearguard actions against rebellious ethnic groups, particularly among the Aymara-speaking polities of the Lake Titicaca basin, and the fiercely independent chiefdoms and petty kingdoms of the Ecuadorian highlands and *selva* regions. Wayna Qhapaq's perpetual military campaigns of reprisal and conquest consumed enormous resources and disrupted the daily lives of countless people conscripted into the Inca armies, required to pay accelerating tribute levies to fund the wars, or forcibly removed from their ethnic homelands and resettled in distant provinces as *mitmaqkuna*. Beneath the glittering surface of imperial splendor, these deep, underlying tensions contributed to a sense of latent instability, a structural condition of political fragility in which an unanticipated event could become a catalyst for catastrophe.

---

[2] Sarmiento (1999:169) claims Wayna Qhapaq ruled for sixty years, ascending to the throne when he was twenty years old.

As fate would have it, that catalyst appeared just over the northern horizon of the Inca Empire in the same year that Wayna Qhapaq was campaigning ferociously in southern Colombia and the Ecuadorian highlands. On November 14, 1524, Francisco Pizarro, a Spanish soldier and well-heeled citizen of the recently established colonial town of Panama, embarked on his first exploratory expedition along the Pacific coast of northwestern South America. During Pizarro's initial foray in search of fame and wealth, his navigator, Bartolomé Ruiz, sailing in the coastal waters off Ecuador ahead of the main military party, commandeered a large ocean-going raft laden with luxury commodities destined for trade. A report of this maritime encounter authored by Francisco de Xerez reveals the potential for vast treasure held by indigenous inhabitants of lands not yet explored by Europeans:

They were carrying many pieces of silver and gold as personal ornaments ... including crown and diadems, belts and bracelets, armour for the legs and breastplates; tweezers and rattles and strings and clusters of beads and rubies; mirrors decorated with silver, and cups and other drinking vessels. They were carrying many wool and cotton mantle and Moorish tunics ... and other pieces of clothing coloured with cochineal, crimson, blue, yellow and all other colors with different types of ornate embroidery, in figures of birds, animals, fish and trees. They had some tiny weights to weigh gold.... There were small stones in bead bags: emeralds and chalcedonies and other jewels and pieces of crystal....They were taking all this to trade for fish shells ... coral-coloured scarlet and white [*Spondylus* shells that were a sign of royalty and an object essential for religious practice throughout the Andes]. (Cited in Hemming 1970:25)

Twenty native crew members manning the raft were killed or captured in this first clash between civilizations in the seas south of the equator. These initial discoveries of jewels, gold, silver, and other luxury goods excited the imagination of Pizarro, who subsequently returned to Spain to raise capital, recruit men, and gain authorization from the Spanish Crown to conquer the new lands that were the source of this treasure.

While Pizarro mobilized resources in Spain for future campaigns that would eventually culminate in an epochal encounter with the Inca some seven years later, the first, and perhaps most devastating weapon of conquest had already been unleashed in the Andes. At some point between 1525 and 1528 a virus, most likely smallpox or measles, or a combination of the two, began to devastate indigenous populations that had no biological immunity to these foreign diseases. European-borne viruses had already infected natives throughout the Caribbean islands, contributing to massive rates of mortality (Figure 7.2). Exposure to these new viruses left the natives profoundly debilitated and vulnerable to a host of grave

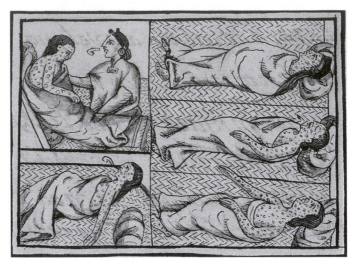

7.2. Aztec smallpox victims portrayed in the Florentine Codex. Throughout the New World, indigenous Americans were decimated by European-brought diseases. (Image © Biblioteca Nazionale Centrale Firenza, Med. Palat. 200, C.460v)

medical complications that included hemorrhagic diarrhea, pneumonia, encephalitis, and corneal scarring leading to blindness. Most natives who contracted the initial wave of viruses weakened and died with terrifying rapidity. Although he had never laid eyes on the Europeans cautiously exploring his Pacific coastal domains, Wayna Qhapaq contracted the virus they had brought to his shores, and, together with many members of his royal court, died of hemorraghic fever in Tumipampa, Ecuador, the place of his birth. His death occurred some five years before Pizarro returned to begin the long-planned conquest of the Inca Empire.

On his deathbed, Wayna Qhapaq designated his son Ninan Kuyuchi as principal heir and successor to the throne. But the officials carrying the news of his selection to the emperor-designate arrived too late: Prince Ninan Kuyuchi had just succumbed to the same epidemic. Before the royal delegation returned to the court with these ill tidings, Wayna Qhapaq was dead. In one swift stroke, the Inca Empire had been decapitated, and the royal succession cast into a state of uncertainty. Even before they began their conquest of the Inca, the Spanish had acquired an invisible, inexorable, and lethal ally. As Wayna Qhapaq's mummy bundle was solemnly borne in a royal litter back to Cuzco for the prescribed mortuary rites, the epidemic continued to rage through the empire, reaching Cuzco well before the dead emperor and his retinue.

These events set in train a devastating civil war that pitted two sons of Wayna Qhapaq, the royal half-brothers Atawallpa and Waskhar, against each other for control of the empire. Before the death of his father, Atawallpa (Figure 7.3) had been in the north for many years campaigning with the battle-hardened veterans of Wayna Qhapaq's armies, including four highly experienced field generals, Challcochima, Quizquiz, Rumiñawi, and Ucumari. Waskhar, in contrast, remained in his luxurious residences in Cuzco, gradually accumulating, in equal measure, political influence and enmity among the nobles and royal *panaqas*. Upon Wayna Qhapaq's death, Waskhar was elected as the new emperor, partially because of the astute political machinations of his mother, Rawa Oqllu. Atawallpa appeared at first to accede to this election, sending gifts from his base in Quito to acknowledge his subordinate position as Waskhar's vassal. But Waskhar remained suspicious of Atawallpa's intentions. When the funeral cortege of the dead emperor neared Cuzco accompanied by high-ranking nobles who had loyally served Wayna Qhapaq during his bitterly contested northern campaigns, Waskhar erupted in fury that they had not brought Atawallpa with them. Like Inca kings before him, Waskhar clearly intended to murder his half-brother and massacre his closest companions to eliminate any potential competitors for the throne. Without Atawallpa in his grasp, Waskhar turned his fury on the nobles accompanying Wayna Qhapaq on his final journey from Quito to Cuzco. Waskhar had them tortured in a fruitless search for military intelligence on Atawallpa's ulterior motives; learning nothing useful, he had some summarily executed and others exiled as *mitmaqkuna* (Betanzos 1996:194). Waskhar's murderous reprisals against high-ranking members of the nobility, many of whom were affiliated with Hanan Cuzco, Atawallpa's and Waskhar's own moiety of birth, generated fear and disgust among Cuzco's elite classes. Waskhar even "commanded that no one consider him a member of the group of Hanan Cuzco, because Atahualpa was of Hanan Cuzco, descended from the lineage of Inca Yupanque, and he no longer wished to be of that lineage.... Henceforth he wished them [the Inca nobility] to recognize him as from Hurin Cuzco because he intended to kill Atahualpa and all his kinsmen and lineage that was of Hanan Cuzco and form a new lineage of Hurin Cuzco" (Betanzos 1996:194). Betanzos relates that in his brief tenure as the Sapa Inca, Waskhar publicly declared his intention to confiscate the properties of the religious foundations and *panaqas* of his royal predecessors: "When he became lord, he went out into the square and declared that henceforth the lands of coca and maize production that had been owned by the Sun and the bodies of the dead rulers, including those of his father, Huayna Capac, would be taken from them. All these he took

ATAHUALLPA. INCA XIIII.

7.3. Portrait of Atawallpa. (Image ©Bildarchiv Preussischer Kulturbesitz/Art Resource, NY-Ethnologisches Museum Staatliche Museen, Germany. Anonymous, 16th-century portrait of Atawallpa)

for himself, saying that neither the Sun nor the dead nor his father who was now dead ate. Since they did not eat, he had need of their lands. This action horrified the lords. And they were saddened because they had permitted him to become lord" (Betanzos 1996:189). By threatening to appropriate the estates of state institutions and *panaqas*, Waskhar was also undermining the religious rationale justifying their functionaries' privileged existence. If the royal mummies curated by the living members of their *panaqa* "no longer ate," this meant that they were incapable of the reciprocal sociality required for membership in the Inca social and political community. Like the *wak'as* purposely destroyed by Inca kings, Waskhar's claims were intended to decommission the royal mummies and their economic and political influence in the community of the living. Waskhar's threats were considered by the Inca nobility to be unprecedented assaults on their economic well-being, as well as a form of religious heresy. Of course, Betanzos's informants were close kin to Atawallpa, and his detailed portrayal of Waskhar's paranoid and vice-ridden personality may seem merely tendentious, reflecting their familial biases. But other sources confirm Waskhar's aggressive attitude toward the Cuzco-based *panaqas* that had initially supported his election (Sarmiento 1999:171) – the testimony of multiple sources implies that Betanzos's account reflects more than strategic rewriting of history from the perspective of self-interested parties. Waskhar's violation of traditional Andean principles of royal power that required personal charisma, religious piety, and conspicuous generosity earned him the deep hatred of a considerable number of the noble houses in Cuzco.

While Waskhar struggled to consolidate his political power in Cuzco, Atawallpa remained in the distant north at his base in Quito and Tumipampa surrounded by his father's powerful army and experienced officer corps. Waskhar's contemptuous rejection of Atawallpa's gifts along with the humiliation and execution of his emissaries precipitated the civil war between the two brothers that devastated the Inca Empire over a period of nearly four years. Waskhar fielded a series of armies in an attempt to capture and defeat Atawallpa. But by all accounts his forces were repeatedly defeated and his field generals either executed or convinced to transfer their loyalty to Atawallpa. The almost preternatural consistency with which Waskhar forces lost battle after battle, even when he had superior numbers on his side, suggests that he did not command the unquestioned loyalty of his followers. Waskhar clearly lacked the personal charisma necessary for effective leadership in the highly factionalized political world of the Inca elite. The course of the war turned decidedly against Waskhar and the dwindling forces from Cuzco that he still commanded. As his armies retreated before Atawallpa's onslaught, Waskhar became increasingly desperate to avoid the fate that awaited him if he were to lose the war to his brother. He consulted oracles and offered sacrifices at the most prominent *wak'as* of the empire, all to no avail. In the end, Waskhar was forced to take personal command of his army as the battles raged ever closer to Cuzco. Waskhar's final attempt to recoup his stunning losses of men and materiel failed. Atawallpa's forces closed in. Through a battlefield ambuscade, General Challcochima tracked Waskhar down on the field of battle, cast him from his litter, and captured him alive. Waskhar was stripped of his magnificent tunic, gold armor, and weapons. His royal standards and the portable *wak'as* carried into battle with him were confiscated so that Atawallpa would "have the honor, as their lord, of treading upon the things and ensigns of enemies who had been subjected" (Betanzos 1996:227). Waskhar was imprisoned in a cage for transport to the Inca town of Cajamarca where

Atawallpa was bivouacked. We can only imagine the festival of pain that Atawallpa was preparing for his vanquished brother.

In the meantime, Atawallpa sent a relative and close confidante, Cusi Yupanki, to Cuzco with instructions to exact retribution on Waskhar's kindred and allies. The terrifying brutality and scope of Atawallpa's revenge underscores the extent to which Inca power politics was not a game for the faint of heart: parricide, fratricide, sororicide, regicide were all common coin of the realm. Atawallpa ordered Cusi Yupanki to

[a]ssemble all of the sons and daughters of my father, Huayna Capac. You must punish and kill all the males you find who know how to use a sling. They were the ones who were there in Cuzco before Huascar brandishing their weapons, saying "Let the *auca* Atahualpa die," and said to Huascar "You are the only lord." Kill them and all those nobles captured in Cuzco. Pay no heed that they are my brothers.... You should also assemble all of the daughters of my father, Huayna Capac. Find all the maidens and send then under strong guard to me. All the others who have known a man, order them killed. Pay no heed that they are my sisters because you should know that ... Huascar has had them as wives, sleeping with him, and in his bed.... With Huascar, they would have called me *auca* and would have approved of the war. Kill all his sons and daughters, making the punishment widely known. (Betanzos 1996:233)

Following these terrible orders to the letter, Cusi Yupanki gathered all of Waskhar's kinsmen, wives, mistresses, and allies together to hear the charges against them and to learn their punishment. He then ordered Waskhar's wives and mistresses to be separated and "commanded that those who were pregnant have their babies torn alive from the womb," and then these along with all of Waskhar's remaining daughters and female relatives were crucified on stakes arrayed along the royal road to Collasuyu, "and the babies taken from their wombs were attached to the hands, arms, and feet of their mothers, who were already hanging on the stakes." The remaining nobles allied with Waskhar were tortured by public whipping and then killed "by smashing their heads to pieces with battle-axes." Additionally, "a great number of the sons and daughters of Huayna Capac were killed, as were all the rest of the main lords of Cuzco and all the children and wives of Huascar. Upon the death of these lords and ladies, Cuxi Yupanque ordered that their flesh and bodies be thrown out, where they would be eaten by birds and foxes" (Betanzos 1996:244).

After this root-and-branch slaughter of Waskhar's lineage and political allies, Cusi Yupanki announced to the surviving nobility that Atawallpa, the new Sapa Inca, had decided to purge Cuzco itself, to displace its accumulated religious and political mystique, and to build his own imperial capital *de novo*. He ordered that the surviving population of the city, along with all the natives living within a ninety-mile circumference of the capital, be taken to Quito "where the new Cuzco will be created" (Betanzos 1996:245). Under protest, but with the memory of Atawallpa's blood-soaked vengeance fresh in their minds, the local *kurakas* began to assemble the resources necessary for their relocation far to the north. So ended the civil war between the two brothers. Just a few years prior, the Inca Empire had been politically unified under the sovereignty of Wayna Qhapaq; now the Realm of the Four Quarters was left in disarray, waiting to see how the new Sapa Inca would refashion the world. The year was 1532.

The dramatic story of Francisco Pizarro's invasion and lightning-fast conquest of the Inca Empire has been often told (Figure 7.4).[3] With considerable justification, the conventional narratives attribute the collapse of Inca authority to the audacity, military acumen, fearlessness, personal toughness, and ferocity of Pizarro and the 168 kinsmen and companions who accompanied him in the conquest of Peru. Yet when Pizarro returned from Spain with the necessary resources and the royal charter to continue his exploration of the Pacific coast, the Inca Empire was not the same as it had been just four years before. Beginning his epochal journey to Cajamarca and his ultimately fateful encounter with Atawallpa, Pizarro's troops witnessed the devastation of the civil war as they passed through the desert coastal and inland settlements that had supported Waskhar in the war. They discovered burned and demolished buildings and whole towns entirely depopulated. In the town of Cajas, Captain Hernando de Soto witnessed "considerable ruin from the fighting that Atahualpa had waged. In the hills were the bodies of many Indians hanging from trees because they had not agreed to surrender: for all these villages were originally under Cuzco [Waskhar], whom they acknowledged as master and to whom they paid tribute" (cited in Hemming 1970:30). Marching to Cajamarca through the treacherous mountain passes might have been a more daunting task for the Spaniards if Atawallpa had not been, precisely at that moment, deeply preoccupied with completing the destruction of Waskhar's faction, eradicating potential traitors, and planning the reorganization of the newly unsettled empire. Pizarro and Atawallpa were aware of each other's presence through a range of intermediaries, diplomatic overtures, and surreptitious intelligence, but each remained uncertain of the other's intentions. This uncertainty played into Pizarro's hands. For a time, Atawallpa evidently considered the possibility that these foreign beings who had

---

[3] See, for instance, William Prescott's magisterial, two-volume *History of the Conquest of Peru* (1874), and John Hemming's definitive *The Conquest of the Inca* (1970).

D.FRAN. PIZAR CONQUIS D. PERU.

7.4. Portrait of Francisco Pizarro. (Image ©Bildarchiv Preussischer Kulturbesitz/Art Resource, NY-Ethnologisches Museum Staatliche Museen, Germany. Anonymous, 19th-century portrait of Pizarro)

erupted into his domain were emissaries of the gods, or perhaps even gods themselves, returning to aid him in reconstituting the empire. The coastal populations evoked the name of Viracocha in referring to these strangers so clearly different from themselves. Yet when an emissary-spy from the court of Atawallpa reported his observations that the Spaniards were obviously men of flesh and blood with the same needs and desires as other mortals, and advised the king to destroy them immediately since they were despoiling the goods and women of his subjects with impunity, Atawallpa hesitated. We do not know why Atawallpa was so irresolute. He had decisively seized power from his enemies with a ferocity that more than matched that of the Spaniards, and, of course, he had a large, disciplined army at his command. The Spanish themselves were puzzled and undoubtedly relieved that Atawallpa took no military action against them as they ascended the narrow, rock-strewn, vertiginous

landscape between the coast and Cajamarca. Hernando Pizarro recol-
lected, "The road was so bad that they could very easily have taken us
there or at another pass which we found between here and Cajamarca.
For we could not use the horses on the road, not even with skill, and
off the roads we could take neither horses nor foot-soldiers" (cited in
Hemming 1970:31).

Atawallpa's indecisiveness may have resulted from a paradoxical combination of fear and overweening pride. He had just completed an epic
victory over Washkar's forces with almost uncanny ease. Who could
argue with Atawallpa's supreme self-confidence and haughty demeanor?
He had proved himself a charismatic, divine king who could treat his
subordinates, even the most highly ranked nobles, as lesser beings,
required to cast their eyes down and bear a token burden on their backs
before entering his presence. Why, then, should he fear a small number of beings on the margins of his empire, even if they were unlike
any others that he had experienced and possessed strange mechanical
instruments and animals never before seen? At the same time, Atawallpa
believed that natural forces circulating through the human world presented considerable risk, and that omens and oracles could influence
one's life for better or worse. At first, Atawallpa must have held back
his military forces wondering if the Spanish were a new form of *wak'a*,
odd, unusual animate beings that he could only make legible through
his deeply ingrained beliefs regarding the supernatural world. Later, his
curiosity and his arrogance contributed substantially to his undoing.
Whatever his psychological motivations, Atawallpa allowed the Spanish
to move unmolested from the coast to Cajamarca where they arrived on
Friday, November 15. Atawallpa had scarcely one more day of freedom
to enjoy his victory and his unquestioned stature as a god-king.

For his part, Pizarro had learned of the Inca's deadly internecine war
that had just reached a definitive conclusion. He witnessed some of the
baleful aftermath of the empire's self-destruction before his own eyes.
Pizarro knew, then, that his plan of conquest would involve manipulating
bitter political divisions to his benefit. But he also grasped the extraordinary obedience and fear that many of Atawallpa's subjects expressed
in their relationships with the Inca king, observing local *kurakas* literally
jump to attention in the presence of Inca authorities acting as delegates
of the god-king. He realized that authority and rule in the empire ultimately emanated from one source, the Sapa Inca, and reasoned that if
that source were seized, so too was control over the empire. In this, he
was no tactical innovator. Pizarro first arrived in the Indies in 1502. By
the time he embarked on his conquest of Peru he was already in his
mid-fifties with a generation of experience observing and living among

native populations. He was fully aware of the military tactics pursued by Spanish conquistadors in the Caribbean, and especially Mexico, where the redoubtable Hernán Cortés had faced similar, daunting odds and achieved his stunning conquest of the Aztecs by audaciously seizing and subsequently executing their king, Moctezuma II. Pizarro enjoyed the considerable advantage over Atawallpa of inside knowledge, even if this was based on analogy to an Indian civilization that had succumbed to the Spanish nearly fifteen years before. For all Pizarro knew, the Inca may have been more accomplished warriors than the Aztecs, and the clear technological superiority of the Spanish, equipped with horses, dogs of war, cannon, crossbows, armor, and steel swords, may not have been sufficient to equalize the demographic advantages presented by Atawallpa's huge and well-seasoned armies. So, as the Spanish ascended the western slopes of the Andes through the desolate landscape of war, observing ghastly battlefield casualties hung from trees, they, too, must have had doubts about their future and their fate. Yet, unlike Atawallpa, Pizarro did know precisely what he intended to do from the very beginning: conquer the Inca and gain even more renown and treasure than that enjoyed by his compatriots who had become Lords of Mexico.

Pizarro and Atawallpa abundantly shared one trait: hubris. But on November 16, 1532, in the principal plaza of Cajamarca, the reckless self-confidence that comes from overweening pride served only one master, and reduced the other to ruin. On that day, Atawallpa deigned to proceed to Cajamarca to meet Pizarro, but not before finishing the celebration of a *taki* together with his kinsmen and allies commemorating his victory over Waskhar. Like all such Inca celebrations, reciprocal toasts and serious drinking went on through the night. The haze of divine drunkenness must have still enveloped Atawallpa as he ascended his litter to be borne into Cajamarca surrounded by his splendid retinue of nobles, bodyguards, warriors, and women. Atawallpa came to Cajamarca not as a battle-hardened warrior, but as a god-king in a state procession that displayed his full magnificence. Pedro Pizarro described the royal spectacle in laconic but revelatory terms: "All the Indians wore large gold and silver discs like crowns on their heads. They were apparently all coming in their ceremonial clothes. In front was a squadron of Indians wearing a livery of chequered colours, like a chessboard. As these advanced they removed the straws from the ground and swept the roadway. They pointed their arms toward the ground to clear anything that was on it.... They were singing a song by no means lacking in grace." Atawallpa proceeded into the plaza with "five or six thousand men, unarmed except that they carried small battle-axes, slings and pouches of stones underneath their tunics." Atawallpa followed behind the vanguard of richly attired though lightly armed warriors riding in "a very fine litter with the ends of its timbers covered in silver.... Eighty lords carried him on their shoulders, all wearing a very rich blue livery.[4] ... His own person was very richly dressed, with his crown on his head and a collar of large emeralds around his neck.... The litter was lined with parrot feathers of many colours and embellished with plates of gold and silver.... Behind it came two other litters and two hammocks in which other leading personages travelled. Then came many men in squadrons with headdresses of gold and silver" (cited in Hemming 1970:38–39).

Atawallpa clearly expected to dominate the alien intruders through the bewildering spectacle of his own majesty. He intended a public demonstration of his personal superiority, of his divinity. A divine king knows no limits, admits no faults, displays no weaknesses. Only the Spanish did not believe in Atawallpa's divinity. They saw, instead, opportunity in the vanity of the Inca king. Pizarro seized the moment. He had concealed his cavalry and foot soldiers in the long, narrow buildings that lined three sides of the plaza and placed his small artillery within the stone *usnu* complex in the center. After Atawallpa arrived with his glittering retinue in the plaza, a Dominican friar, Vicente de Valverde, emerged, missal in hand, accompanied by a young interpreter attached to the forces of Pizarro (Figure 7.5). Valverde engaged Atawallpa with an explanation of the superiority of the Christian faith and declaimed a version of the *Requerimiento*, a formal demand that the Inca submit to the sovereignty of the king of Spain and accept the presence of Christian missionaries to teach the articles of the faith. According to the logic of the *Requerimiento*, if Atawallpa refused to accept these demands, the Spanish were legally authorized to use lethal force against the natives, to kill or enslave them, and to confiscate all of their worldly goods. For a time, reading the *Requerimiento* to an uncomprehending or even absent audience (the tract was often read offshore from the decks of ships, on desolate beaches, or to empty villages) provided the Spanish conquistadors with legal and moral cover for their violent subjugation of native populations in the Americas, until the inherent hypocrisy of the exercise appalled even the most cynical minds of the Spanish court and its use was abolished in 1556. But, in the early evening of November 16, 1532, Pizarro had all of the justification he needed for the premeditated slaughter that he had prepared. When Atawallpa contemptuously threw Valverde's missal to the ground and rose up in his litter to finally confront the Spanish, Pizarro and his men erupted into the packed plaza

---

[4] Indigo, which became a precious commodity for the Spanish colony.

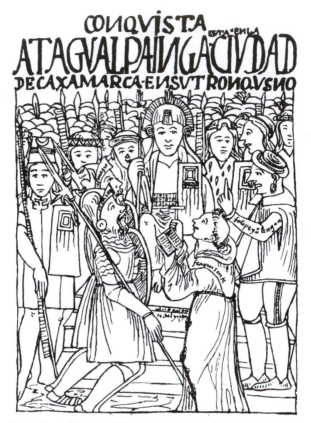

7.5. Atawallpa and Pizarro meet in the central plaza of Cajamarca, accompanied by an indigenous interpreter and a Spanish priest. (Adapted from Guaman Poma de Ayala 1615)

on their stallions of war and brandishing steel swords that could slice through any native armor with devastating result. Pizarro's men discharged the small artillery and arquebuses from their hiding place in the *usnu* to add to the terror of Atawallpa's assembled warriors, who were clearly unprepared for this sudden, vicious assault. The Spanish soldiers gave no quarter: they had no intention of capturing any Inca warrior alive, except for one – the reigning Sapa Inca. Pizarro himself moved single-mindedly to seize Atawallpa, who remained standing in his litter in the midst of the chaos. Pizarro's men slashed through the masses of nobles surrounding Atawallpa, cutting off the hands of the litter bearers who desperately surged in wave after wave to sustain the god-king aloft on his portable throne. Despite their self-sacrifice, they failed in the effort when several mounted Spaniards wrenched the litter onto its side, hurling Atawallpa to the ground.

Eyewitness accounts of the ensuing massacre reveal the terrible incomprehension of Atawallpa concerning the kind of enemy he faced. With trumpets blaring, artillery reverberating, armored warhorses studded with clanging rattles, and the conquistadors shouting their holy battle cry to Saint James, the Incas' initial shock at the assault was quickly overwhelmed by visceral fear. Any military discipline the Inca may have had on an open battlefield dissolved in an instant into sheer panic as their warriors, close-packed in the plaza and lightly armed, became like cattle put to slaughter. Their fear was so great they broke down an enclosure wall in a desperate attempt to flee the charging Spanish, who continued to lance natives in the surrounding fields into nightfall. Clad in protective chainmail, the mounted Spanish relentlessly pressed their advantage. Within the space of two hours, thousands of corpses littered the plaza and surrounding fields. Upon witnessing the butchery erupting around them, the battalions of Atawallpa's troops remaining outside Cajamarca fled in utter dismay. Many Inca nobles, influential provincial elites, and allied war chiefs perished in the massacre. With their god-king fallen into captivity, the Inca Empire as a political project came to a catastrophic end.

The narrative of the conquest of Peru has been frequently told, but the perennial question remains: how could Pizarro and his small military force so quickly subjugate the largest and most powerful empire ever forged by native Americans? Conventional explanations attribute the rapidity of the Inca Empire's collapse to a combination of the devastating effects of superior technology, Pizarro's astute military strategy, and the inflexibility of the Inca's hierarchical political structure. From this perspective, guns, steel-tipped lances, full-body armor, Toledo steel swords, and warhorses gave the Spanish an insuperable "shock and awe" technological advantage over their adversaries. The psychological impact on the native Andeans of the swift, pitiless slaughter of what seemed to be the most powerful military force in their world surely did contribute to the house-of-cards collapse of the Inca Empire. Pizarro's lightning-fast seizure of the god-king also gave pause to any potential resistance. For a time, Atawallpa continued to communicate with his subjects through various lieutenants and surreptitiously gave commands, most notably ordering the assassination of his vanquished half-brother, Washkar, who was, at that moment, imprisoned in a cage being dragged to Cajamarca for his ultimate punishment at the hands of the victor.

Ironically, Atawallpa was now also imprisoned, a hostage awaiting his fate. But he still acted as an imperious god-king, attempting to save his own life and seeking any means to return to power. Concerted resistance to the Spanish forces was hamstrung while Atawallpa remained alive and seeming to direct the response of his subjects to the violent, avaricious foreigners. The aura of divinity – and divine power – that surrounded Atawallpa did not dissipate in an instant, as is evident from the eyewitness testimony of his Spanish captors. They observed with great fascination and not a little envy the extreme deference and personal service rendered to the Inca god-king even in his humiliating captivity. Servant girls and noble women attended to his daily needs, dressing him in luxurious tunics, ceremonially presenting his food on gold and silver platters, collecting the remains of meals, discarded clothes and every object that the god-king had touched with his holy hands to preserve them in leather chests. According to Pedro Pizarro, the natives explained to him that "anything that had been touched by the rulers, who were the sons of the sun, had to be burned, reduced to ashes and thrown to the air, since no-one was allowed to touch it" (cited in Hemming 1970:50). Another eyewitness to Atawallpa's captivity, Juan Ruiz de Arce, recounted that the god-king "did not spit on to the ground when he expectorated: a woman held out her hand and he spat into it. The women removed any hairs that fell on his clothing and ate them. We enquired why he did that in spitting, [and learned that] he did it out of grandeur. But with the hairs he did it because he was very frightened of sorcery: he ordered them to eat the hairs to avoid being bewitched" (cited in Hemming 1970:50–51). In at least the initial stages of his captivity, Atawallpa still retained the unquestioned power of divinity, and with so many potential alternative leaders slaughtered in the streets of Cajamarca, effective native resistance to Pizarro's invasion remained paralyzed and in states of fear, confusion, and disarray. The downside of charismatic rule became painfully clear for the empire: no alternative leader could emerge to organize resistance to the invasion while the god-king remained alive and still possessed of the aura of divinity.

These straightforward explanations help us understand the rapidity of the empire's collapse at the level of the highest political authorities who were either murdered en masse in Cajamarca or still in politico-religious thrall to their imprisoned god-king. But, of course, they are not the entire story. Many historical and structural factors converged to unleash the apocalypse that destroyed the Inca Empire. As we have seen, the empire itself had reached logistical limits of governability just prior to the advent of the European invasion. In 1525, Wayna Qhapaq may even have contemplated breaking the empire into two parts, north and south, one governed from Quito and the other from Cuzco, in acknowledgment of the difficulties of sustaining a single government apparatus over such a vast and internally diverse territory. That year he was struggling to extend Inca control in the far north, while quelling repeated rebellions in the vast, recalcitrant territories of the Lake Titicaca basin. Internal resistance to the accelerating tribute demands of the Inca and the central government's deepening involvement in local political and economic affairs began to generate considerable tension in the early years of the sixteenth century. During this time, Wayna Qhapaq intensified and sought to centralize Inca control over subject ethnic groups. He reorganized tribute assessments into the decimal system of administration and imposed new *kurakas* with principal obligations and loyalties to the Inca aristocracy, and not to the subject ethnic groups themselves. Massive programs of forced population resettlement through the *mitmaq* system increased during Wayna Qhapaq's tenure, as did expansion of the *yana* social status that removed substantial numbers of people from the authority of their home communities and absorbed them as retainers into the households of the Inca aristocracy. This gradual erosion of local autonomy inevitably engendered hostility among the traditional authorities of the subject ethnic groups. Wayna Qhapaq's attempts to restructure traditional patterns of authority, to break down the kin-based loyalties of subjects to their natal communities, and to reorient religious, political, and economic practices toward the centralized, patrimonial government of which he was the head were insufficiently consolidated by the time of Pizarro's invasion. That is, Wayna Qhapaq's ambitious program of nation building, of forging by force and persuasion the one-world *ayllu* in which all of the subjects of the empire were to be incorporated, had only begun when the epochal encounter with the Spanish intervened.

Not insignificantly, this encounter was presaged by waves of devastating epidemics that killed, maimed, and psychologically terrorized native Andeans even before they laid eyes on the alien intruders who came to dominate their world. The sudden deaths by disease of Wayna Qhapaq and his designated heir further destabilized the already fragile fabric of Inca governance. All prospects for empire-wide unity evaporated during the ensuing bitter civil war between the factions of Waskhar and Atawallpa. The internecine warfare among the Inca that raged as the Spanish established their beachheads on the Pacific coast was a serendipitous stroke of luck for the invaders, a historical accident that rendered Francisco Pizarro's plans for conquest infinitely more plausible. As Pedro Pizarro wrote, "[H]ad Huayna Capac been alive when we Spaniards entered this land it would have been impossible to win it, for he was greatly loved by his subjects ... also if the land had not been divided by the wars of Huascar and Atahualpa, we could not have entered or conquered it unless over a thousand Spaniards had come simultaneously. But it was impossible at that time to assemble even five hundred" (Pizarro [1571], cited in Hemming 1970:55). Whether Wayna Qhapaq was truly so well loved by his subjects as Pizarro claims does not alter the conclusion that the relative coherence of the empire under his rule was deeply compromised by the "wars of Huascar and Atahualpa." Pizarro's comments underscore another truth regarding the conquest of the Inca: even if the empire had been unified at the time of the invasion, it was only a matter of time before it fell before the onslaught of the relentless and technologically superior forces of Spain. Perhaps five hundred Spaniards could not have conquered a unified Inca Empire under the command of a single ruler, yet the many thousands more that ventured out into the Americas in the subsequent years of Spanish exploration and world conquest surely would have. But in the actual historical circumstances of 1532, the Inca Empire was divided into bitter factions and already suffering the devastating impact of lethal pandemics that caused both biological and political havoc among its populations. Francisco Pizarro had technology, audacity, fortunate circumstance, and lethal microbes on his side.

Atawallpa remained in captivity in Cajamarca for some eight months as the Spanish sent out small reconnaissance parties to Cuzco and the great oracle of Pachacamac on the Peruvian coast near Lima in search of treasure and military intelligence. In return for sparing his life, Atawallpa had promised Pizarro enormous quantities of gold and silver, engendering the now much burnished story of Atawallpa's "ransom." Until Pizarro understood the political conditions outside of Cajamarca, he needed to keep Atawallpa alive and in communication with his subjects. So the slow assembly of Atawallpa's ransom served both their purposes: Atawallpa remained alive, certainly with the idea still in his mind that he might regain his liberty and power, while Pizarro temporized, sending for reinforcements to stabilize his still-precarious military position. These reinforcements arrived from Panama under the leadership of Pizarro's lieutenant Diego de Almagro in April 1533 and set in train the denouement of Atawallpa's brief reign as the Sapa Inca.

As gold and silver flowed into Cajamarca, Almagro and Pizarro debated the fate of Atawallpa. They had no intention of unconditionally releasing Atawallpa after his "ransom" had been collected. Almagro, in particular, believed that Atawallpa had to be dispatched immediately or else the Spanish risked placing themselves in mortal danger from concerted native resistance to their nascent enterprise of conquest. Pizarro appears to have hesitated in agreeing to this strategy, believing that holding Atawallpa hostage offered the Spanish protection from his subjects since Atawallpa held such apparent, unquestioned authority over the natives. But, in the end, with Spanish military superiority consolidated by Almagro's reinforcements, Pizarro decided to execute the Inca king. Once this decision was made, Pizarro faced a final obstacle: in the eyes of the Spanish king, on what legal grounds could Pizarro execute Atawallpa, the sovereign lord of a native empire? The principle of the divine right of kings was at stake if Pizarro, not himself a king, could summarily order the murder of the Inca sovereign. These grounds were found in an unsubstantiated rumor that Atawallpa had surreptitiously ordered Rumiñawi, one of his generals who had remained in command of an intact native army in Quito, to exterminate the Spanish invaders. Once this claim was made, Almagro demanded Atawallpa's murder under the pretext of his "treasonous" intentions to kill Christians. With palpable fear of organized native reprisals circulating among the Spanish forces and with this gossamer legal justification for regicide in hand, the conquerors tied Atawallpa to a stake in the principal plaza of Cajamarca on the evening of July 26, 1533. In lieu of being burned to death, Atawallpa accepted baptism into the Christian faith under the instruction of Friar Vicente de Valverde, the same priest whose missal Atawallpa had contemptuously thrown to the ground on the fateful day of his capture at the hands of Pizarro. Atawallpa was garroted, and subsequently his corpse, clad in his royal tunic, was partially burned. His singed remains were left on display through the night. On Sunday morning, July 27, 1533, the memory of Atawallpa was honored with all the pomp and circumstance of a Christian funeral presided over by his executioners. But Atawallpa's body did not linger long in a Christian grave: his surviving relatives clandestinely removed his remains and spirited them away to final repose in a location that has never been discovered. Soon after Atawallpa's execution, Pizarro led his expeditionary forces to Cuzco to take formal possession of the Realm of the Four Quarters.

The narrative of the Inca Empire does not entirely end with the murder of Atawallpa. While Pizarro marched on Cuzco, Atawallpa's armies under the leadership of his generals Rumiñawi, Quizquiz, and Challcochima still remained at large, even though without the benefit of a supreme commander who could coordinate resistance to the European invaders. For his part, Pizarro, in the presence of assembled *kurakas* who survived the massacre of Cajamarca, quickly appointed Tupac Wallpa, a son of Wayna Qhapaq and Waskhar's younger brother, as a puppet ruler. Pizarro's astute installation of a member of Waskhar's faction as the new Sapa Inca instantly gained him a considerable force of native allies who had been opposed to Atawallpa and his usurpation of the throne from their patron. As Pizarro moved south toward Cuzco, pressing the attack on remnants of Atawallpa's forces, he also received the military support of various ethnic groups such as the Wanka of the central Peruvian highlands and the Kañari of Ecuador who bitterly resented their own conquest by the Inca. So the Spanish invaders were no longer merely a small, though technologically superior, martial force. They had rapidly become a powerful alternative force of dispositive military and political authority. After occupying Cuzco on November 15, 1533, exactly one year after their first glimpse of Cajamarca, the Spanish quickly moved to establish a provisional government in the Andes in which they were the dominant players. When Tupac Wallpa suddenly died of a viral infection in Xauxa on the road to Cuzco, Pizarro chose as his next puppet-king yet another son of Wayna Qhapaq who had been a fugitive from Atawallpa's forces in their determined attempt to exterminate the members of Waskhar's lineage and all his political allies. This ambitious new Inca monarch, Manco Capac, eagerly allied himself with Pizarro to extract revenge against Atawallpa's faction for their savage attacks on his family and, most likely, with the ultimate intent of consolidating all of the traditional lineaments of political power enjoyed by his royal predecessors. The newly enthroned Manco marshaled large native armies to help the Spanish eradicate the persisting military threat presented by Rumiñawi, Quizquiz, and Challcochima. Pizarro and Manco collaborated in ridding the realm of Atawallpa's generals and their remnant native forces.

While the final military conquest of the Inca Empire proceeded, Pizarro began to establish new governing bodies and municipalities structured by Spanish principals of authority. He also distributed the fruits of conquest to his companions and allies, and to the Spanish Crown, initially melting down vast hoards of metallic loot extracted from the vanquished Inca Empire. Pizarro expropriated valuable city properties in Cuzco, Xauxa, and Cajamarca and created others in newly founded cities, such as the Ciudad de los Reyes, or, as it is known today, Lima. More importantly for his loyal Spanish compatriots who had accompanied him in the conquest, Pizarro began to distribute vast *encomiendas*, grants of native vassals obligated to work for their European overlords. Some of the conquistadors received as many as forty thousand natives for their personal labor service. The Spanish Crown, too, initially benefited from this system of forced labor until appalling abuses of the natives forced some reforms in the name of humanitarianism. These reforms were often made over bitter protest from the original conquerors, who felt that they had the right to enjoy the unfettered menial service of the people they had subjected. Such tensions among the original conquistadors and between the initial conquistadors and the Spanish Crown generated more misery for the native populations, who were drawn into a new civil war, in this case among the Spanish themselves.

By 1535, Manco Capac's illusion that he could exert a substantive measure of authority in collaboration with Pizarro and the Spanish melted away under the rapid concentration of wealth, land, urban property, and labor sources in the hands of the foreign invaders. During the charade of his coregency of the Inca Empire, Manco was increasing subjected to personal humiliation at the hands of Pizarro's younger brothers, Juan and Gonzalo Pizarro, who among others had been left in command of Cuzco. Manco also became fully aware of the atrocities perpetrated on native populations by roving bands of Spaniards who were arriving in increasing numbers to exploit this new land of opportunity. According to the testimony of Cristóbal de Molina, a Spanish priest who accompanied the exploratory expedition of Diego de Almagro into the old southern reaches of the Inca Empire in present-day Chile:

Any natives who would not accompany the Spaniards voluntarily were taken along bound in ropes and chains. The Spaniards ... led them by day heavily loaded and dying of hunger ... [and the porters] worked without rest all day long, ate only a little roast maize and water, and were barbarously imprisoned at night. One Spaniard on this expedition locked twelve Indians in a chain and boasted that all twelve died in it. When one Indian died, they cut off his head, to terrify the others and to avoid undoing their shackles or opening the padlock on the chain. (Molina 1873, cited in Hemming 1970:178–179)

The revolting sadism of these acts, along with the futility of Manco's political position, finally alienated him from his Spanish patrons. By the autumn of 1535, Manco decided to end his collaborationist policy. After one abortive attempt to surreptitiously leave Cuzco that resulted in even further physical abuse and humiliation, Manco successfully escaped Spanish authorities on April 18, 1536. He fled into the fortified landscapes around Ollantaytambo to organize his rebellion against the foreigners who had by now amply revealed their intent to permanently subjugate the indigenous populations of the Andes.

Manco quickly amassed a large native army. However, most of the participants in the rebellion were not professional soldiers, but rural farmers called up during the rainy season after their crops were already in the ground. Manco raised a massive siege of Cuzco, relying not so much on military prowess as on sheer numbers. Manco's forces attacked the ancient capital with a ferocity borne of desperation. They rained down sling stones, bolas, boulders, and burning faggots on the besieged Spaniards. They diverted streams and canals to create impassable mud morasses outside of the city to disable the Spanish cavalry.

7.6. The monumental complex of Saqsawaman above Cuzco. (Image courtesy of author)

They barricaded streets with adobes and cut stones from collapsed buildings, at times engaging in hand-to-hand combat with the Spanish, even though possessing vastly inferior weapons. They seized the great, fortified temple complex of Saqsawaman (Figure 7.6), which presented them with their only real tactical advantage. In the end, the Spanish counterattacked in the company of many native allies who had chosen not to join Manco's rebellion, most likely judging correctly that the foreigners would eventually prevail. Despite heavy casualties, including the death of Juan Pizarro, younger brother of Francisco, the Spanish retook Saqsawaman and put to death the entire contingent of native defenders, many of whom committed suicide by jumping from the high walls of the temple rather than be slaughtered at the hands of the vengeful Spaniards and their native allies. The high priest of the Inca, the Villac Umu, along with other generals of Manco Capac, attempted to regain Saqsawaman and fiercely fought on for three more days, but had no hope for dislodging the Spanish, who had now firmly garrisoned this strategic complex. While the siege of Cuzco raged on, Manco incited rebellions elsewhere in the empire with some initial success, and even assaulted the new Spanish city of Lima where Francisco Pizarro had established his coastal headquarters. In the end, Manco Capac's attempt to expel the Spanish from the empire failed, as new reinforcements poured in from the coast to counter the native offensive. Open rebellion faded into protracted resistance and guerrilla warfare as Manco Capac retreated further into the maquis of the Vilcabamba wilderness, eventually establishing a neo-Inca state that persisted for almost forty years under the leadership of his son Titu Cusi and Titu Cusi's brother Tupac Amaru. The political resistance of the Inca royal dynasty finally ended with the execution of Tupac Amaru on September 24, 1572, in the main plaza of the now thoroughly Hispanicized city of Cuzco. On that day, the imperial narratives of the native lords of Cuzco came to a bloody end.

If the superior military technology, improvisational skill in pursuing their strategic goals, and diplomatic dexterity in acquiring native allies of the Spanish conquerors and the internal disunity of the Inca played major roles in the collapse of the Inca Empire, the continuing biological trauma wrought by virulent pandemics that swept the Andes destroyed the demographic base of native Andean civilization. Mortality from warfare was certainly high, but the epidemics of measles, typhus, plague, and hemorrhagic smallpox in a population not previously exposed to these diseases quickly produced desolate ghost towns throughout the Andes. Spanish eyewitness accounts graphically record the terrible mortality among indigenous populations and lament the economic impact that this mass die-off had on the labor supply essential to Spanish colonization of the New World. The precise rate of native mortality is difficult to establish, but plausible estimates from census records indicate appalling losses among the native population, particularly in the first traumatic years of Spanish contact with the Americas. As early as the late 1530s, entire regions of the desert coast and highlands were virtually depopulated. By the mid-sixteenth century, the native population had declined by 25–90 percent, depending on location and degree of isolation from European contact. Epidemics, harsh tribute extractions, malnutrition, forced labor on Spanish *encomiendas* and in the hellish silver and mercury mines of Potosí and Huancavelica, physical abuse, and systematic use of capital punishment at the hands of European overlords all contributed to what we should not hesitate to call an American holocaust. A contemporary report sent by Hernando de Santillán, an official of the Spanish court, to the Audiencia of Lima, graphically conveys the life situation of mid-sixteenth-century Andean natives as they adapted to the oppressive conditions of Spanish colonization:

Even if it freezes or if their cereals and other foods are dried up and lost, they are forced to pay their tribute in full. They have nothing left over from what they

7.7. Francisco Pizarro sets fire to the home of Guaman Poma's father. (Adapted from Guaman Poma de Ayala 1615)

can produce. They live the most wretched and miserable lives of any people on earth. As long as they are healthy, they are fully occupied only in working for tribute. Even when they are sick, they have no respite, and few survive their first illness, however slight, because of the appalling existence they lead.... They are deeply depressed by their misery and servitude ... and have come to believe that they must continue to work for the Spaniards for as long as they or their sons or descendants live, with nothing to enjoy for themselves. Because of this, they despair; for they ask only for their daily bread and cannot have even that. (Cited in Hemming 1970:353)

By best projections, the native populations of the Americas, both North and South, did not recover in numbers until the late twentieth

7.8. Spanish abuse of indigenous Andeans in the mines. (Adapted from Guaman Poma de Ayala 1615)

century, and, for many Andean natives, under life conditions only marginally better than their sixteenth-century ancestors (Figures 7.7, 7.8, and 7.9).

Some scholars of the Inca Empire refer to a continuing legacy from the Inca past, a kind of imagined memory that still courses through contemporary political debates and electoral contests. Although contemporary cultural and political discourses about the Inca still do animate Peruvian society, the truth is that the Spanish conquest represents a uniquely tragic rupture in native Andean historical experience. Subsequent centuries of systematic oppression and interaction with European colonizers have so thoroughly transformed the historical consciousness of native

7.9. Priests and *encomenderos* alike physically abused indigenous
Andean men and women. (Adapted from Guaman Poma de Ayala
1615)

Andeans that the achievements of the Inca Empire have become for
them little more than convenient myths useful as political propaganda.
Any true legacy of the Inca Empire that still exists resides in the testimony of archaeology and in the historical record, not in the minds of the
native populations of the Andes.

Glossary of Foreign Terms

All terms are Quechua, unless otherwise noted. "Sp." indicates a Spanish term. Alternate spellings are given in parentheses.

ají: a hot pepper domesticated in the Andes and grown in low-altitude areas. Important in the pre-Hispanic world as a spice and trade item.

altiplano: high-altitude, expansive plateau region, primarily located in modern Bolivia and southern Peru.

aqlla (aclla) (pl. *aqllakuna*): a "chosen woman" selected from the provinces as a young girl and cloistered in a state-sponsored facility. *Aqllakuna* brewed *chicha* and wove fine garments for the state.

aqllawasi (acllahuasi): "house of the *aqlla*"; the facility in which *aqllakuna* lived together and produced *chicha* and garments for the state.

ayllu: a multiscalar concept referencing any unit within a nested set of social groups. The *ayllu* claimed access to productive resources on the basis of kinship via descent from a shared, jointly venerated, ancestor.

Cacique (Sp.): "chief"; a Spanish term derived from Arawak.

camay: the vitalizing, creative power understood by the Inca to bring life to and animate all material things.

chakra: an agricultural field.

chapa: an irrigation district (one of ten) outside of Cuzco, comprised of primary, secondary, and tertiary canals radiating from a primary water source.

charki (charqui): dried meat (jerky).

chaski (chasqui): runners who carried information, often encoded in *khipu*, along the Qhapaq Ñan.

chicha: maize beer.

chuño: a freeze-dried potato.

cuy (pl. *cuis*): a guinea pig.

encomienda (Sp.): grants of indigenous residents obligated to work for Spanish overlords and settlers in the early colonial period.

hanan: the upper, higher-status section of ranked, complementary dual social units, such as the *ayllu* or the city of Cuzco.

hatun runa: commoners.

haylli: a martial song of triumph analogizing warfare to agricultural activity and sung during planting ceremonies.

huaccha concha: descendants of a king and his secondary wives, ineligible for kingship but often appointed to imperial administrative positions.

hurin: the lower, lesser-status section of ranked, complementary dual social units, such as the *ayllu* or the city of Cuzco.

kamayuq (camayoc) (pl. *kamayuqkuna*): a full-time laborer for the state, specializing in a craft occupation.

khipu (quipu): a system of knotted, multicolored cords used for recording figures and narrative information.

khipu kamayuq (quipu camayoc) (pl. *khipu kamayuqkuna*): a specialist able to record and read the *khipu.*

kuraka: a community political leader; a "chief."

llacta kamayuq (llactacamayoc) (pl. *llacta kamayuqkuna*): a state specialist managing administrative information related to the governance of the community (*llacta*).

mamakuna (pl.) (*mamacona*): alternative term for *aqllakuna.*

mindalá: a long-distance trader of the northern Andes.

mit'a: a form of taxation that entailed rotating labor obligations to the state.

mitmaq (mitima) (pl. *mitmaqkuna*) (*mitimaes*): a population of colonists removed from their indigenous territory and relocated to other provinces of the Inca Empire for political, defensive, or economic reasons.

mullu: crushed shells of the thorny oyster (*Spondylus princeps*). *Mullu* were highly valued by the Inca as a symbol of divinity and elite status.

orejones (Sp.): literally, "big ears"; Inca nobles whose status was marked by large earplug ornaments.

pacarina (Hispanicized version of Quechua *paqarisca*): "place of dawning"; a type of landscape *wak'a* that served as the origin point from which a community emerged.

panaqa (panaca): "royal *ayllu*"; the relatives and descendants of a king who maintained his mummy and estate in perpetuity.

piña: a war captive who became his or her captor's personal servant.

puna: high-altitude, treeless plateau (above 4,000 m), often utilized for camelid herding and the cultivation of tubers.

Qhapaq Ñan: system of state roads extending throughout the Inca Empire.

qhapaq ucha (*capac hucha; capa cocha*): ritual of "royal obligation," usually entailing the sacrifice of children, often performed on mountains, following a pilgrimage to and away from Cuzco.

qollqa (*collca*): a state-owned storehouse.

qoya (*coya*): a queen.

Sapa Inca: "unique lord"; the reigning Inca monarch.

Saqsawaman: a fortified religious complex immediately north of the city of Cuzco.

señorío (Sp.): a term used to indicate the form of government of the formerly autonomous polities that were incorporated into the Inca Empire.

suyu: term used to indicate any kind of segment of a larger whole.

taki (*taqui*): a ceremony that entailed large-scale feasting, drinking, dancing, and spectacle.

tampu (*tambo*): a way station for supplies and temporary lodging; *tampus* were distributed regularly along the Qhapaq Ñan.

Tawantinsuyu: "the four quarters together"; the Incas' name for their empire.

tokrikoq: a provincial governor.

usnu (*ushnu*): a ceremonial stone "throne" and the physical proxy of the Inca king, associated with a receptacle for libations and located in the central plaza.

wak'a (*huaca*): a sacred object strongly infused with *camay*. It could be a shrine, a fixed point of the landscape, or any unusual or extraordinary object, place, or person.

wawqi (*huauque*): "object-brothers" of the Inca king; these stood in for the physical presence of the king and were venerated in perpetuity, in much the same way as was his actual mummy.

yana (pl. *yanakuna*) (*yanacona*): a "personal retainer" attached to a noble household. *Yanakuna* owed allegiance to these households rather than to their natal communities, and were exempt from the tributary obligations associated with their community of origin.

zeq'e (*ceque*): a system of landscape shrines (*wak'as*) distributed along forty-one idealized sight lines that radiated out of the Qorikancha precinct in Cuzco.

Works Cited

Acosta, José de. 2002[1590]. *Natural and Moral History of the Indies*. F. López-Morillas, trans., and J. Mangan, ed. Durham, NC: Duke University Press.

Ascher, Marcia, and Robert Ascher. 1981. *Code of the Quipu: A Study in Media, Mathematics and Culture*. Ann Arbor: University of Michigan Press.

Bastien, Joseph. 1978. *Mountain of the Condor: Metaphor and Ritual in an Andean Ayllu*. St. Paul, MN: West.

Bauer, Brian. 1992. *The Development of the Inca State*. Austin: University of Texas Press.

Bauer, Brian. 1996. Legitimization of the state in Inca myth and ritual. *American Anthropologist* 98(2):327–337.

Bauer, Brian. 1998. *The Sacred Landscape of the Inca: The Cuzco Ceque System*. Austin: University of Texas Press.

Bauer, Brian. 2004. *Ancient Cuzco: Heartland of the Inca*. Austin: University of Texas Press.

Bauer, Brian, and Alan Covey. 2002. Processes of state formation in the Inca heartland (Cuzco, Peru). *American Anthropologist* 104(3):846–864.

Bauer, Brian, and David Dearborn. 1995. *Astronomy and Empire in the Ancient Andes: The Cultural Origins of Inca Sky Watching*. Austin: University of Texas Press.

Bauer, Brian, Lucas Kellett, and Miriam Aráoz Silva. 2010. *The Chanka: Archaeological Research in Andahuaylas (Apurimac), Peru*. Los Angeles: Cotsen Institute of Archaeology Press, University of California.

Bauer, Brian, and Charles Stanish. 2001. *Ritual and Pilgrimage in the Ancient Andes: The Islands of the Sun and the Moon*. Austin: University of Texas Press.

Berdan, Frances. 1985. Markets in the economy of Aztec Mexico. In *Markets and Marketing*. Monographs in Economic Anthropology 4. S. Plattner, ed., pp. 339–367. New York: University Press of America.

Betanzos, Juan de. 1996[1557]. *Narrative of the Incas*. R. Hamilton and D. Buchanan, eds. and trans. Austin: University of Texas Press.

Bloch, Marc. 1965. *Feudal Society*. L. A. Manyon, trans. London: Routledge.

Bray, Tamara, Leah Minc, María Constanza Ceruti, José Antonio Chavez, Ruddy Perea and Johan Reinhard. 1995. A compositional analysis of pottery vessels associated with the Inca ritual of capacocha. *Journal of Anthropological Archaeology* 24(1):82–100.

Cabello Balboa, Miguel. 1951[1586]. *Miscelánea antárctica: Una historia del Perú antiguo*. Lima: Universidad Nacional Mayor de San Marcos.

Chepstow-Lusty, A., M. Frogley, B. Bauer, M. Leng, K. Boessenkool, C. Carcaillet, A. Ali, and A. Gioda. 2009. Putting the rise of the Inca Empire within a climatic and land management context. *Climate of the Past Discussions* 5:771–796.

Cieza de León, Pedro. 1976[1553]. *The Incas*. H. de Onis, trans., and V. von Hagen, ed. Norman: University of Oklahoma Press.

Cobo, Bernabé. 1979[1653]. *History of the Inca Empire: An Account of the Indians' Customs and Their Origin, Together with a Treatise on Inca Legends, History, and Social Institutions*. R. Hamilton, trans. Austin: University of Texas Press.

Cobo, Bernabé. 1990[1653]. *Inca Religion and Customs*. R. Hamilton, trans. and ed. Austin: University of Texas Press.

Coe, Michael. 2005. *The Maya*. New York: Thames and Hudson.

Comaroff, Jean, and John L. Comaroff. 1991. *Of Revelation and Revolution*. Vol. 1: *Christianity, Colonialism, and Consciousness in South Africa*. Chicago: University of Chicago Press.

Cook, David Noble. 2004. *Demographic Collapse: Indian Peru, 1520–1620*. Cambridge: Cambridge University Press.

Covey, Alan. 2006. *How the Incas Built Their Heartland: State Formation and the Innovation of Imperial Strategies in the Sacred Valley, Peru*. Ann Arbor: University of Michigan Press.

D'Altroy, Terence. 1992. *Provincial Power in the Inka Empire*. Washington, DC: Smithsonian Institution Press.

D'Altroy, Terence. 2002. *The Incas*. Malden, MA: Blackwell.

Dean, E. M. 2005. "Ancestors, Mountains, Shrines, and Settlements: Late Intermediate Period Landscapes of the Southern Vilcanota Valley." Ph.D. diss., University of California, Berkeley.

Demarest, Arthur. 1981. *Viracocha: The Nature and Antiquity of the Andean High God*. Peabody Museum Monographs, no. 6. Cambridge, MA: Harvard University Press.

Demarest, Arthur. 2004. *Ancient Maya: The Rise and Fall of a Rainforest Civilization*. Cambridge: Cambridge University Press.

Descola, Philippe. 1994. *In the Society of Nature: A Native Ecology in Amazonia*. Nora Scott, trans. Cambridge: Cambridge University Press.

Descola, Philippe. 1996. *The Spears of Twilight: Life and Death in the Amazonian Jungle*. J. Lloyd, trans. New York: New Press.

Diamond, Alan, ed. 1991. *The Victorian Achievement of Sir Henry Maine: A Reappraisal*. Cambridge: Cambridge University Press.

Díaz del Castillo, Bernal. 1844[1632]. *The Memoirs of the Conquistador Bernal Díaz del Castillo Written by Himself Containing a Full and True Account of the Discovery and Conquest of Mexico and New Spain*. J. Ingram Lockhart, trans. London: J. Hatchard and Son.

Duviols, Pierre. 1973. Huari y llacuaz: agricultores y pastores: Un dualismo prehispánico de oposición y complementaridad. *Revista del Museo Nacional* 39:153–193.

Duviols, Pierre. 1979. La dinastía de los inca: ¿Monarqui o diarquía? Argumentos heurísticos a favor de una tesis estructuralista. *Journal de la Société des Americanistes* 66:67–83.

Eisenstadt, S. N. 1996. *Japanese Civilization: A Comparative View.* Chicago: University of Chicago Press.

Elias, Norbert. 1983[1969]. *The Court Society.* E. Jephcott, trans. Oxford: Blackwell.

Falcón, Francisco. 1918 (ca. 1580). *Representación hecha por el Lic. Falcón en concilio provincial, sobre los daños y molestias que se hacen a los Indios.* Colección de libros y documento referentes a la historia del Perú, Serie I, Vol. 11. Lima: Imprenta y Librería Sanmartí.

Foucault, Michel. 1979. *Discipline and Punish: The Birth of the Prison.* New York: Vintage Books.

Foucault, Michel. 1982. *Michel Foucault: Beyond Structuralism and Hermeneutics.* H. Dreyfus and P. Rabinow, eds. Chicago: University of Chicago Press.

Friedrich, Paul. 1989. Language, ideology, and political economy. *American Anthropologist* 91:295–312.

Garcilaso de la Vega, Inca. 1961[1609]. *The Incas: The Royal Commentaries of the Inca.* María Jolas, trans. and A. Gheerbrant, ed. New York: Avon Books.

Garnsey, Peter. 1988. *Famine and Food Supply in the Graeco-Roman World: Responses to Risk and Crisis.* Cambridge: Cambridge University Press.

Gasparini, Graziano, and Luise Margolies. 1980. *Inca Architecture.* Bloomington: Indiana University Press.

Gelles, Paul. 1995. Equilibrium and extraction: Dual organization in the Andes. *American Ethnologist* 22(4):710–742.

Gose, Peter. 1996. Oracles, divine kingship, and political representation in the Inka state. *Ethnohistory* 43(1):1–32.

Gramsci, Antonio. 1971. *Selections from the Prison Notebooks of Antonio Gramsci.* Q. Hoare and G. Newell Smith, eds. New York: International Publishers.

Gutiérrez de Santa Clara, Pedro. 1905[1603]. *Historia de las guerras civiles del Perú (1544–1548).* Madrid: V. Suárez.

Hassig, Ross. 1985. *Trade, Tribute, and Transportation: The Sixteenth-Century Political Economy of the Valley of Mexico.* Norman: University of Oklahoma Press.

Heffernan, K. 1989. "Limatambo in Late Prehistory: Landscape Archaeology and Documentary Images of Inca Presence in the Periphery of Cuzco." Ph.D. diss., Australian National University.

Heffernan, K. 1996. *Limatambo: Archaeology, History, and the Regional Societies of Inca Cusco.* BAR International Series 644. Oxford: British Archaeological Reports.

Hemming, John. 1970. *The Conquest of the Incas.* New York: Harvest-Harcourt Brace Jovanovich.

Hernández Príncipe, Rodrigo. 1923. Mitología andina: Idolotrías en Recuay. *Revista Inca* 1(1):25–78.

Hocart, A. M. 1970[1936]. *Kings and Councillors.* Chicago: University of Chicago Press.

Hodge, Mary, and Michael E. Smith, eds. 1994. *Economies and Polities in the Aztec Realm.* Albany: Institute for Mesoamerican Studies, State University of New York at Albany.

Hyslop, John. 1990. *Inka Settlement Planning.* Austin: University of Texas Press.

Isbell, Billie Jean. 1978. *To Defend Ourselves: Ecology and Ritual in an Andean Village*. Austin: Institute of Latin American Studies, University of Texas.

Isbell, William. 2008. Wari and Tiwanaku: International identities in the Central Andean Middle Horizon. In *Handbook of South American Archaeology*. H. Silverman and W. Isbell, eds., pp. 731–760. New York: Springer.

Isbell, William, and Gordon McEwan, eds. 1991. *Huari Administrative Structure: Prehistoric Monumental Architecture and State Government*. Washington, DC: Dumbarton Oaks.

Joyce, Arthur. 2010. *Mixtecs, Zapotecs, and Chatinos: Ancient Peoples of Southern Mexico*. Malden, MA: Wiley-Blackwell.

Julien, Catherine. 1982. Inca decimal administration in the Lake Titicaca region. In *The Inca and Aztec States, 1400–1800: Anthropology and History*. G. Collier, R. Rosaldo, and J. Wirth, eds., pp. 119–151. New York: Academic Press.

Julien, Catherine. 1988. How Inca decimal administration worked. *Ethnohistory* 35(3):257–279.

Julien, Catherine. 2000. *Reading Inca History*. Iowa City: University of Iowa Press.

Kantorowicz, Ernst. 1981. *The King's Two Bodies: A Study in Medieval Political Theology*. Princeton, NJ: Princeton University Press.

Kendall, A. E. 1984. Archaeological investigations of Late Intermediate Period and Late Horizon Period at Cusichaca, Peru. In *Current Archaeological Projects in the Central Andes*. BAR International Series 210. A. Kendall, ed., pp. 247–290. Oxford: British Archaeological Reports.

Kendall, A. E. 1988. Inca planning north of Cuzco between Anta and Machu Picchu and along the Urubamba Valley. In *Recent Studies in Precolumbian Archaeology*. BAR International Series 421. N. Saunders and O. de Montmollin, eds., pp. 457–488. Oxford: British Archaeological Reports.

Kolata, Alan. 1990. The urban concept of Chan Chan. In *The Northern Dynasties: Kingship and Statecraft in Chimor*. M. Moseley and A. Cordy-Collins, eds., pp. 107–144. Washington, DC: Dumbarton Oaks.

Kolata, Alan. 1993. *The Tiwanaku: Portrait of an Andean Civilization*. Cambridge, MA: Blackwell.

Kolata, Alan. 1996. Principles of authority in the native Andean state. *Journal of the Steward Anthropological Society* 24:61–84.

Kolata, Alan. 1997. Of kings and capitals: Principles of authority and the nature of cities in the native Andean state. In *The Archaeology of City States: Cross-Cultural Approaches*. D. L. Nichols and T. H. Charlton, eds., pp. 234–254. Washington, DC: Smithsonian Institution Press.

Kolata, Alan. 2003. The social production of Tiwanaku: Political economy and authority in a native Andean state. In *Tiwanaku and Its Hinterland: Archaeology and Paleoecology of an Andean Civilization*. Vol. 2: *Urban and Rural Archaeology*. A. Kolata, ed., pp. 449–472. Washington, DC: Smithsonian Institution Press.

Kosiba, Steven. 2009. "Becoming Inka: The Transformation of Political Place and Practice during Inka State Formation." Ph.D. diss., University of Chicago.

La Barre, Weston. 1948. *The Aymara Indians of the Lake Titicaca Plateau, Bolivia*. J. Alden Mason and D. Donath, eds. Menatha, WI: American Anthropological Association.

Laclau, Ernesto, and Chantal Mouffe. 1985. *Hegemony and Socialist Strategy: Towards a Radical Democratic Politics*. Winston Moore and Paul Cammack, trans. London: Verso.

Lockhart, James. 1992. *The Nahuas after the Conquest: A Social and Cultural History of the Indians of Central Mexico, Sixteenth through Eighteenth Centuries*. Stanford, CA: Stanford University Press.

MacCormack, Sabine. 1991. *Religion in the Andes: Vision and Imagination in Early Colonial Peru*. Princeton, NJ: Princeton University Press.

MacCormack, Sabine. 2000. Processions for the Inca: Andean and Christian ideas of human sacrifice, communion and embodiment in early colonial Peru. *Archive für Religionsgeschichte* 2(1):1–31.

Maine, Sir Henry. 1895[1871]. *Village Communities in the East and West: Six Lectures Delivered at Oxford*. London: John Murray.

Maine, Sir Henry. 1982[1861]. *Ancient Law*. Birmingham, AL: Legal Classics Library.

Marx, Karl. 1852. *The Eighteenth Brumaire of Louis Bonaparte*. E. Paul and C. Paul, trans. New York: International Publishers.

McEwan, Colin, and Maarten van de Guchte. 1992. Ancestral time and sacred space in Inca state ritual. In *The Ancient Americas: Art from Sacred Landscapes*. R. Townsend, ed., pp. 359–373. Chicago: Art Institute of Chicago.

McEwan, Gordon, ed. 2005. *Pikillacta: The Wari Empire in Cuzco*. Iowa City: University of Iowa Press.

Molina, Cristóbal de. 1873[1575]. *Narrative of the Rites and Laws of the Yncas*. C. Markham, ed. and trans. New York: Burt Franklin.

Morris, Craig. 1992a. The technology of highland Inka food storage. In *Inka Storage Systems*. T. Levine, ed., pp. 237–258. Norman: University of Oklahoma Press.

Morris, Craig. 1992b. Foreword. In *Inka Storage Systems*. T. Levine, ed., pp. ix–xiii. Norman: University of Oklahoma Press.

Morris, Craig, and Donald Thompson. 1985. *Huánuco Pampa: An Inca City and Its Hinterland*. London: Thames and Hudson.

Moseley, Michael. 1992. *The Incas and Their Ancestors: The Archaeology of Peru*. London: Thames and Hudson.

Murra, John. 1960. Rite and crop in the Inca state. In *Culture in History*. S. Diamond, ed., pp. 393–407. New York: Columbia University.

Murra, John. 1962. Cloth and its functions in the Inca state. *American Anthropologist* 64(4):710–728.

Murra, John. 1972. El "control vertical" de un máximo de pisos ecológicos en la economía de las sociedades andinas. In *Formaciones económicas y políticas del mundo andino*, pp. 59–115. Huánuco, Peru: Universidad Hermilio Valdizán.

Murra, John. 2002. *El mundo andino: Población, medio ambiente, y economía*. Lima: Instituto de Estudos Peruanos, PUCP.

National Research Council, Advisory Committee on Technology Innovation, Board on Science and Technology for International Development. 1989. *Lost Crops of the Incas: Little-Known Plants of the Andes with Promise for Worldwide Cultivation*. Washington, DC: National Academy Press.

Niles, Susan. 1999. *The Shape of Inca History: Narrative and Architecture in an Andean Empire*. Iowa City: University of Iowa Press.

Ocampo, Baltasar de. 1907[1610]. *History of the Incas, by Pedro Sarmiento de Gamboa, and the Execution of the Inca Tupac Amaru, by Captain Baltasar de Ocampo*. Sir Clements Markham, ed. and trans. Cambridge: The Hakluyt Society.

Orlove, Benjamin. 1977. *Alpacas, Sheep, and Men: The Wool Export Economy and Regional Society of Southern Peru*. New York: Academic Press.

Ossio Acuña, Juan. 1996. Symmetry and asymmetry in Andean society. *Journal of the Steward Anthropological Society* 24(1–2):231–248.

Pärssinen, Martti. 1992. *Tawantinsuyu: The Inca State and Its Political Organization*. Helsinki: SHS.

Patterson, Thomas. 1991. *The Inca Empire: the formation and disintegration of a pre-capitalist state*. Oxford: Berg.

Pease, Franklin. 1978. *Del Tawantinsuyu a la historia del Perú*. Lima: Instituto de Estudios Peruanos.

Pease, Franklin. 1981. *Los últimos Incas del Cuzco*. Lima: P. L. Villanueva.

Pease, Franklin. 1982. *El pensamiento mítico*. Lima: Mosca Azul Editores.

Pizarro, Pedro. 1921[1571]. *Relation of the Discovery and Conquest of the Kingdoms of Peru*. P. Ainsworth Means, trans. New York: Cortes Society.

Platt, Tristán. 1982. *Estado boliviano y ayllu andino: Tierra y tributo en el norte de Potosí*. Lima: Instituto de Estudios Peruanos.

Polo de Ondegardo, Juan. 1916–1917[1571]. *Informaciones acerca de la religión y gobierno de los Incas*. Lima: Sanmartí.

Poma de Ayala, Guaman. 2002[1615]. *El primer nueva corónica y buen gobierno*. Copenhagen: Museum Tusculanum Press, University of Copenhagen.

Posnansky, Arthur. 1945. *Tihuanacu, the Cradle of American Man*. New York: J. J. Augustin.

Prescott, William. 1874. *History of the Conquest of Peru, with a Preliminary Review of the Civilization of the Incas*. Philadelphia: J. B. Lippincott.

Quilter, Jeffrey, and Gary Urton, eds. 2002. *Narrative Threads: Accounting and Recounting in Andean Khipu*. Austin: University of Texas Press.

Reinhard, Johan. 1992. An archaeological investigation of Inca ceremonial platforms on the Volcano Copiapo, Central Chile. In *Ancient America: Contributions to New World Archaeology*. N. Saunders, ed., pp. 145–172. Oxford: Oxbow Monographs, no. 24.

Reinhard, Johan. 1993. Llullaillaco: An investigation of the world's highest archaeological site. *Latin American Indian Literatures Journal* 9(1):31–65.

Reinhard, Johan. 1996. Peru's ice maidens. *National Geographic* 189(6):62–81.

Reinhard, Johan. 1998. *Discovering the Inca Ice Maiden: My Adventures on Ampato*. Washington, DC: National Geographic Society.

Reinhard, Johan, and María Constanza Ceruti. 2000. Sacred mountains, ceremonial sites, and human sacrifice among the Incas. *Archaeoastronomy* 19:1–43.

Rostworowski de Diez Canseco, María. 1960. Succesion, cooption to kingship, and royal incest among the Inca. *Southwestern Journal of Anthropology* 16:417–427.

Rostworowski de Diez Canseco, María. 1970. Mercaderes del valle de Chincha en la época prehispánica. *Revista Española de Antropología Americana* 5:135–178.

Rostworowski de Diez Canseco, María. 1983. *Estructuras andinas del poder: Ideología religiosa y política*. Lima: Instituto de Estudios Peruanos.

Rostworowski de Diez Canseco, María. 1989. *Costa peruana prehispánica*. Lima: Instituto de Estudios Peruanos.

Rostworowski de Diez Canseco, María. 1999. *History of the Inca Realm*. H. Iceland, trans. Cambridge: Cambridge University Press.

Rowe, John H. 1945. Absolute chronology in the Andean area. *American Antiquity* 10:265–284.

Rowe, John H. 1946. Inca culture at the time of the Spanish Conquest. In *Handbook of South American Indians*. Bureau of South American Ethnology, Bulletin 143, vol. 2. J. Steward, ed., pp. 183–330. Washington, DC: Smithsonian Institution Press.

Rowe, John H. 1948. The Kingdom of Chimor. *Acta Americana* 6:26–59.

Rowe, John H. 1967. What kind of a settlement was Inca Cuzco? *Ñawpa Pacha* 5:59–75.

Rowe, John H. 1979. An account of the shrines of Ancient Cuzco. *Ñawpa Pacha* 17:2–80.

Rowe, John H. 1982. Inca policies and institutions relating to the cultural unification of the empire. In *The Inca and Aztec States, 1400–1800: Anthropology and History*. G. Collier, R. Rosaldo, and J. Wirth, eds., pp. 83–118. New York: Academic Press.

Rowe, John H. 1986. Probanza de los Incas nietos del conquistadores. *Histórica* 9(2):196–245.

Sahlins, Marshall. 1985. *Islands of History*. Chicago: University of Chicago Press.

Sahlins, Marshall. 2004. *Apologies to Thucydides: Understanding History as Culture and Vice Versa*. Chicago: University of Chicago Press.

Sahlins, Marshall. 2005. Preface. *Ethnohistory* 52(1):3–6.

Sahlins, Marshall. 2010. The whole is a part: Intercultural politics of order and change. In *Experiments in Holism: Theory and Practice in Contemporary Anthropology*. T. Otto and N. Bubandt, eds., pp. 102–126. Malden, MA: Wiley-Blackwell.

Salomon, Frank. 1985. The dynamic potential of the complementarity concept. In *Andean Ecology and Civilization: An Interdisciplinary Perspective on Andean Ecological Complementarity*. S. Masuda, I. Shimada, and C. Morris, eds., pp. 431–511. Tokyo: University of Tokyo Press.

Salomon, Frank. 1986. *Native Lords of Quito in the Age of the Incas: The Political Economy of North Andean Chiefdoms*. Cambridge: Cambridge University Press.

Salomon, Frank. 1991. Introductory essay: The Huarochirí Manuscript. In *The Huarochirí Manuscript: A Testament of Ancient and Colonial Andean Religion*. F. Salomon and G. Urioste, trans., pp. 1–38. Austin: University of Texas Press.

Salomon, Frank. 2004. *The Cord Keepers: Khipus and Cultural Life in a Peruvian Village*. Durham, NC: Duke University Press.

Sancho de la Hoz, Pedro. 1917[1543]. *Documents and Narratives Concerning the Discovery and Conquest of Latin America: An Account of the Conquest of Peru*. P. Ainsworth Means, trans. New York: Cortes Society.

Sarmiento de Gamboa, Pedro. 1999[1572]. *History of the Incas*. B. Bauer and V. Smith, trans. and eds. Austin: University of Texas Press.

Schobinger, Juan. 1995. *Aconcagua: Una enterratoria incaico a 5.300 metros de altura*. Mendoza, Argentina: Inca Editorial.

Schobinger, Juan. 2001. *El santuario incaica del Cerro Aconcagua*. Mendoza, Argentina: Universidad Nacional de Cuyo.

Schreiber, Katharina. 1992. *Wari Imperialism in Middle Horizon Peru*. Ann Arbor: University of Michigan Press.

Scott, James C. 1990. *Domination and the Arts of Resistance: Hidden Transcripts*. New Haven, CT: Yale University Press.

Scott, John. 2001. *Power*. Malden, MA: Blackwell Publishers.

Seddon, Matthew. 1998. "Ritual, Power, and the Development of a Complex Society." Ph.D. diss., University of Chicago.

Sherbondy, Jeanette. 1982. "The Canal System of Hanan Cuzco." Ph.D. diss., University of Illinois, Urbana-Champaign.

Sherbondy, Jeanette. 1986. *Mallki: ancestros y cultivos de árboles en los Andes*. Documento de trabajo 5, Proyecto FAO/Holanda: Lima, Peru.

Sherbondy, Jeanette. 1987. The Inkaic organization of terraced irrigation in Cuzco, Peru. *British Archaeological Reports International Series* 359(1):365–371. Proceedings of the 45th Annual Congress of Americanists, Bogotá, Columbia, 1985, Pre-Hispanic Agricultural Fields in the Andean Region, Part I.

Sherbondy, Jeanette. 1992. Water ideology in Inca ethnogenesis. In *Andean Cosmologies through Time*. R. Dover, K. Seibold, and J. McDowell, eds., pp. 46–66. Bloomington: Indiana University Press.

Sherbondy, Jeanette. 1996. Panaca lands: Re-invented communities. *Journal of the Steward Anthropological Society* 24(1–2):173–202.

Shimada, Izumi. 1985a. La cultura Sicán: Caracterización arqueológica. In *Presencia Histórica de Lambayeque*. E. Mendoza, ed., pp. 76–133. Lima: Editorial e Imprenta DESA, S.A.

Shimada, Izumi. 1985b. Perception, procurement, and management of resources. In *Andean Ecology and Civilization: An Interdisciplinary Perspective on Andean Ecological Complementarity*. S. Masuda, I. Shimada, and C. Morris, eds., pp. 357–399. Tokyo: University of Tokyo Press.

Silverblatt, Irene. 1978. Andean women in the Inca Empire. *Feminist Studies* 4(3):36–61.

Silverblatt, Irene. 1987. *Moon, Sun, and Witches: Gender Ideologies and Class in Inca and Colonial Peru*. Princeton, NJ: Princeton University Press.

Silverman, Helaine. 1992. Review of *Provincial Power in the Inka Empire*, by Terence D'Altroy. *The Americas* 50(1):119–121.

Smith, Michael E. 1980. The role of the marketing system in Aztec society and economy: Reply to Evans. *American Antiquity* 45(4):876–883.

Smith, Michael E. 2004. *The Aztecs*. Malden, MA: Blackwell.

Spalding, Karen. 1984. *Huarochiri: An Andean Society under Inca and Spanish Rule*. Stanford, CA: Stanford University Press.

Stern, Steve J. 1982. *Peru's Indian Peoples and the Challenge of Spanish Conquest: Huamanga to 1640*. Madison: University of Wisconsin Press.

Tomlinson, Gary. 2007. *The Singing of the New World: Indigenous Voice in the Era of European Contact*. Cambridge: Cambridge University Press.

Torero, Alfredo. 2002. *Idiomas de los Andes: Lingüística e historia*. Lima: IFEA.

Urton, Gary. 1998. From knots to narratives: Reconstructing the art of historical record keeping in the Andes from Spanish translations of Inka *khipus*. *Ethnohistory* 45(5):409–438.

Urton, Gary. 2001. A calendrical and demographic tomb text from northern Peru. *Latin American Antiquity* 12(2):127–147.

Urton, Gary. 2003. *Signs of the Inka Khipu: Binary Coding in the Andean Knotted-String Records*. Austin: University of Texas Press.

Van Buren, Mary. 1997. Continuity or change? Vertical archipelagos in southern Peru during the early colonial period. In *Approaches to the Historical Archaeology of Mexico, Central and South America*. J. Gasco, G. Smith, and P. Fournier-García, eds., pp. 155–164. Los Angeles: Institute of Archaeology, University of California.

Van de Guchte, Maarten. 1990. "Carving the World: Inca Monumental Sculpture and Landscape." Ph.D. diss., University of Illinois, Urbana-Champaign.

Wachtel, Nathan. 1982. The mitimas of the Cochabamba Valley: The colonization policy of Huayna Capac. In *The Inca and Aztec States, 1400–1800: Anthropology and History*. G. Collier, R. Rosaldo, and J. Wirth, eds., pp. 199–229. New York: Academic Press.

Weber, Max. 1958. Politics as a vocation. In *From Max Weber: Essays in Sociology*. H. H. Gerth and C. Wright Mills, eds., pp. 77–128. New York: Oxford University Press.

Weber, Max. 1978[1914]. *Economy and Society: An Outline of Interpretive Sociology*. G. Roth and C. Wittich, eds. Berkeley: University of California Press.

Wernke, Steven. 2006. The politics of community and Inka statecraft in the Colca Valley, Peru. *Latin American Antiquity* 17(7):177–208.

Wernke, Steven. 2007. Negotiating community and landscape in the Peruvian Andes: A transconquest view. *American Anthropologist* 109(1):130–152.

Wilson, Andrew, Timothy Taylor, María Constanza Ceruti, José Antonio Chávez, Johan Reinhard, Vaughan Grimes, Wolfram Meier-Augenstein, Larry Cartmell, Ben Stern, Michael P. Richards, Michael Worobey, Ian Barnes, M. Thomas, and P. Gilbert. 2007. Stable isotope and DNA evidence for ritual sequences in Inca child sacrifice. *Proceedings of the National Academy of Sciences* 104(42):16456–16461.

Zárate, Augustín de. 1968[1555]. *The Discovery and Conquest of Peru*. J. M. Cohen, trans. Baltimore: Penguin Books.

Zuidema, R. Tom. 1964. *The Ceque System: The Social Organization of the Capital of the Inca*. Leiden, Netherlands: E. J. Brill.

Zuidema, R. Tom. 1977/1978. Shafttombs and the Inca Empire. *Journal of the Steward Anthropological Society* 9(1–2):133–178.

Zuidema, R. Tom. 1982a. Myth and history in ancient Peru. In *The Logic of Culture*. I. Rossi, ed. South Hadley, MA: J. F. Bergin.

Zuidema, R. Tom. 1982b. Bureaucracy and systematic knowledge in Andean civilizations. In *The Inca and Aztec States, 1400–1800: Anthropology and History*. G. Collier, R. Rosaldo, and J. Wirth, eds., pp. 419–458. New York: Academic Press.

Zuidema, R. Tom. 1983a. Hierarchy and space in Incaic social organization. *Ethnohistory* 30(2):49–75.

Zuidema, R. Tom. 1983b. The lion in the city: Royal symbols of transition in Cuzco. *Journal of Latin American Lore* 9(1):39–100.

Zuidema, R. Tom. 1983c. Llama sacrifices and computation: The roots of the Inca calendar in Huari-Tiahuanaco culture. In *Acts of the Congress on Ethnoastronomy.* Washington, DC.

Zuidema, R. Tom. 1986. Inka dynasty and irrigation: Another look at Andean concepts of history. In *Anthropological History of Andean Polities.* J. Murra, N. Wachtel, and J. Revel, eds., pp. 177–200. Cambridge: Cambridge University Press.

Zuidema, R. Tom. 1989a. The Inca kinship system: A new theoretical view. In *Reyes y guerreros: Ensayos de cultura andina.* M. Burga, ed., pp. 54–116. Lima: FOMCIENCIAS.

Zuidema, R. Tom. 1989b. The moieties of Cuzco. In *The Attraction of Opposites: Thought and Society in the Dualistic Mode.* D. Maybury-Lewis and U. Almagor, eds., pp. 255–275. Ann Arbor: University of Michigan Press.

Zuidema, R. Tom. 1990. *Inca Civilization in Cuzco.* Jean-Jacques Decoster, trans. Austin: University of Texas Press.

Index